In 1982 Prime Minister Pierre Trudeau realized his life's ambition: the repatriation of the Canadian constitution and the enshrinement of a Charter of Rights and Freedoms. At the same time he dealt a severe blow to his arch-enemies, the Quebec nationalists who believed that a significant and rewarding partnership with Canada was possible without renouncing their identity as Quebecers. In *Trudeau and the End of a Canadian Dream* Guy Laforest argues that Trudeau's constitutional reforms destroyed the dualistic vision of the Canadian federation developed in Quebec through the twentieth century.

Laforest reveals that Trudeau betrayed the trust of the people of Quebec during the 1980 referendum on sovereignty-association and contends that the whole repatriation exercise, completed without the consent of Quebec, is not legitimate in that province. He also holds Trudeau responsible for the ultimate rejection of the "distinct society" clause in the Meech Lake Accord, which had given a glimmer of hope to Quebec federalists.

Trudeau and the End of a Canadian Dream shows how constitutional reform, and the political culture it fostered, shattered the hopes of those who believed that being both a Canadian and a Quebecer was possible.

GUY LAFOREST is associate professor of political science, Université Laval.

Trudeau and the End of a Canadian Dream

Guy Laforest

Translated by
Paul Leduc Browne
and Michelle Weinroth

McGill-Queen's University Press
Montreal & Kingston • London • Buffalo

© McGill-Queen's University Press 1995
ISBN 0-7735-1300-0 (cloth)
ISBN 0-7735-1322-1 (paper)

Legal deposit second quarter 1995
Bibliothèque nationale du Québec
Printed in Canada on acid-free paper

McGill-Queen's University Press is grateful to the
Canada Council for support of its publishing program.

Canadian Cataloguing in Publication Data

Laforest, Guy, 1955–
Trudeau and the end of a Canadian dream.
Translation of: Trudeau et la fin d'un rêve canadien.
Includes bibliographical references.
ISBN 0-7735-1300-0 (bound) –
ISBN 0-7735-1322-1 (pbk.)
1. Federal-provincial relations – Canada. 2. Federal
government – Canada. 3. Trudeau, Pierre Elliott,
1919–   . 4. Quebec (Province) – History –
Autonomy and independence movements.
5. Nationalism – Quebec (Province).
I. Title.
JL65.1992.L3313 1995   971.064'6   C95-900100-X

Typeset in Palatino 10/12
by Caractéra production graphique, Quebec City

This book is a translation of *Trudeau et la fin d'un rêve
canadien*, published by Septentrion, 1992.

Cover illustration:
The signing of the constitution,
17 April 1982.
Photo by John McNeill.
The Globe and Mail, Toronto.

Contents

Preface to the English Edition

The writing of this book in French was completed before the Charlottetown Accord was drafted in the summer of 1992. I voted No in the referendum of October 1992, essentially because I saw in the Charlottetown package only a different visage of the one-nation idea of Canada. The main argument of this book is that the constitutional reform of 1982 and the failure of the Meech Lake Accord mean the end of the dualistic dream for Canada as it has been formulated in Quebec throughout the twentieth century. Nothing that has occurred in the past couple of years has made me change my mind on this fundamental point.

This book does not provide an analysis of either the Charlottetown saga itself or the international context that impinges on the Canada-Quebec crisis. Alone, or with others, I have tried to do that in various publications.[1] Reflecting on the content of this work, with its bright spots and also with its weaknesses, I feel the need to add only one remark. I recognize that the two-nations thesis is an unsatisfactory symbolic proposition for contemporary Canada. I do not deny the existence of an element of myth in that vision of the country. Native leaders, such as Ovide Mercredi and Matthew Coon-Come, have every right to denounce it. However, the official vision of Canada, the one that is presented to the world, continues to be the one-nation approach of Pierre Elliott Trudeau. It should be as unacceptable to the First Peoples as it is to Quebec.

At Laval, McGill, and the University of Calgary, many colleagues have helped me refine my ideas. I thank them all. I dedicate this book to my father and to the memory of my mother, Gisèle Brunet Laforest. She taught me respect for good spelling and sound grammar, first in French and from there to all languages.

Introduction

For the past thirty years, the beginning of each decade has signalled a quickening of the historical process in Quebec. The Quiet Revolution began in 1960 with the victory of Jean Lesage's Liberals. Ten years later, the October Crisis swept us into the turmoil of the fear of insurrection, the War Measures Act, the death of Pierre Laporte, and the exacerbation of the malaise pervading Quebec society. Then came the referendum campaign and that fateful day of 20 May 1980, which once and for all killed the momentum that Quebec had enjoyed on the Canadian political stage. For some, the result of the referendum meant the rejection of autonomy and seemed a symbol of political immaturity. For others, it came forth draped in the colours of a renewed federalism and exhibited all the signs of a magnificent confidence. Both parties – and I shall underscore this theme repeatedly in the course of this book – could legitimately claim roots in Quebec nationalism. Their rivalry at the time concealed common values and a common rallying ground, foreshadowing the struggles to be waged on shared turf, in a more or less distant future, against identical foes. In 1994, as I write these lines, it seems to me that the political circumstances in Quebec still lend themselves to such a reconciliation.

In 1990, ten long years after the referendum, history suddenly began to quicken its pace again. Of course, this did not occur in our society alone. Europe rose up in the autumn of 1989. Communism collapsed in the East, Germany took the first steps towards reunification, and entire peoples broke the chains that dictatorial regimes had maintained for more than forty years. In the USSR an immense empire began to disintegrate before our eyes, while another grew more rigid in China. In Quebec, as everywhere else in the world, people were stunned, astounded by all these upheavals. But no sense of wonder or amazement at the historical process unfolding abroad can exempt us from confronting our own history here at home. In Canada and Quebec, the political and constitutional crisis brought on by the Meech Lake Accord, and more specifically by its pitiful failure in June 1990, has constituted the underlying web of this dynamic historical development.

Throughout history, the heralds of successive crises have contemplated the possibilities brought into being by political storms. Crises have quickly become "opportunities." This was the case twenty-five years ago with the Royal Commission on Bilingualism and Biculturalism. In its preliminary report, published in March 1965, the commission, which was jointly chaired by Davidson Dunton and André Laurendeau, declared that Canada was unwittingly passing through the deepest crisis of its history. In the same thrust, it set in motion a process of analysis intended to endow Canada with institutions that would be more representative of the peoples and cultures that had founded it. This preliminary report compelled our English-speaking fellow citizens to ponder the fate of the country, to engage in introspection. History will recall that Pierre Elliott Trudeau's election as leader of the country in 1968 corresponded to the sudden end of this period of introspection.

Ten years later, on the day after the Parti québécois victory, the Task Force on Canadian Unity, led by Jean-Luc Pepin and John Robarts, took up this discourse of crisis and "opportunity." The first volume of their report, published in January 1979, laid the foundations of a genuine restructuring of Canadian federalism in a way that was sensitive to the decentralizing demands of the regions and of Quebec. But history will recall that the Pepin-Robarts Report was swiftly relegated to oblivion by Mr Trudeau and his government.

If there is a crisis today, and if I perceive it as the dawning of a certain "opportunity," it is in part because the Canadian political system, faithful to Pierre Elliott Trudeau's vision, is headed towards the rejection of duality, one of the great principles the two commissions shared in their understanding of federalism.[1] If there is a crisis, it is fundamentally because Mr Trudeau was victorious in his battle against the dualist ideas of Quebec politicians and intellectuals. The end of duality, in my mind, portends the end of the Québécois' Canadian dream.

The failure of the Meech Lake Accord in June 1990 confirmed the idea that duality – a pivotal factor in the interpretation of Canadian federalism within French-Canadian and, subsequently, Quebec historiography – has become impossible. It has become unrealistic to hope that the dualist vision of federalism as an agreement between two distinct societies – between two nations, or two founding peoples – can wield significant power within the Canadian constitutional infrastructure. A Canadian dream has ended, and this is a source of great sadness.

French Canadians (the majority of whom have regarded themselves as Québécois since the Quiet Revolution) invested a great deal in the dream of two equal collectivities. It was the project of Etienne Parent, Louis-Hippolyte LaFontaine, and George-Etienne Cartier, of Henri Bourassa and André Laurendeau, of Daniel Johnson Sr and Claude Ryan. These great figures of our history did not all attribute the same meaning to duality. Nonetheless, duality in its various guises was always the indispensable factor that enabled them to embrace a certain form of Canadian patriotism. This patriotism was possible as long as it permitted French Canada, Quebec, to remain itself – as long as it did not demand that the Québécois categorically renounce their primary allegiance to the society in which they were born. My hypothesis in this book is that Canadian institutions have imposed such a renunciation on us since 1982.

The Canadian patriotism of the Québécois was a legitimate fact for more than a century. To claim the contrary, as the sovereigntists have done, is rather cynical. Solange Chaput-Rolland, Robert Bourassa, and Claude Ryan campaigned for the No vote during the May 1980 referendum on sovereignty association, promising to renew Canadian federalism on the basis of a recognition of duality and Quebec's need for increased powers. They could reasonably draw on a historical and political tradition whose fidelity to French Canada and Quebec was flawless. I am, however, well aware of the existence of another school of thought, which is graced with as much legitimacy as the first and which holds that it is not possible to reconcile the affirmation of Quebec society with the demands of Canadian nationalism; in the wake of the Conquest and the Act of Union, and by virtue of their pessimistic interpretation of the federal union of 1867, historians such as Maurice Séguin and Michel Brunet, worthy representatives of the Ecole Historique de Montréal, have deemed equality impossible. I leave to others the task of sorting out who is right in the historiographical arena. I shall restrict myself in these pages to seeking the meaning of the contemporary situation in Quebec for those who believed in duality.

The failure of the Meech Lake Accord dealt a fatal blow to the traditional Canadian patriotism of Quebecers – the patriotism of Henri Bourassa and André Laurendeau, a blend of idealism and nobility, with maybe a dash of naiveté. With duality becoming impossible, this meant the end of the Canadian dream, which a large proportion of the people and élites of Quebec have nurtured from generation to generation. In emphasizing a certain number of political events since the referendum and in highlighting the contributions of a sample of intellectuals and politicians, I shall attempt in this book to identify the main factors that led to the death of this Canadian dream. For the moment, though, I merely wish to offer the reader a symbolic prefiguration of them.

On 9 June 1990, at the end of an incredible week of negotiations in Ottawa, a fine session of "national" reconciliation was organized to celebrate the eleventh-hour compromise that was supposedly going to save the Meech Lake deal. In reality, of course, there was no unanimous agreement, no compromise. The Manitoban leaders signed the document knowing full well that there would be a procedural tangle in their provincial legislature and that it would be very difficult to sign the agreement before 23 June. Clyde Wells, for his part, did not commit himself to working for ratification of the compromise. Buttressed by his adamant convictions and supported by a large part of English-Canadian public opinion, he did not go down under the enormous pressure that must have been exerted on him.[2] When he spoke that night, he said more or less the following to an increasingly livid Robert Bourassa: "You Quebecers, too, must be Canadians first and foremost." For Wells and the Trudeauite political forces that he represents, duality of allegiances had become impossible, even assuming that it was ever otherwise. The festive melodies that played in Ottawa that evening of 9 June were therefore a sham, for the fate of the Meech Lake Accord in no way altered the fact that a Canadian dream was dying in the hearts of many Quebecers.

I am writing this book specifically for those who, like myself, occasionally believed in this dream, or who continue to believe in it or cannot bring themselves to abandon it. The projects built around this dream have not been in vain, and there is certainly no need to feel any shame for having participated in it. Quite the contrary. Our ancestors worked themselves into the ground throughout North America for nearly four centuries. They explored Canada from sea to sea, leaving behind unforgettable tracks. This country remains in large part theirs as well as ours. Today, one million French Canadians still live outside Quebec. These people are our brothers, said André Laurendeau during one of his pilgrimages through Canada at the time of the Royal Commission on Bilingualism and Biculturalism. And he was right. One probably ought to go further and add that for many Quebecers, the brothers and sisters referred to are not only anonymous individuals belonging to the same nation; for many of us, they are literally our brothers and sisters. It was wrong to neglect this facet of the Québécois allegiance to Canada. For French- or English-speaking Quebecers, there is a political price to pay for living in the same country as our brothers and sisters who live in the other Canadian provinces. Until recently, a majority of the citizens of Quebec remained willing to pay this price – the referendum of May 1980 proved it – but I would argue that the price to be paid is henceforth too great. The very logic of the Canadian federal system indicates a will to crush the collective dimension of the Québécois identity. As a result, our Canadian dream has become outmoded, and duality has become impossible. I aim to show how this logic works and to demonstrate all the ways in which it threatens Quebec.

In this book, I would like to delineate some of the historical and theoretical reasons that underpin the coming together that I wish to see between sovereigntists and those who are both Quebec nationalists and supporters of federalism. Over the last decade, Canadian politics have been dominated by the spectre of duality. Historians, politicians, and intellectuals in French Canada and Quebec are just about unanimous in believing that two founding peoples, two nations, two distinct societies, two majorities gave birth to Canada in 1867. This belief is deeply anchored in the Québécois psyche; it dominates public perception at different levels of abstraction and conceptualization in all walks of life. In the wake of the 1980 referendum, the federal government of Pierre Elliott Trudeau engaged in a systematic attempt to eliminate this dualist interpretation once and for all. Enormous efforts were made to cobble together a single Canadian identity that would be uniformly valid from coast to coast. Quebec has been and still is the main target of this campaign. If my hypothesis proves correct, I will have demonstrated the negative character of the whole affair. In the end, it is simply an attempt to subordinate fidelity to Quebec to allegiance to Canada.

Quebec public opinion and those who influence it are not sufficiently aware of this dimension of federal policy and of the significant support it has gained in English Canada. They do not realize the consequences of this policy – of this truly obsessive fear of duality – in metropolitan Montreal, the battleground that will determine the fate of Quebec's French experience of modernity in the twenty-first century. Symbols of identity define the general aspect of this battle, whose outcome will no doubt be decided at the end of the present decade. Since 1980, various federal governments, including that of Brian Mulroney, have focused their attacks on these symbolic questions. The federal proposals of September 1991 and the Beaudoin-Dobbie Report of February 1992, which were intended to renew the Canadian political system, are equally subject to this dynamic. In

Montreal even more than elsewhere, a panoply of legislation contributes to shaping and remodelling civic identity in the cause of Canadian nationalism, with a view to dispensing with duality once and for all. The Constitution Act, 1982, with its Charter of Rights and Freedoms, naturally contributes to this, but it is not unique. Federal legislation on citizenship, official languages, and multiculturalism has the same effect.

Many intellectuals and politicians have spoken out since the autumn of 1989 to underline the need either for a bipartisan alliance between the Liberal Party of Quebec and the Parti québécois or the existence of a historical common front around the idea of a distinct society, or to stress the urgency of rallying together the vibrant forces of Quebec. In the most animated moments of the debate on the ratification of the Meech Lake Accord, in May 1990, this idea was omnipresent. The search for a consensus that would transcend party differences was, moreover, at the heart of the Bélanger-Campeau Commission's work on the political and constitutional future of Quebec. In the intellectual world, similar arguments were defended by people such as Louis Balthazar, Edouard Cloutier, and Christian Dufour. There is thus no great originality in repeating them in these pages, but I would like to restate them more systematically than others have done, by encompassing in a single analysis the significant moments of Canadian and Quebec politics of the last fifteen years, from the referendum to the crisis provoked by the failure of the Meech Lake Accord. The originality I hope to lend this analysis will stem from the methods adopted, which are those of political philosophy and the history of political ideas. They cast the most direct light on the assault that Pierre Elliott Trudeau and his troops have conducted against duality since 1980.

Those who devote themselves to political philosophy and the history of political ideas often work as antiquarians, as curators of the philosophical heritage of our civilization. However, they do much more than this. They are citizens, too, who are almost invariably involved in public debate and want to raise the beacons of tradition in order to illuminate the political deliberations of their respective communities. Thus, not only Aristotle, Machiavelli, and Locke, but also Fichte, Hegel, and Herder will appear in these pages as references whose philosophical and political experiences are likely to guide our choices. This list of philosophers is neither artless nor neutral. It is because of these thinkers that I believe I have arrived at a better understanding of the person who has embodied the struggle against duality during the past fifteen years: Pierre Elliott Trudeau. With the help of these philosophers, I shall therefore attempt to produce a critical analysis of Trudeau's thought and actions since the referendum. At a later date, a more general account of the relationship between Trudeau and political thought will be necessary.

In Canada and in Quebec, as much if not more than elsewhere, political and intellectual leaders have had a determining influence on the orientation of their communities at critical moments of history. When the time came to make fundamental political choices, the people were rarely consulted. In this respect, the unbelievable week of deliberations behind closed doors over the Meech Lake Accord in June 1990 is no exception. It conforms roughly to the precedents established during the previous round in 1981–82 and during the discussions leading to the British North America Act in 1867. In Canada, until the 1992 referendum on the Charlottetown Accord, the people remained at a remove from constitutional negotiations and did not ratify them. The exception was of course the Quebec referendum of May 1980, when the people were genuinely consulted on an issue of great importance. After such collective affirmation, it would be very difficult for anyone to deny the existence of the Québécois people, whatever the Stephen Scotts and William Johnsons of this world may say. Because the people of Quebec had already been consulted about their collective destiny, they would hardly have consented if their leaders had tried to dispense with a referendum in 1992. Nonetheless, the task of building bridges between Canada's two great cultural and linguistic communities has traditionally fallen to politicians and intellectuals.

Readers will therefore not be surprised to learn that intellectuals will be granted a substantial place in this book. In a certain sense, this is because of my occupation, since some of my courses deal with the political commitment of intellectuals in Canada and Quebec since 1945. But there are other reasons to justify my delving into certain chapters from the history of ideas. Intellectuals can be seen as microcosms, as ideal types of the Canadian-Québécois experience in its totality – the experience of two solitudes brought together by rational voluntarism but holding together uneasily, perpetually tempted to yield to incomprehension. I shall especially emphasize the paradigmatic figures of Léon Dion, André Laurendeau, Ramsay Cook, F.R. Scott, and, of course, Pierre Elliott Trudeau. I am well aware that there are dozens of others, but I intend to do them justice in other works, if possible.

Trudeau straddles recent history like a colossus. Obsessed with the dangers of duality, he submitted his reason and that of the central state to his efforts to transcend duality – the two solitudes – in order to engender a Canadian identity that would be resolutely homogeneous, despite the value attributed to cultural and linguistic pluralism. From the referendum battle to the Meech Lake debate,

Trudeau was so ubiquitous that one almost forgets the silence in which he cloistered himself from 1984 to 1987. In 1980 his interventions in the referendum campaign were solemn and, in the eyes of many observers, decisive. He was the great architect of the 1982 constitution, which the Quebec authorities continue to regard as illegitimate. From 1987 to 1990, he was really the first to sound the alarm against the Meech Lake Accord, and he tirelessly resumed his attacks on it at the most opportune moments. In addition, the most memorable moment of the 1992 referendum on the Charlottetown package was Trudeau's speech at the Maison Egg Roll in Montreal. Those who believe that this uncanny man has finally uttered his last word are harbouring illusions. One can fault him with everything but inconsistency.

This study must therefore include a careful scrutiny of Trudeau's trajectory in the 1980s. Three chapters will be directly devoted to this. The first will bring out the thorny question of Trudeau's intentions, both in his actions and in his referendum speeches of 1980. The second chapter will re-examine the 1981–82 patriation of the constitution from the perspective of concepts borrowed from one of the great masters of liberal philosophy, John Locke. If I have correctly read Locke and the applicability of his ideas to our situation, the reader may well make some surprisingly radical discoveries in these pages. Another chapter – the fifth – will deal with Trudeau's reactions to the Meech Lake Accord. I see it as a fine example of the usefulness of Machiavelli in illuminating the behaviour of the co-founder of *Cité libre*.

It is easy to yield to the temptation of polemical nastiness when crossing swords with Trudeau, and in fact such a style is not entirely foreign to him. However, it seems preferable to shift the debate to the level of what is best in Trudeau, to an analytical effort based on political philosophy. On this level, a critic must be both honest and merciless. Those who would take offence at such an absence of consideration or tact should reread Trudeau's long introduction to a collective work that caused quite a stir in the 1950s, *La grève de l'amiante* ("The Asbestos Strike"). This is considered to be the most important antinationalist manifesto of that era. The reader will notice that Trudeau did not pull any punches against the bards of traditional nationalism:

The lack of realism of our Catholic social thought corresponded perfectly to the lack of realism of our nationalist thinking, of which it was only a predicate. Both were characterized by the same ensconcement within "truth," the same retrograde "orthodoxy," the same dearth of inventiveness, the same passivity in the face of appeals to authority, the same fear of adventure. And their intellectual scaffolding inevitably erected clericalism and reaction, one in the area of religion, the other in politics.[3]

Another aim of this study will therefore be to gain a better understanding of Trudeau's role in our political life during the last decade by identifying the ins and outs of his thought during this period and by providing the material for a critique of his political involvement. Trudeau, a giant with feet of clay? Possibly – and I shall try to prove it by searching for cracks in the armour of this nonetheless formidable jouster. In the sixth chapter, which is devoted to the Canadian political culture promoted by the Canadian Charter of Rights and Freedoms, we will see that after 1980, Trudeau renounced the systematic antinationalism that had typified his thought in the 1960s. The eighth chapter will deal with transcending the legacy of 1763. In it, I shall identify certain weaknesses of Trudeau's liberalism, particularly with respect to the question of rights and national minorities. The spectre of Lord Durham will hover over this chapter.

As important as Trudeau may be in my discussion, he will not take up the whole stage. Throughout this study, I claim that the institutions Trudeau bequeathed us scarcely leave room for linguistic and cultural duality, for the vision that a pact between two founding peoples gave birth to Canada. Yet historians, in Quebec as much as in the rest of Canada, persist in maintaining that the difficult dialogue between French and English Canadians, between a predominantly French-speaking Quebec and a predominantly English-speaking Canada, represents the most fundamental characteristic of Canada as a country. If Canada has been able to lay claim to being a distinct country in North America, it is principally because of this feature – and to what else if not that? According to Gordon Robertson, who was clerk of the privy council under the Trudeau government, the preservation of this dialogue constitutes Canada's transcendental objective, its principal contribution to history.[4] The seventh chapter of this book will analyse the Allaire and Bélanger-Campeau reports, as well as the federal proposals of September 1991 and February 1992, and it will show that while Quebec did not renounce national duality, the federal government carried forward the torch of a single national Canadian identity, which Trudeau had handed it.

Two intellectuals, André Laurendeau and F.R. Scott, offer fine examples of the dialogue which, according to Gordon Robertson, has given the Canadian political odyssey its specific character. Here are two remarkable men, both writers and politicians, both artists and teachers, two nationalists who articulated visions of Canada that are totally representative of French-Canadian and Québécois opinion on the one hand and English-Canadian majority opinion on the other. Laurendeau and Scott, taken together, with their respective visions, embody the notion of duality that characterizes Canada. This is what I shall try to demonstrate in the third chapter. There I shall also suggest that the Meech Lake Accord would have benefited from being viewed as a compromise between the visions of Laurendeau and Scott. To be sure, one might question how balanced that compromise was. Nonetheless, it was a genuine compromise. The recognition of Quebec as a distinct society would have introduced a profoundly dualist element into a constitutional structure in which centralism and Canadian nationalism have held sway since 1982. Would this compromise have been sufficient for Quebec? What would have been the consequences for Quebec's future as a distinct society? In the final analysis, how should one interpret the failure of this agreement and the new possibilities that are open to us? No one can answer these questions once and for all. But the analysis that follows should provide instruments for deeper thought on the matter.

There is one more point I should like to make about Laurendeau and Scott. In recent years, there has been renewed interest in Laurendeau in Quebec and in Scott in English Canada. I believe that the various events, books, and conferences devoted to one or other of these men have missed the essential point. During a vigorous debate on the state of schooling in Quebec some twenty-five years after the reforms of the 1960s, a conference explored the question of how education could be thought through with André Laurendeau, a teacher who saw no conflict between universalism and rootedness in a particular society. On another occasion, during a series of conferences on the political leaders of contemporary Quebec, a gathering of politicians and intellectuals, including the cabinet minister Claude Ryan, recognized their debt towards Laurendeau and pointed to his relevance to contemporary Quebec nationalism and the problems it faces. This relevance comes to light in a remarkable fashion in the log Laurendeau kept during his years with the Royal Commission on Bilingualism and Biculturalism.[5] This diary, which was published in 1990, is particularly instructive about the relations between Laurendeau and Trudeau, but for my purposes in this study, the dialogue between Laurendeau and Scott is especially enlightening. Theirs is the exchange that appears most likely to educate, develop, or reform the political intelligence of Quebecers.

Quebecers have thus to study the relationships between Laurendeau and Scott in order to complete their political education. It is in this specific sense that we need to think education through with André Laurendeau, the veritable paradigm of the Québécois intellectual in modern times, according to essayist Jean Larose.[6] What discoveries does this dialogue harbour? First, Laurendeau offers one of the finest formulations – perhaps the definitive synthesis – of the duality that is so fundamental for Quebec. Secondly, Scott increasingly voices distrust of duality and resists it more and more, deeming it potentially dangerous to Canadian nationalism. One slowly gathers that it is not enough for Quebec and its representatives to brandish the flame of duality in order to win the day during major constitutional negotiations. Duality is not self-evident. On the contrary, it has always been a problem. The difficulties encountered by Laurendeau and Scott in their dialogue are very revealing in this respect.

The later aspects of their dialogue are equally instructive for Quebec. Scott, that symbol of English Canada on the Royal Commission on Bilingualism and Biculturalism, did not wish to recognize Quebec as a nation or as a distinct society in the 1960s. Since 1971, the dialogue has shifted onto other stages. I shall argue that the Meech Lake Accord represented the culmination of twenty years' worth of efforts in this direction. For Laurendeau's heirs, for those who worked with the Task Force on Canadian Unity between 1977 and 1979 and produced the Pepin-Robarts Report, for those who conceived the beige paper of the Liberal Party under the leadership of Claude Ryan in January 1980, and for those who struggled for renewed federalism during the referendum period, the recognition of Quebec as a distinct society would have amounted to a great victory. The hydra of duality resurfaced in the distinct society clause – to Pierre Trudeau's great displeasure. In every pedagogical exercise there are crucial, decisive lessons: genuinely formative experiences, to use the words of the German philosopher Hegel. These lessons perfect a process of transmitting knowledge within a specific field. The odds are that Quebecers had a similar experience in the Meech Lake saga. They witnessed the foundering of their dualist dream.

Laurendeau and Scott were unable to agree. Since then, many politicans and intellectuals, both French- and English-speaking, have pursued the course of action left hanging by their predecessors. In the fourth chapter of this book, I would like to study one of them, Professor Léon Dion. I have chosen Dion because his intellectual and professional life seems to be characterized by a wish to succeed where Laurendeau and Scott failed, namely, in arriving at a definition of the political community as a synthesis of French and English Canada, while still lucidly accepting duality. In particular, I shall focus on Dion's debt to the German philosopher J.G. Fichte. There are intellectuals and academics in English Canada who have led the same fight in favour of duality as Dion did, for example, John Meisel and

Ronald Watts of Queen's University. However, they seem less representative of Canada in the 1980s than a man who was influenced by Pierre Elliott Trudeau – historian Ramsay Cook of York University. In the eighth chapter, which is about overcoming the legacy of 1763, I shall portray Cook as a symbol of the antidualist evolution of English Canada's intellectual and political classes. The fight for duality led by Laurendeau, Dion, and Ryan seems to me to have been irrevocably lost.

In 1992, Canadians celebrated the 125th anniversary of Confederation as well as the tenth anniversary of the Constitution Act, 1982, and the Charter of Rights and Freedoms. However, both the magnanimous spirit and the recognition of the specific character of Quebec that prevailed in the compromise of 1867 now lie at the bottom of Meech Lake. Moreover, the substance of the 1982 reform and the way in which it was executed have resulted in this: by endowing itself with a new constitution, Canada has ceased, in the eyes of Quebec, to be a country worthy of the name. In sum, we have no cause for rejoicing. This book will endeavour to show how we arrived at our present situation, but also – so as not to end on a negative note – how it is still possible to dream politically beyond Pierre Trudeau and his triumph over Quebec's dualist imagination.

CHAPTER ONE

Trudeau and the Referendum

The political upheavals of the spring of 1980 might have sealed the fate of Quebec and Canada once and for all. For many people, the very flow of the seasons was interrupted. Many are the intellectuals and observers of the political scene who relive the debates of that period almost daily. These memories were of course stirred up once again by the failure of the Meech Lake Accord, which brought the federal Canadian system to a political impasse, thus giving rise to all kinds of questions. Among the many facets of the referendum campaign, there is one that has not ceased to arouse controversy: the notorious issue of the role played by Prime Minister Pierre Elliott Trudeau. The subject has been aired publicly in letters to the editor. These exchanges carry forward a dialogue that has been raging between Trudeau and his fellow intellectuals since the end of the Second World War.[1]

Roughly speaking, there are two conflicting interpretations of Trudeau's actions and speeches during the referendum year. Some people believe that Trudeau deliberately lied, that he duped the population of Quebec when he solemnly promised to reform the structure of Canadian federalism. According to this argument, the former prime minister hastened to put these promises aside immediately after the referendum when he embarked on a remarkably well-orchestrated strategy of unilateral action on the constitutional front.[2] Mr Trudeau and his supporters obviously reject such a reading. They claim that the Liberal leader, who owes his enviable reputation to rigorous reasoning and steadfast ideas, was wholly true to himself both in the form and the content of his promises about renewed federalism. The urgency of repatriating the Canadian constitution and the need to include in it a charter of rights and freedoms for individuals did not mysteriously appear from nowhere to dominate

Trudeau's thought following the referendum.[3] His ideas on the matter had been well known since the Quiet Revolution had taken off in the early 1960s. The general outlines of his federalist creed had remained the same.

It is logically impossible to endorse both interpretations at the same time, but it is possible that both are partially wrong, for one can claim, in the same breath, that Trudeau did not lie and that he shrewdly remained ambiguous. In the final analysis, how should Trudeau's political and ideological behaviour during the referendum campaign be judged? In this chapter, I shall try to furnish a satisfactory answer to this extremely complex question. Reflection on such a subject does not occur exclusively in the sheltered serenity of the academic world. When the Meech Lake Accord was ratified in the spring of 1987, the battle over the meaning of Trudeau's interventions ceased to belong only to researchers and intellectuals. As of that moment, the debate was caught in the tentacles of politics.

The advocates of the Meech Lake agreement struggled to show that promises had been made to Quebec in 1980 and that Trudeau and others had broken their word. The price of patriating the constitution, they argued, was Quebec's isolation. It was therefore necessary to find a way of closing the chasm that had opened up in the legitimacy of federal political institutions so that Quebec could be brought into the heart of the Canadian constitutional family with honour and enthusiasm. This vocabulary is easy to identify. It belongs to the discourse of "national reconciliation" that was used by the federal Conservative Party and its leader, Mr Brian Mulroney, starting with the electoral campaign of the summer of 1984. This idea of redress was at the heart of the famous Meech Lake compromise.

The Meech Lake Accord challenged several aspects of Pierre Elliott Trudeau's concept of Canadian federalism. Although it recognized the federal government's spending power and its capacity to intervene in spheres of exclusive provincial jurisdiction, it imposed limits on them. It also granted the provinces the right to veto any changes made to federal institutions such as the Senate. Moreover, the sphere of provincial power was increased in the area of immigration and in the nominating procedures to the Senate and the Supreme Court of Canada. In the eyes of a centralist such as Trudeau, this amounted to a lot of provincial power. Yet worse was to come.

The Meech Lake Accord included an interpretive clause that recognized Quebec as a distinct society within Canada. For the co-founder of *Cité libre*, this meant nothing less than the re-emergence of the hydra of special status for Quebec.[4] I think Trudeau is correct in this, but with one proviso: the agreement carefully and meticulously opened doors to an indirect form of special status.[5] Whatever the case may be, it was predictable that Trudeau would break the silence he had kept for more than three years, in order to assail the Meech Lake Accord. True to his style, he did it with an audacity skilfully blended with an innate sense of polemics. In embarking on an almost desperate undertaking to thwart ratification of the accord, Trudeau opened wounds that had scarcely healed. His article of 27 May 1987 in the pages of *La Presse* and the *Toronto Star* was like a brick lobbed into the relatively tranquil waters of Meech Lake. It amounted to a re-evaluation of his years in power and his attitude during the referendum campaign.[6]

Trudeau's articles in the daily press, his speeches and interventions before the joint parliamentary committee and before the Senate, and the books he published between 1988 and 1990 deserve to be analysed with the utmost care. That is why I am devoting a later chapter exclusively to Trudeau and Meech Lake. His many interventions compel us to see him as the twentieth century's most important promoter of Canadian nationalism. In the present chapter, in an analysis based on the concepts of ambiguity and confidence, I shall restrict myself to interpreting Trudeau's role in 1980, a matter that belongs unquestionably to the ongoing debate on the political and constitutional future of Quebec. The aim of clarifying the meaning of Trudeau's interventions during the referendum campaign seems to be justified in itself, but it will acquire ever greater relevance if it can help us map out the political situation better.

BEYOND THE HORIZON OF INTENTIONS

The question of Trudeau's true intentions in his referendum speeches resurfaced in the spring of 1989 in the pages of the Montreal daily, *La Presse*. Besides Trudeau himself, Marcel Adam, a veteran journalist at *La Presse*, and the former Péquiste minister Claude Morin contributed to the debate. Adam opened the hostilities by emphasizing that the Meech Lake Accord had been made necessary by the treatment inflicted on Quebec in 1981. According to him, Quebec had been duped during that year's constitutional negotiations.[7] He even spoke of fraud in describing Trudeau's attack, which after the referendum produced results that were wholly different from the commitments he had previously made to Quebec.[8]

The reply was not long in coming. Trudeau strongly objected to being accused of fraudulent actions. He claimed never to have made a secret of his visceral opposition to any hint of special status for Quebec. He did not deny having promised, during the referendum campaign, to bring an end to the constitutional review process that the premiers of Ontario and Quebec, John Robarts and Daniel

Johnson, had initiated in 1967. From the fall of 1967, when, as federal
minister of justice, he had clearly articulated his position on these
questions, to the 1980 referendum, his thinking and priorities had not
changed: they embodied patriation of the constitution, equality
between francophones and anglophones, a charter of rights, and an
amending formula granting a right of veto to Quebec.[9] Trudeau
added that René Lévesque had not been wrong in thus interpreting
the meaning of his promises four days before the referendum.
Lévesque had not been duped. Nor had the people of Quebec.

This answer enabled Adam to go to the heart of the matter and
ask a question that I ask here too: How did the people of Quebec
really interpret Trudeau's promises? As Adam correctly pointed out,
this question deserves as much attention as the question of Trudeau's
true intentions. Adam reasoned as follows. In the first place, the
referendum campaign clearly was punctuated by solemn declarations
that held out to Quebecers the promise of radical reforms of the
workings of federalism. In the second place, one must consider that
what counts in such a context is the impact of these declarations on
ordinary citizens, whose everyday lives are not taken up with constitutional questions. Since Jean Lesage, every premier of Quebec has
demanded radical renewal of the constitution. Trudeau's promise,
draped in the language of "renewed federalism," could only suggest
that he was disposed to commit himself to paths already blazed by
the political leaders of contemporary Quebec. In addition, the polls
taken before the referendum revealed that a large number of those
who were poised to vote Yes fundamentally desired renewed federalism. If one is to believe Adam, Trudeau attempted to make voters
think twice by giving them promises that were rendered ever more
enticing by virtue of their very imprecision.[10]

I think that Adam was right to accuse Trudeau of consciously
planning to be ambiguous. It would no doubt be an exaggeration to
speak of lies or of fraud, given the precise meaning that one must
attribute to those words. However, what actually happened seems
even worse, as I shall explain after sketching the ideological and
political context of 1978–80 in Canada and Quebec.

Shortly after the first exchange, Claude Morin leaped into the fray
to corroborate Marcel Adam's interpretation. According to Morin,
Trudeau had misled the people, had brilliantly played on words,
inasmuch as "renewed federalism" was a traditional aspiration of
Quebecers.[11] While Trudeau persisted in stating that, since 1967, the
people of Quebec had known full well what he meant by "renewed
federalism", Morin retorted that Trudeau could not have been igno-
rant of the nature of the reforms that had been associated with the

renewal of federalism by the people of Quebec and their governments since the Quiet Revolution. These reforms included revamped
political structures as well as a new division of powers between the
federal government and the provinces, especially between Ottawa
and Quebec.

Trudeau fought back with an article revealingly entitled "That's No
Way to Write History." In a key passage, he reproached Morin for
having suggested that the uneducated were not shrewd enough to
understand that the kind of constitutional reform tirelessly promoted
by Liberal governments since 1968 would be the order of the day
after the referendum.[12] According to Trudeau, Morin's statement
betrayed a deep contempt for the people of Quebec. The battle
became even livelier with the publication of another article by Morin:
"Let's Try to Have Done with May 1980." In this article, Morin
pointed out that the leaders of the No camp had proclaimed that
Trudeau's speeches genuinely endorsed Quebec's traditional
demands, and he asked why they were not immediately reprimanded
for their erroneous reading.[13] Morin claimed to have searched in vain
for a satisfactory answer to this question. I share his view. In the
overall debate, when the time came to study the positions of intellectuals and politicans who had fought the referendum battle
equipped with the meaning usually ascribed to renewed federalism,
with its themes of decentralization and accrued power for Quebec,
Trudeau chose evasion. He put an end to the polemic by invoking
the virtues of honour and openness in his political struggles:

In games of love and of luck, the rules are relentless; but their results are
seldom known in advance, precisely because of the luck factor. The players
are simply honour-bound not to cheat and to accept graciously their victory
or their defeat.

In politics, the same applies. It means putting all your cards on the table
and competing, so to speak, with your visor up. And trusting in chance as
much as in skill.[14]

The discussions between Adam, Morin, and Trudeau took place in
the spring of 1989, at a time when opposition to the Meech Lake
Accord was being consolidated in English Canada. A book contain-
ing their contributions, as well as Trudeau's main speeches and writings against the deal, was published in early November 1989, in the
days preceding the premiers' conference on the economy and the
constitution. This inevitably links any analysis of Trudeau's involvement in the referundum with the debate over the Meech Lake
Accord. By illuminating his role in the referendum, we gain a new

perception of the political and constitutional swamp in which we are
still mired today.

There are those who doubt Trudeau's sincerity when he undertakes
to rectify the account of his intentions during the referendum campaign. In my view, the discussion cannot be restricted to questions
about the nature and purity of overt or tacit intentions. Over the past
twenty years, the works of two British professors, Quentin Skinner
and John Dunn of Cambridge University, have brought new methodological insight to the history of political ideas. They have perfected the study of the meaning of political documents, texts, and
speeches, which they regard as so many complex speech acts.[15] The
important speech Trudeau delivered at the Paul Sauvé Centre on
14 May 1980, in which he solemnly promised to renew federalism,
belongs intrinsically to the family of texts and "speech acts" that one
can better comprehend as a result of this new methodological
approach.

An author's declared intentions are clearly a starting point for
textual intepretation. The meaning attributed to the words themselves, to sentences and clauses, constitutes a further element. However, according to Skinner, these elements leave out a question of
crucial importance. What is the author doing in writing his texts?
What, for instance, was Trudeau actually doing on the night of
14 May in delivering his speech? When the prism of analysis is
limited to explicit intentions, sentences, and clauses, an essential
dimension is lost. In the philosophy of language, this dimension is
referred to as the illocutionary power of a text or speech. When the
author of a political speech places a certain number of statements
side by side, he is not merely saying things; he is also performing
one or more acts. Movement and power shine forth from every
serious linguistic performance, quite apart from the intentions and
latent meaning of the words uttered.[16]

What was the illocutionary force of Trudeau's most famous foray
into the referendum campaign? To assess this requires an understanding of the discursive context and the ideological and political contexts
within which his performance occurred. One must ask, What did the
expression "renewed federalism" mean in the late 1970s and early
1980s in the intellectual and ideological life of Canada and Quebec?
According to Skinner, this type of question is always an urgent one
for intellectual historians: "To understand what any given writer may
have been *doing* in using some particular concept or argument, we
need first of all to grasp the nature and range of things that could
recognisably have been done by using that particular concept, in the
treatment of that particular theme, at that particular time."[17]

To grasp the meaning of a text, to understand a speech as an ideological act, one must know the conventional meaning of the most important concepts within a particular context. For example, to speak of renewed federalism in Quebec in 1980 did not mean the same thing as it would have meant in the Soviet Union in 1991. Furthermore, all authors operate in a practical, political context over and above their ideological environment. Thus, in the case of Trudeau, one must also delineate the political circumstances surrounding his actions in 1979–80 in order to bring out their character as political manœuvres. My analysis will develop in three stages. First, I shall consider the political context of 1979–80, stressing the federal elections of May 1979 and February 1980. I shall then study the main documents of the time that claimed to articulate "renewed federalism." Finally, I shall examine the referendum campaign and the role Trudeau played in it. His 14 May speech will occupy a special place in my analysis.

IDEOLOGICAL AND POLITICAL CONTEXTS

Two federal elections took place in Canada in the twelve months preceding the referendum. Pierre Trudeau's fortunes were poles apart in them. Moreover, the form and content of his behaviour were very different from one election to the other. When he embarked on the spring 1979 election campaign, Mr Trudeau had occupied the prime minister's chair for almost eleven years. Despite the fact that his leadership and government had aroused much opposition, he could boast of being one of the most experienced leaders in the Western world. The question of leadership was the leitmotif of the 1979 campaign. At first, Trudeau fell back into some of his bad habits. He insulted many people from one end of the country to the other. Starting in April, he returned to his favourite theme, the promotion of a strong central government, expressing apprehension at the balkanizing tendencies inherent in some provincial policies. Even though he was strongly advised against it, in the last weeks of the campaign Trudeau stressed national unity and the need to reform the constitution. He made important speeches in Toronto and Montreal, demanding a clear mandate to meet again with his provincial counterparts and to obtain their consent for patriating the constitution.[18]

While showing a willingness to devote a lot of energy to gaining a consensus after the election, the prime minister of Canada equally underscored his intention to act unilaterally should the need arise. On this question, Trudeau was the most direct of politicians. In the spring of 1979, he laid all his cards on the table and openly revealed his most important objectives to the voters, telling them clearly what he would try to achieve if he was brought back to power. But Trudeau and the Liberals lost the election, and Joe Clark and the Progressive Conservative Party formed a minority government. Scarcely six months later, on 21 November 1979, Pierre Elliott Trudeau announced his desire to resign the leadership of the Liberal Party of Canada.

At a press conference, Mr Trudeau recalled that there were times in one's life when one simply had to choose one's fate.[19] He believed he had reached such a crossroad and announced that he would return to Montreal to see to his sons' education. The Liberal Party, he said, needed a new leader to restructure its organization and to wage the battle for national unity that would continue for several years after the referendum. He promised Canadians that he would fight with all his might during the referendum campaign to safeguard the integrity of the country. When all was said and done, analysts called on to examine the Trudeau era in Canadian political history concluded on a mixed note. They lauded him for his clear thinking and lucidity, for his determination and perseverance, but they recalled that he had failed on an essential issue.[20] He was giving up the reins of power without having accomplished what he prized most: to get rid of Quebec nationalism and its threat to Canada, and to patriate the constitution. On both these fronts, he had achieved only mediocre results.

Scarcely a month later, Trudeau was once again in the midst of an election campaign, and once more as leader of the Liberal Party. As he recalled in his polemic against Morin and Adam, politicians have to count as much on fortune as on ability. In the language of Niccoló Machiavelli, to whom I shall frequently turn in the chapter on Trudeau and Meech Lake, the fate of politicians rests as much on *Fortuna* as on their own *Virtú*.[21] At the end of 1979, fortune held out one last "opportunity" to Mr Trudeau. The Conservative minority government bungled its first budget speech, causing its own downfall during a confidence vote at a time when Joe Clark's party was trailing in the polls. Fortune, in her magnanimity, had opened the door for Pierre Trudeau's return to the political stage. Trudeau claimed that he had no choice but to return to do his duty and rid Canadians of such a miserable government.

Trudeau's announcement that he was shelving his retirement plans brings out clearly the contrast between his behaviour during the election campaign of the spring of 1979 and that of the winter of 1979–80. He stressed the Conservatives' chronic dithering and their unfitness to govern. He presented western alienation and Quebec separatism as equal problems.[22] He did not even allude to the constitution. This gave a foretaste of the kind of election campaign he was preparing to wage. Enjoying a considerable lead in the polls and anxious not to upset anyone, the Liberals kept a low profile. They spoke about economic issues such as energy. Trudeau's speeches were repetitious and monotonous. The pace of his campaign was a lot less hectic than during preceding elections. Strange as it may seem, Quebec was almost completely ignored by the Liberal leadership. Trudeau visited Quebec only on rare occasions. From the early days of the campaign, he revealed that he would not grant more importance than was necessary to the national unity issue.[23] After the election there would be ample time to deal with the question of the referendum and related constitutional problems. Trudeau said this in early January 1980, just before the publication of the Quebec Liberals' beige paper, a major manifesto on the renewal of federalism. This created the impression that Trudeau was not prepared, in the context of an election campaign at least, to pit his ideas against the views of his coming allies in the Quebec referendum.

Mr Trudeau's main adversary did not show the same restraint. Joe Clark and the Conservatives published a document outlining the operation of a task force on renewed federalism. Under the chairmanship of Senator Arthur Tremblay, this task force would be mandated to produce a green paper for the fall of 1980, and it would seek inspiration in the spirit and regionalist tendencies of the Task Force on Canadian Unity, which had submitted its report in 1979. Short of conceding special status to Quebec, Canada would be conceived as a community of communities, thus recognizing the provinces' right to be the principal architects of their own development. In the pages of Le Devoir, Michel Roy wrote that the Clark government seemed eager to satisfy some of Quebec's traditional demands by means of a system of intergovernmental delegation.[24]

The francophone press was not alone in its surprise over Trudeau's silence on many subjects. In the Gazette, Richard Gwyn compared Trudeau's failure to discuss national unity and the repatriation of the constitution to "newspeak," referring to George Orwell's novel 1984.[25] Also writing in the Gazette, Ian MacDonald claimed that Trudeau had clearly shown at the start of the campaign that he preferred to avoid the Quebec question.[26] A few weeks later, MacDonald had in no way changed his view: "It is evident that Pierre Trudeau, who has made his career on the Quebec question, now intends to bring it up as little as possible – if at all – in the winter campaign."[27] In MacDonald's eyes, this was a strange turnaround, to say the least. In another article, MacDonald compared Trudeau's campaign to Clark's. He called attention to the fact that the Conservative leader did not avoid the constitutional question, that he came regularly to Quebec, and that he frequently used French during his speeches in English Canada. The contrast with Trudeau was striking; silent on the constitution, Trudeau had spent barely two days in Quebec during eight weeks of campaigning and was tightfisted in his use of French: "By contrast Trudeau has been loath to utter more than a perfunctory chers amis outside Quebec."[28] William Johnson, who worked for the *Globe and Mail* at the time, corroborated MacDonald's analysis. He argued that Trudeau was taking refuge in English Canada's indifference as his explanation of why the constitutional question was relegated to oblivion. According to Johnson, Canadians would soon know Joe Clark's constitutional position. As for Pierre Trudeau, he most certainly had one; however, he was careful not to rekindle the voters' memory of it in any way.[29]

Only in the last days of the campaign, during speeches delivered in Toronto and Vancouver, did Trudeau return to his preferred themes – a great Canadian nation and a strong central government. In an interview with *Le Devoir*, he gave his own interpretation of coming events in Quebec. The people of Quebec would first have to state clearly whether they were in favour of independence, whether they wished Quebec to separate from the rest of Canada.[30] He felt that this must happen before any genuine discussions on the renewal of federalism could occur, and he specified that the discussions would be virtually impossible as long as René Lévesque and the Parti québécois were at the helm in Quebec. Yet the reader will note that barely three months later, with the cinders of the referendum battle still smouldering, Trudeau urgently requested that discussions on the constitution begin.

In my opinion, the February 1980 election represents a turning point in Trudeau's attitude towards the constitution. Until then, he truly deserved his reputation as a lucid and trenchant analyst of federalism and of the mechanism he favoured for policy making in this area. But the closer the referendum deadline approached, the more he tended towards imprecision, towards ambiguity. As I have tried to demonstrate, his behaviour in the political context of 1979–80 confirms this interpretation. The same is true of his activity in the ideological sphere, as can be seen if we look more closely at the theme of "renewed federalism."

Ideological activity in the field of renewed federalism was dominated in 1979–80 by the publication of two reports. Formed in the months following the Parti québécois' rise to power, and co-chaired by John Robarts and Jean-Luc Pepin, the Task Force on Canadian Unity released the first volume of its report in January 1979. The

Constitutional Committee of the Quebec Liberal Party offered its beige paper for criticism in January 1980.

The Pepin-Robarts approach was reminiscent of the Laurendeau-Dunton Commission's *Preliminary Report* (1965). It simultaneously acknowledged the existence of a crisis and the emergence of a new "opportunity." The overall view was broadened, however, to take into account the social evolution of Canada. While reiterating that duality remained the principal challenge facing the country, the task force's report, *A Future Together*, noted that regionalist divisions were increasingly becoming a priority. With advice from political analysts and constitutional experts of the calibre of Léon Dion, John Meisel, Edward McWhinney, and Ronald Watts, the task force hoped to reach a historic agreement with the modern Quebec that had emerged from the Quiet Revolution. Its report really went a long way towards recognizing the distinct character of Quebec society, listing a whole series of elements constituting this specificity: Quebec's history, the French language, the legal system, the population's ethnic origins, individual and collective outlooks, and the shift in the political identity of francophones, henceforth defined in terms of their majority status in Quebec, rather than their minority status within Canada as a whole. *A Future Together* recognized Quebec's right to self-determination sixteen months before the 1980 referendum. It also proposed that the preamble of any new constitution should recognize, among other things, the distinct character of Quebec and the existence of a historic partnership between English and French Canadians. The spirit that prevailed in the writing of the report is well summed up in the following passage:

Nevertheless if we perceive the Canadian duality in a political perspective as the expression of two realities, neither of which is superior to the other, then to recognize the distinctiveness of each is not to confer upon either of them a "special" or "privileged" status. Each is as special as the other: the only special feature is that one of the dualities is expressed politically at the level of provincial governments by nine and the other by one ...

Let us put our conviction strongly: Quebec is distinctive and should, within a viable Canada, have the powers necessary to protect and develop its distinctive character; any political solution short of this would lead to the rupture of Canada."[31]

The co-signatories of *A Future Together* shared the view that the recognition of diversity, as well as the modernization of our political institutions, would pave the way for a strengthening of Canadian identity. Their recommendations, had they been adopted, would have meant the beginning of a fundamental review of the Canadian federation. Their proposals included the abolition of the federal government's powers of disallowance and reservation, the transfer of residual powers to the provinces, curtailment of the federal spending power gradually accrued in areas of provincial jurisdiction, and the need for any constitutional reform to be ratified by a referendum, with majority support in each of the four regions of the country as the condition of amendment. The report also recognized Québec's special responsiblity to promote its culture and its distinct national heritage. All the provinces – not only Quebec – would have enjoyed greater powers in the social and cultural fields. Another recommendation involved the abolition of the Senate, which was to be replaced by a House of the Federation made up of sixty representatives named by the provinces. The Supreme Court was to be modified too: five judges out of a total of eleven were to be experts in civil law, and the provinces would be consulted systematically on the nomination of these judges. Finally, it should be noted that the report proposed to add sixty new members to the House of Commons, elected under a system of proportional representation. This, by and large, was what the Task Force on Canadian Unity meant by renewed federalism in the winter of 1979.

Like all constitutional reform projects, the Pepin-Robarts Report had to experience the pangs of criticism, of public reception. Pierre Elliott Trudeau described it as a "landmark contribution." However, he guarded himself well against officially ratifying any of the task force's recommendations. Considering that Mr Trudeau was the elected prime minister in 1979 and that during the federal election of that year he openly campaigned in favour of his own ideas on national unity and constitutional reform, it is reasonable to claim that he clearly dissociated himself from the Pepin-Robarts Report. In other words, the document was shelved by the federal government. Nonetheless, the ideas put forward in *A Future Together* received great support in Quebec. Those intellectuals and politicians who persisted in wanting to reconcile Québécois nationalism and Canadian federalism (for instance, Léon Dion, and also Solange Chaput-Rolland and Gérald Beaudoin, both of whom were members of the task force) interpreted the report as a symbol of the federal system's flexibility.[32]

Some four months before the 1980 referendum, yet another public document sketched out the features of renewed federalism. *A New Canadian Federation*, the Report of the Constitutional Committee of the Quebec Liberal Party, led by Claude Ryan, unquestionably belonged to the same intellectual family as the Pepin-Robarts Report. Like the members of the federal task force, the Quebec Liberals had adopted the vocabulary popularized by André Laurendeau in the 1960s. The basic premise of this report (which has come to be known as the "beige paper") was made clear in its first pages: "Within the Canadian political family, Quebec society has all the characteristics of a distinct national community."[33] Like the task force, the authors of the beige paper foresaw in this crisis an opportunity to renew Canadian federalism. They recognized that the Canadian experience had generally been quite positive, especially regarding the protection of freedom. They stressed, however, that Quebec occupied a very special position in Canada and in North America as a whole, being the only predominantly francophone society, and they added that the people of Quebec were urgently seeking a form of federalism that would be flexible enough to make room in its institutions for Quebec's legitimate aspirations.[34] The objectives stated in the beige paper show that the authors wished to find a compromise between Québécois nationalists, on one side, and Mr Trudeau's government and those of the English-Canadian provinces on the other. These objectives included affirmation of the equality of the two founding peoples, the granting of guarantees that would satisfy Quebec without contradicting the principle of equality among all partners of the federation, and recognition of the judicial primacy of individual rights and fundamental freedoms.

Thus, Mr Trudeau and the authors of the beige paper saw eye to eye with respect to enshrining a charter of rights in the constitution. However, the beige paper distanced itself considerably from the prime minister in advocating radical decentralization of the Canadian political system. This was to begin with the abolition of the Senate, as it had existed since 1867, and its replacement by a new Federal Council, made up of delegates chosen by the provinces. This new legislative body would be called on to ratify the use of the federal government's emergency and spending powers, as well as the nomination of judges to the Supreme Court. On questions relating to duality, the new council would assume the form of a standing committee made up of an equal number of English and French delegates. Short of going as far as the Pepin-Robarts Report in reshaping the Supreme Court, the beige paper nonetheless proposed that the latter operate as a dualist constitutional court in particular circumstances. It also recommended that several of the central government's unilateral powers be eliminated: the powers of reservation and disallowance, the declaratory power, and the possibility of legislating the protection of peace, order, and good government in an unlimited fashion. The beige paper also advocated the transfer of residual powers to the provinces. The decentralizing effect would have been heightened by the reinforcement of provincial autonomy in the areas of education and culture, and by the devolution of increased responsibilities in the areas of social security and unemployment insurance.

Given Quebec's exclusion in 1982 and the context leading up to the derailment of the Meech Lake Accord in 1990, it is useful to note that the beige paper recommended that the federal government and the legislatures of all the provinces, without exception, ratify a new constitution. Claude Ryan's Liberals also demanded Quebec's right to veto any further changes pertaining to the division of powers, the Charter of Rights, and the status of official languages. In conclusion, the authors of the beige paper alluded directly to the political context in Quebec on the eve of the referendum:

A majority of Quebecers undoubtedly prefer to continue to be part of the whole Canadian federation. However, to pursue this option, even the most moderate of them now demand that the Canadian federal framework reflect more faithfully the political and social realities of today. Above all they demand that it recognize and guarantee, in a more explicit manner, the desire for equality of Francophones and Quebec. To fulfil this expectation, major changes are needed at the constitutional level. No simple replastering or cosmetics will suffice.[35]

With such a document to back him up, Claude Ryan had everything he needed to become a champion of renewed federalism in the referendum debate. Pierre Elliott Trudeau was not long in responding to the publication of this manifesto. According to him, it was conceived in a constructive spirit and represented an extremely serious basis for further discussions. He refused, however, to be part of a debate on its specifics. He argued that there would be ample time for such discussions after the February federal election.[36] Barely two weeks later, Mr Chrétien, who was soon to become Claude Ryan's shadow in the referendum campaign, displayed much greater enthusiasm, hailing the unprecedented appearance of an option formulated by a Quebec leader, an option that could serve as a springboard for real negotiations.

Pierre Trudeau never explicitly dissociated himself from the beige paper. As we have just seen, he remained utterly silent on the subject during the federal election campaign of January and February 1980. His silence must be compared to the studied precision of the supporters of renewed federalism in Quebec, from the members of the Task Force on Canadian Unity to the authors of the beige paper. The work of the Constitutional Committee of the Quebec Liberal Party and that of the Pepin-Robarts group were the source of numerous discussions in political and intellectual circles in Quebec. To cite but one example, the beige paper was severely criticized for having knelt excessively before the altar of regionalism, and this at the expense of Quebec's sacrosanct specificity. The authors were blamed for having chosen a systematic decentralization of powers for all the provinces rather than special status for Quebec. These discussions did not create a consensus in favour of any of the reform projects then circulating. However, they did clearly circumscribe the meaning that "renewed federalism" could take on in Quebec at that time.

This brief retrospective enables us to conclude that after the federal election, some three months before the referendum deadline, Mr Trudeau's position remained ambiguous. The great spring battle that was soon to begin would allow all the participants who so wished to lay all their cards on the table and confront each other openly.

THE REFERENDUM CAMPAIGN

As prime minister of Canada, Pierre Elliott Trudeau was careful not to involve himself in the daily skirmishes of the referendum campaign. He entrusted his minister of justice, Jean Chrétien, with the task of accompanying Claude Ryan in his tours throughout Quebec. Trudeau thus remained above the fray, targeting his interventions so as to achieve maximum effect. His first major speech was delivered to the House of Commons on 15 April 1980. It came after Lise Payette's error of judgment provoked the emergence of the "Yvettes" movement, thus breaking the momentum that the Yes camp had gained during the debate in the National Assembly. As usual, Trudeau was brilliant, incisive, unequivocal: sovereignty association would lead to an impasse, since the federal government and the governments of the English-Canadian provinces would refuse to negotiate an economic association with the Péquiste government.[37] The prime minister added that even a positive response to the referendum question would not give René Lévesque a precise mandate to achieve sovereignty, especially since Trudeau knew he did not have a mandate to negotiate Quebec's independence. At the dawn of the campaign, the message from Ottawa had the merit of being clear: a Yes vote would lock Quebec within the status quo. Ten days later, Mr Trudeau wrote an open letter to his compatriots in Quebec, warning them not to expect miracles if the No camp triumphed on the evening of 20 May; real reforms would be impossible as long as a government bent on the destruction of federalism held power in Quebec. Trudeau nevertheless promised to devote all his energies to the project of renewing the constitution.[38]

Readers will remember that Mr Trudeau's polemical responses to Marcel Adam and Claude Morin openly extolled frankness and candour as virtues of political debate, as the course of honourable adversaries who come out into the open and lay their cards on the table. He spoke this language of clarity and honesty on 2 May 1980 in Montreal, during his first real foray into the referendum campaign. There he praised such early leaders of the independence movement as Pierre Bourgault and André d'Allemagne for having courageously defended an idea that did not lack nobility. Trudeau said that although he believed they were mistaken, he saw them as idealists endowed with a certain sense of honour.[39] They were honest and courageous people, he said – decidedly different from their successors, who spoke of sovereignty association in ambiguous terms and timidly requested a mandate to negotiate, promising that there would be a second referendum in any event. These manœuvres masked a faint-hearted strategy, according to Trudeau.

In this May 2 speech to the members of the Montreal Chamber of Commerce, Mr Trudeau made direct reference to Quebec as an autonomous political community within Canada, as well as to the people of Quebec taken as a whole. He pointed out that this community and its people would most likely be humiliated if the Yes camp triumphed in the referendum and the English-Canadian provinces then refused to negotiate an economic association with Quebec, as their premiers kept telling Quebecers they would. Trudeau criticized Lévesque and other sovereigntist leaders for proposing an option that left the responsibility of deciding Quebec's fate to others.[40] The theme of renewed federalism took a back seat in this speech. Trudeau insinuated that an independent Quebec would resemble Cuba or Haiti, and he found time to wonder aloud whether René Lévesque would agree to negotiate the renewal of federalism in good faith, should his side lose in the referendum.

On 7 May, in Quebec City, the themes of courage and moral strength were on the menu of a speech Trudeau delivered at a huge No rally. The federal leader shared the limelight that evening with Jean Lesage – the living symbol of modern Quebec and the Quiet Revolution – as well as with Claude Ryan, who was not only leader of the Quebec Liberal Party and of the opposition to the PQ, but was also the successor of André Laurendeau as editor of Le Devoir and éminence grise of renewed and asymmetrical federalism in Quebec. At a time when the polls registered that three-quarters of Quebec citizens felt a deep sense of belonging to Canada, the real question, according to Mr Trudeau, was whether these people were willing to abandon their Canadian identity.

Of all Trudeau's interventions, this was the most emotionally charged. He recalled that several great French Canadians had led the country, men such as Laurier and St Laurent, who had known how to work to build Canada with Quebec leaders of the calibre of Taschereau, Duplessis, and, of course, Jean Lesage. He said he found it much more courageous to fight for Canada, to preserve the right to what had always been and still was the whole of "our territory," rather than to retreat behind the walls of Quebec. Honour, pride, and true patriotism were on Canada's side. Finally, Trudeau reaffirmed his belief in his own ability to conduct successful negotiations on Quebec's place within Canada, and he concluded that it would therefore be pointless to break up the country.

The determining event of the campaign, and no doubt one of the decisive moments in Pierre Trudeau's political life, occurred on 14 May 1980 at Montreal's Paul Sauvé Centre, where Trudeau and other leaders of the No camp gave speeches before a crowd of more than ten thousand enthusiastic supporters. One could feel the euphoria of people who know that victory is at hand. A week away from the historic encounter, Trudeau finally consented to clarify the meaning of his message. Until then, he had devoted most of his efforts to recalling what a Yes vote would signify, namely, the impossibility of renewed federalism and eventually the destruction of Canada. Although he had sporadically commented on his own plans, they had not so far really caught the attention of the media or public opinion. But that night, profiting from the rather extraordinary nature of the occasion, Trudeau behaved as if he really wanted to act through the medium of his words, thus endorsing Skinner's and Austin's pragmatic approach, which I mentioned in the first pages of this chapter. He delivered his speech with the intelligence of a person determined to "hook" his audience. His target seems self-evident: he was aiming essentially at the undecided voters, those who were preparing to vote Yes for reasons of pride, solidarity, or because they did not truly understand the question, or else because they wished to strengthen Quebec's position as the inevitable negotiations with the rest of Canada drew near. In the solemn and pressing atmosphere that only such a rally could produce, Trudeau soared into an unforgettable and fateful flight of oratory:

I know because I spoke to the [Liberal] MPs this morning, I know that I can make the most solemn commitment that following a No, we will start immediately the mechanism of renewing the Constitution, and we will not stop until it is done. We are staking our heads, we Quebec MPs, because we are telling Quebecers to vote No, and we are saying to you in other provinces

that we will not accept having a No interpreted as an indication that everything is fine, and everything can stay as it was before. We want change, we
are staking our seats to have change.[41]

This could only signify the firmest commitment to change. In any
event, that was the interpretation given by the press and the elec-
tronic media. The next day, *Le Devoir* did not hesitate to run the
headline "Trudeau Is Committed to Renewing Federalism Immediately."[42] Concrete developments along these lines were to be expected
in the days and weeks following the referendum. This reading was
reinforced by Mr Trudeau's very last speech of the campaign, a
speech broadcast on television to all the people of Quebec forty-eight
hours before the referendum. The prime minister seemed to regain
his serenity as leaders and public opinion from the rest of Canada
accepted the need for change. The nation's population, he argued,
had finally understood both the urgency of the moment and Quebec's
aspirations. Yes, federalism would be renewed.

In his writings on the methodology of intellectual history, Quentin
Skinner attempts to reconcile principles that could, prima facie,
appear contradictory: the importance of considering an author's
explicit intentions in order to interpret the meaning of his texts,
coupled with the need, in certain circumstances, to reject the author's
account of his own intentions in order to get to the heart of the matter.
What the author has to say must be clearly defined. But according to
Skinner, an author may fail to recognize or reformulate the meaning
of words uttered in the past.[43]

I would not dare accuse Pierre Elliott Trudeau of incompetence. I
think, however, that I have sufficient evidence to ignore his contemporary remarks and those of my colleague Max Nemni regarding his
forays into the referendum campaign. Let us remember that in his
exchanges with Adam and Morin, Mr Trudeau posed as the apostle
of candour in political struggles. On numerous occasions he claimed
that leaders should not underestimate the judgment and intellectual
abilities of the ordinary citizen. Rather than scorning the people's
intelligence, one had to explain things as one saw them, without
diminishing their complexity. Trudeau maintained that he had
detected – and deplored – just such a contemptuous attitude among
the advocates of sovereignty association, who were unable to
acknowledge openly that their goal was indeed Quebec's independence. In his heart of hearts, Trudeau believed – and no doubt
continues to think – that he avoided succumbing to the temptation
of contempt and deceit. According to him, from 1967 until the referendum, he relentlessly stated that the renewal of federalism would

mean repatriating the constitution, in conjunction with the creation of a charter of rights and consolidation of the central government's powers. To claim the contrary would be tantamount to rewriting history.

In my opinion, it is Pierre Elliott Trudeau who perpetuates and promulgates a shameless distortion of history. During the federal election that preceded the referendum, he scarcely disclosed any of his constitutional plans. This was a complete contrast to the campaign of the spring of 1979, which was marked by resounding pleas for patriation and national unity. During the federal campaign of January and February 1980, Mr Trudeau was careful to avoid the continual repetition of his constitutional proposals. In fact, during all those weeks, he did not even deign to discuss the two documents that were intended as symbols and beacons of renewed federalism in Quebec, namely, the report of the Task Force on National Unity and the Quebec Liberals' beige paper. And to think that this man has the gall to taunt others about fighting openly!

These two reports were not identical, of course, but both gave expression to the conventional meaning of renewed federalism that had, in a certain sense, crystallized in Quebec during the years 1979–80. The two reports had much in common. Both advocated enshrining Quebec's specificity within the constitution; both recommended involving the provinces more in the operations of federal institutions such as the Supreme Court and the Upper House; and both advocated abandoning or considerably reducing a whole panoply of special powers that make the Canadian federation a quasi-unitary political system, according to Donald Smiley.[44] To paraphrase Trudeau's televised speech of two days before the referendum, these two reports displayed an undeniable sensitivity to the aspirations that Quebec had nurtured since the Quiet Revolution, for they at least partly promised that federalism would be rebuilt according to dualist and bicultural parameters.

It may happen that some people will read these lines at a time when Quebec is once more caught in the throes of a referendum. I would like those readers to recall that during the entire year preceding May 1980, Mr Trudeau chose to abstain from discussions regarding the various facets of renewed federalism in Quebec. Yet in the last week – indeed, even in the last days of the campaign – he did not hesitate to step onto ideological and conceptual ground that had been prepared by persons other than himself. He stated unequivocally that a Yes vote would result in the status quo, that he would work fervently to bring about changes, and that it took courage to promote the cause of Canada. I would like readers to remember that in 1980 we were indeed promised that Quebec's demands would be satisfied, that there would be reforms, and that the leaders of the federation – Mr Trudeau, first and foremost – were committing themselves to this in the most solemn fashion. These reforms, we were told, would get under way immediately after the referendum.

In this context, I believe that the illocutionary force of Mr Trudeau's actions and speeches, and in particular his intervention at the Paul Sauvé Centre, become quite clear. What was Pierre Trudeau doing when he expressed to his audience the desire to work on a speedy transformation of the Canadian constitution? In reality, he was trying, I believe, to convince undecided voters to support the No camp. To achieve this, he multiplied his ambiguous references to renewed federalism and the vocabulary associated with it. If I understand Skinner's methodological nuances correctly, to throw light on Trudeau's rhetorical manœuvres is to discover some of his intentions. When a statement has been adequately inserted into its political and ideological contexts, we learn much about the meaning of the message that an author or orator transmits to his public. The facts clearly show that Trudeau intended to speak ambiguously. Everything he has said on the matter over the last few years is indisputably interesting, but that is not necessarily more important than the real story behind the whole affair. I do not harbour illusions about my own contribution, and I know that I will certainly not succeed in closing the debate on Trudeau and the referendum; nevertheless, I will at least have shown readers another way of addressing this chapter of our history.

CONCLUSION

It is impossible to overemphasize the importance of the referendum of May 1980 in the history of the Quebec people. On the political level, the referendum was an act of self-determination, but to this must be added the ontological dimension of the referendum campaign. It belonged to the type of collective action that consolidates the existence of a people, a nation, in the minds of its members as well as in the minds of observers who, living abroad, might entertain doubts about the future of this particular political community. In 1980, for the first time in their history, Quebecers, the heirs of the British Conquest, were invited to express themselves as a people on the question of their membership in a political system. According to the British philosopher John Locke, on whose thought I shall base the next chapter, only explicit consent, such as Quebecers granted in 1980, can crown institutions with legitimacy. But legitimacy is not eternal. In the spirit of our institutions, which owe much to Locke, elected representatives must act in such a manner as to preserve the trust invested in them.

During the 1980 referendum, the people of Quebec renewed their trust in Pierre Elliott Trudeau and Canadian federalism without thereby giving blind approval to all later actions of those who wielded political authority. In a representative democracy, there is no such thing as a blank cheque. Hindsight makes clear the whole extent of Quebec's remarkable show of confidence in 1980. Less than two years later, the principal beneficiary of this trust, Pierre Elliott Trudeau, imposed a new constitution on Canada and Quebec, without the latter's consent and in defiance of the will of the National Assembly and the Government of Quebec. Let us examine the meaning of Trudeau's actions more closely.

So far, I have claimed that Trudeau knowingly remained ambiguous in 1980. But it is not enough to leave it at that. If I am correct, one can say that Trudeau's actions fostered greater ideological ambiguity about the nature of renewed federalism, for they instilled doubt in the minds of some citizens. What proportion of the electorate was affected by these remarks? We shall never really know, and in truth it hardly matters. The essential point is to be sought elsewhere.

It is not unusual for a politician to be vague or imprecise and to benefit from the electorate as a result. Some realistic observers would go so far as to claim that it is always thus. In a certain sense, Trudeau merely followed in the footsteps of his predecessors. Like the gardener who carefully tends his spring flowers even though he knows they are ephemeral, Trudeau nurtured his favourite flower, his doubt concerning the nature of renewed federalism. For him as for every gardener, the flower's vulnerability did not diminish its worth. However, the spring of 1980 was exceptional. The referendum cannot be compared with the elections that regularly punctuate the political life of a people. It is not enough, therefore, to say that Trudeau veiled his statements with ambiguity. To determine the real impact of his actions, one must consider the chosen time and place of their occurrence, as well as their specific political context. As a son of Quebec and the most important political leader of the Canadian federation, Pierre Elliott Trudeau chose to be ambiguous at what was clearly the most crucial moment in the history of the Quebec people. On 14 May 1980, at that temple of Quebec nationalism, the Paul Sauvé Centre, in an atmosphere laden with solemnity, Trudeau promised to renew Canadian federalism. He went so far as to lay his career and those of his Liberal colleagues on the line. And he did all this less than a week before the referendum. To my knowledge, never before in

Canadian history were a politician's statements uttered in such grave
circumstances. I wager that more than one reader remembers those
events as though they happened yesterday.

Politicians have a duty, just as gardeners have with their crops. The
trust that the citizens – their compatriots – temporarily invest in them
must be cherished above all else. This trust is not a buttonhole that
one wears and then discards at the end of the day. In all likelihood,
Pierre Elliott Trudeau did not lie in the spring of 1980. However, he
was unworthy of the trust that the people of Quebec placed in him.
He neglected that trust, though he was its supreme guardian. As we
shall see more fully in the next chapter, when such a flower fades,
the stalk upon which a political system rests begins to wither. At the
time of the referendum on sovereignty association, it was already
possible to foresee the storms that were to shake Canadian federalism
in the 1990s.

This reading of Trudeau's course of action during the referendum
puts another complexion on the debate surrounding the ratification
of the Meech Lake Accord. The relationship of trust between Trudeau
and the Quebec electorate began to wilt in 1980. It deteriorated
further in 1981–82 when the constitution was modified without Quebec's consent. Peter Leslie, a political analyst who worked that year
in Joe Clark's task force on constitutional affairs, not long ago recognized the gravity of violating the fundamental principle that a government's legitimacy rests on the citizens' consent. According to
Leslie, such a violation "offends against democracy and imperils the
political stability of a country whose people are committed to democracy."[45] Donald Smiley, the late political analyst, who was one of the
greatest experts on Canadian federalism, ventured even further:

In general, then, an exercise in constitutional review and reform whose
alleged objectives were to create more harmonious relations between Quebec
and the wider Canadian community has involved a betrayal of the Quebec
electorate, a breach of fundamental constitutional convention, a recrudes-
cence of Quebec nationalism, and an even more serious Quebec challenge
than before to the legitimacy of the Canadian constitutional order.[46]

Pierre Elliott Trudeau's assault on the Meech Lake Accord, to
which I shall return in chapter 5, assumed several forms. Trudeau's
most fundamental criticism appears be that, basically, the Meech Lake
operation was totally pointless; he believed he had promised to
renew federalism during the referendum and had subsequently
delivered the goods. The 1981–82 repatriation of the constitution and
enactment of the Canadian Charter of Rights and Freedoms had been

heralded for years. There was thus no abuse of power, no breach of trust, and no collapse of legitimacy.

The participants in the Meech Lake debate stood in one or the other camp, according to their acceptance or refusal of Trudeau's rhetoric. I am among those who believe that the former prime minister rewrote history by emphasizing continuity and untrammelled trust in his interpretation of the referendum. In 1980, Pierre Elliott Trudeau's buttonhole wilted. Let us now consider how the constitutional reform of 1981–82 dried up the dualist flower bed of the Canadian federalist garden.

CHAPTER TWO

John Locke and the Constitutional Deadlock between Canada and Quebec

Nineteen eighty-nine marked the bicentenary of the French Revolution, an event widely celebrated in France as everywhere else in the world.[1] The mystique that continues to surround the French Revolution has helped to erase the anniversary of another political upheaval, one that is particularly significant for Canadian and Quebec institutions: England's Glorious Revolution of 1688–89. The Glorious Revolution culminated in the emergence of a limited, constitutional monarchy, which respected the principle of the "rule of law" and was more aware of the function of Parliament.

A detailed analysis of the historical and legal context of the Glorious Revolution is still relevant in itself. It fosters a better understanding of the origins of the political liberalism that typifies modern democracies. Closer to home, we find that some of the work that the Glorious Revolution has inspired in the area of political theory furnishes the key to a more lucid analysis of the constitutional and political impasse prevailing in Canada. John Locke's political thought between 1680 and 1690 can help shed new light on the turbulent 1980s, a decade highlighted by the referendum campaign and the debate around the Meech Lake Accord. Locke's ideas will also help us understand what a national referendum meant for Quebec in 1992, during the Canada round of constitutional negotiations, and what it might well mean in the near future.

THE NATURE OF THE GLORIOUS REVOLUTION AND THE POLITICAL THOUGHT OF JOHN LOCKE

What in fact happened in England some three centuries ago, in 1688–89? Those years were marked by the accession of William of Orange and his wife Mary to the throne that James II had occupied since 1685. This transition was neither smooth nor ordinary. During his short reign, the very Catholic James II had united virtually the whole country against him. He had strengthened his position through the expedient of a permanent army and had unilaterally modified the rules of parliamentary elections, as well as annulling the Test Act and the criminal laws against Roman Catholics. The birth of his son in 1688 drove even the most ardent defenders of the monarchy within the nobility and the Church of England to act against him. Tories and Whigs alike urged William of Orange to avert the triumph of absolutism and papism in England.

William landed at Torbay in November 1688; and James II, fearing the worst for his family and himself, hastily fled to the continent. In February 1689, William and Mary accepted the Declaration of Rights, thus recognizing the crucial significance of parliamentary prerogatives. This step clearly represented the disappearance of absolute monarchy and its replacement with the system of limited government. In the weeks that followed the solemn reading of the Declaration of Rights before the new monarchs, the philosopher John Locke put an end to his exile in Holland. He had fled the country some years earlier after the aborted plots against Charles II. On his return to England, Locke began publishing his works on psychology, religion, and politics – works that would soon bring him great fame.

For a long time, historians of political thought believed (and several still do) that John Locke wrote and published *Two Treatises of Government*[2] in order to justify the events linked to the Glorious Revolution. They considered Locke to be the official ideologue of the system of limited constitutional monarchy. A good example of this interpretation is the comment of André Jardin, De Tocqueville's biographer, who wrote that Locke wished to legitimize the moderate institutions that enable individual rights to flourish in the finest tradition of political liberalism.[3] Intellectual historians have often associated this moderation with Locke's personality. In the nineteenth century, Macaulay stressed that Locke's empiricist and prudent philosophical temper would have made him most unwilling to participate in the conspiracies that marked the fate of English politics during the 1680s.[4] And in a recent edition of the *Second Treatise*, Simone Goyard-Fabre, a French intellectual historian reknown for the rigour and seriousness of her work, endorsed the belief that "Locke's life was not punctuated by extraordinary events. It was modest and ruled by work."[5]

Over the past twenty years, an extraordinary wave of renewal has swept through the Anglo-American cultural sphere of Lockean studies.[6] The arguments of a Canadian philosopher, Crawford Brough Macpherson, have served as a starting point for most of the work done by this revisionist school. Two of the salient themes in this research pertain directly to the issues just raised: that it would be wrong to believe that Locke was the ideologue of the Glorious Revolution, and that his life did not in fact unfold at a remove from the extraordinary events that rocked England in his day.

For fifteen years, Locke was secretary and adviser to Lord Shaftesbury, the most important opposition politician of Restoration England. Beginning in 1666–67, when they first met, Locke fought at Shaftesbury's side against Catholicism and absolute monarchy, and for religious tolerance and civil liberties. During Shaftesbury's lifetime, Locke's pamphlet writing and opposition to Charles II's policies cost him four years of exile in France. After Shaftesbury's death, in 1683, the activity of Locke and the radicals intensified. They went so far as to plot to kidnap and assassinate the king, for they had lost all hope of being able to prevent the Catholic Duke of York, the future James II, from ascending the throne. They were sure that James would miss no opportunity to hurl England into the arms of absolutism and of Louis XIV, king of France. The plot was discovered and Locke once more went into exile. Some of his fellow conspirators were less fortunate and perished on the scaffold. Locke spent five years among English dissidents in Holland, during which time he and his comrades sat by helplessly as the Catholic and absolutist stranglehold tightened all over Europe. The reader will recall how, in 1685, Louis XIV revoked the Edict of Nantes, which had guaranteed the rights of the French Protestants, the Huguenots. Exile did not destroy the dissidents' morale, however. They pursued the struggle against James II, and Locke was involved in preparing an expedition commanded by the Duke of Monmouth, which proved to be a miserable failure.[7]

The philosopher only returned to England in February 1689, after James II's departure and William of Orange's accession to the throne. His famous *Letter on Toleration* was published the same year, followed by the appearance of *An Essay concerning Human Understanding* and *Two Treatises of Government* in 1690.[8] In view of all this, one can hardly claim that Locke led a quiet life before becoming the official ideologue of the Glorious Revolution and its constitutional and political legacy.

Inasmuch as the Glorious Revolution can rightly be considered the starting point of political liberalism in modern times, we must recognize that Locke's thought had much in common with it. In *Two Treatises of Government*, he eloquently stressed the virtues of a limited government in which legislative and executive power ought not be entrusted to one and the same person. He spent much time lauding the importance of the legislative body, that true soul of the political community, where elected representatives must constantly remember that they are to work for the public good as keepers of the voters' trust.[9]

This notion of trust is crucial to Locke's political thought. To disturb this trust is probably the worst political error one could possibly commit. In advocating representative democracy, modern liberal systems of government have inherited from Locke and the Glorious Revolution a certain distrust of political participation. Locke himself did not hesitate to consider it a burden.[10] In the spirit of the Glorious Revolution, he was inclined to trust governments and, for example, to leave the executive branch considerable room for manœuvre. The common spirit that linked Locke to the events of 1688–89 also included the principle of the "rule of law." Locke abhorred the personalization of power; it was synonymous with absolutism and arbitrary power. He thought that human beings had consented to the emergence of civil society, of political community, in order to preserve their property, which was understood to be the right to life, liberty, and the possession of material goods. Contrary to Hobbes – the absolutist English philosopher, whose main works were published between 1640 and 1655, during the turmoil of the Civil War – Locke claimed that the preservation of property required the government's submission to the laws that it established and applied.

One can gain a better understanding of the thrust of Locke's works in the last two decades of the seventeenth century if one considers the Glorious Revolution in the more general context of European affairs. Even though he was by no means wholly satisfied with the compromise of 1689 between the English Parliament and William of Orange, Locke resolutely sided with the British crown in the struggles it sought to engage in on various fronts in Europe. Short of vindicating religious tolerance as strongly as he had hoped, William must be credited with making England a fortress against abolutism and Catholic imperialism. Locke thus participated in the administrative consolidation of the English state.[11]

Locke's efforts in the 1690s were directed towards safeguarding and promoting England's national interests. This makes it harder to grasp the surprisingly radical character of his political thought in *Two Treatises of Government*. In sum, one may claim without too much risk of error that Locke was on the side of the merchant and industrial classes. He participated in England's struggle to win commercial supremacy in Europe, in its efforts to dominate non-European populations and exploit their resources. In short, his cause was that of English imperialism.

Nonetheless, Locke's lucidly stated political theory, which comes across with exceptional clarity in his *Second Treatise of Government*, is one of the most remarkable expressions of liberal radicalism at the dawn of the modern era. Between 1679 and 1681, English politics had been dominated by the exclusion crisis. Three parliamentary elections had taken place within two years, and the same theme dominated them all. The party in opposition, to which Shaftesbury and Locke belonged, wanted to bar the Duke of York from succeeding to the throne, because they feared his Catholic proselytizing. Participation in these elections was extremely high; in fact, it was during this crisis that the Whig party was born as a result of the opposition's forces rallying together.[12] The Whigs won on three occasions, and each time King Charles II dissolved the new Parliament as swiftly as he could. After the failure of this reformist strategy, which had held to the existing institutional structure, the Whig movement became more radical. Locke wrote the *Two Treatises of Government* primarily to justify this hardening of attitude.

Locke's political thought was built around the notion of trust. He was willing to grant this trust generously, but he could become just as merciless in his judgment when he felt that the trust had been abused. At the dawn of modern times, Locke developed a political theory favouring both the individual and popular sovereignty. In so far as he believed that the passage from the state of nature to civil society, to the political community, required individual consent expressed in the form of a contract, he is to be ranked among the advocates of individualism, not to mention political atomism.[13] The precondition of this consent enables the community to endow itself with a proper government. Thanks to a majority vote, the community delegates its authority to the wielders of legislative and executive power. Locke's radicalism arises out of the notion that sovereign authority returns to the people when government has abused its power, when it has broken the pact of trust that ties it to the citizens as a whole. Such a breach of trust is tantamount to a dissolution of government, annulling the people's obligation to obey and respect that authority:

In these and the like cases, when the Government is dissolved, the People are at liberty to provide for themselves, by erecting a new legislative, differing from the other, by the change of Persons, or Form, or both as they shall find it most for their safety and good. For the Society can never, by the fault of another, lose the Native and Original Right it has to preserve itself, which can only be done by a settled legislative, and a fair and impartial execution of the laws made by it.[14]

John Locke wrote *Two Treatises of Government* between 1680 and 1683 to provide a manifesto to a Whig movement that was becoming so disillusioned with Charles II that it was ready to opt for a revolutionary strategy and to relinquish reformism.

Locke was quite well disposed towards the British constitutional tradition of executive prerogative. He was in favour of its capacity to act vigorously, in the public interest, "because it is impossible to foresee, and so by laws to provide for, all Accidents and Necessities."[15] In his time, as indeed in ours, the convening and dissolution of Parliament came under this executive prerogative. Yet one of the Whigs' great charges against Charles II was the repeated dissolution of Parliament during the exclusion crisis, which they believed precipitated the collapse of the government:

It may be demanded here, What if the Executive Power being possessed of the Force of the Commonwealth, shall make use of that force to hinder the meeting and acting of the legislative, when the Original Constitution, or the publick Exigencies require it? I say using Force upon the People or without Authority, and contrary to the Trust put in him, that does so, is a state of War with the People, who have a right to reinstate their legislative in the Exercise of their Power.[16]

For the Shaftesbury Whigs, it was patently clear that Charles II was the real rebel and hence that he had declared war on his people. He belonged to that group of ferocious beasts, to use Locke's vocabulary, who threaten the citizens' liberty and property.

When Locke's manuscript was completed in 1682–83, he did not publish it. The Whigs' resistance was eroding, and Locke had to go into exile. He did not seriously reflect on *Two Treatises of Government* again until five years later, in the midst of the Glorious Revolution. As we saw above, James II had left England, and William of Orange was in the process of accepting the conditions of Parliament. Locke was very displeased with the unfolding political situation. Under James II, just as under Charles II, if not more so, the conditions had been present for a genuine dissolution of the government, with a constituent authority devolving on the people. James II had attacked the legislative branch, the very basis of any political community. By annulling the Test Act, by smashing the criminal laws against Catholics, by unilaterally modifying the electoral laws, and by accepting the authority of a foreign power, the papacy, he had perverted the social pact. Trust had been shattered, and the people were freed of their obligations. Locke therefore fought for the election of an expanded constituent assembly, which in his view was the only type of body that would be able to respect Shaftesbury's political testament: the struggle for civil liberties and religious tolerance.

When the government had been dissolved, Locke preferred to trust the people. He did not wish to leave matters in the hands of intermediary bodies.[17] Parliamentary sovereignty would not suffice. In this, he was considerably ahead of his time. *Two Treatises of Government*[18] was regarded as a radical manifesto, and Locke was not heeded. He found himself marginalized even within the Whig movement. To appeal to the people, to grant them the right of resistance, smacked too much of democratic radicalism. To allow artisans, shopkeepers, and small-scale property owners to participate in decisions as fundamental as those concerning the nation's constitution seemed unrealistic and foolhardy in 1689. Yet this is unquestionably what Locke desired when he published his manuscript: "Upon the Forteiture of their Rulers, or at the Determination of the Time set, it reverts to the Society, and the People have a Right to act as Supreme, and continue the Legislative themselves, or erect a new Form, or under the old form place it in new hands, as they think good."[19]

The constitutional compromise of 1689 meant failure for John Locke and his doctrine of popular sovereignty. Parliamentary traditions and distrust of popular judgment won the day. However, the Lockean concepts of consent, trust, resistance, constituent power, and devolution can act as guideposts in the constitutional imbroglio of Canada and Quebec.

DISSOLUTION OF GOVERNMENT IN CANADA IN THE 1980S

Since 17 April 1982, Canada has possessed all the attributes of sovereignty. On that day, the last judicial and colonial ties with Great Britain were broken. The Constitution Act, 1982, enabled Prime Minister Pierre Elliott Trudeau to realize one of his great political dreams, namely, to patriate our constitution and to enrich it by way of a charter of rights and freedoms. Ever since then, the federal government has used the new constitution to strengthen allegiance to Canada and to promote Canadian identity. Thanks to the intervention of the federal bureaucracy, 17 April has become Citizenship Day. The patriation process has taken its toll. From a strictly Lockean point of view, I venture to say that the events of the fall of 1981 and the spring of 1982 have marred the legitimacy of Canadian government institutions. For the people of Quebec, 17 April marks another day of defeat. Those who view it as an occasion for rejoicing are rare.

The events of the early part of the decade are well known.[20] In February 1980, Pierre Elliott Trudeau and the Liberal Party overthrew Joe Clark's Conservative minority government in a campaign that hardly touched on the constitution. Shortly thereafter, on 14 May, in the midst of the referendum campaign, Mr Trudeau solemnly promised that he and his supporters would work towards renewing Canadian federalism if the bid for sovereignty association was defeated. The promise was ambiguous. Did it mean acceptance of the program detailed in the Quebec Liberal Party's beige paper and advanced by Claude Ryan as leader of the No forces? Or was it an allusion to Mr Trudeau's ideas, which inclined towards a strong central government and towards a patriated constitution accompanied by a charter of rights and freedoms? The answer came swiftly in the days following the referendum. Mr Trudeau engaged in a massive constitutional offensive, with the intention of acting unilaterally if necessary. René Lévesque and the Parti québécois were re-elected in April 1981, and from the first days of their mandate they aligned themselves with a common front of eight provinces that were opposed to unilateral repatriation.

In hindsight, it is no doubt rather facile to claim that the PQ's strategy was destined to fail. Nevertheless, I still wonder how one can avoid seeing that Quebec's renunciation of its right of veto was a terrible mistake. In the autumn of 1981, the Supreme Court ruled that the federal initiative was legal but illegitimate. Substantial provincial consent was required, given our constitutional conventions. The Supreme Court did not reach a decision at that time on Quebec's right of veto, on political duality. It left that to the politicians. The federal government and the nine English provinces found a path of compromise on the night of 4 and 5 November 1981. This is the compromise we find expressed in the Constitution Act, 1982.

The Quebec government was excluded from the constitutional negotiations of 1981–82. The accord was formulated in its absence, and Quebec did not consent to it. At the National Assembly, a very large majority of both main parties opposed what had just transpired. In some circles, it was claimed that the federal government did not have any choice, that René Lévesque's party would never have consented to genuine reform of federalism. That is possible, though one cannot prove it. Those who require certainty must seek it elsewhere. What is certain is that no Quebec government would have signed that constitutional document in its present form.

Since 1982, Quebec has remained isolated, refusing to play along with any dialogue on further reforms to the constitution as long as certain conditions remain unsatisfied. In a general sense, one can say that no Quebec government will sign such a document until the distinct character of Quebec is recognized and until the institutional mechanisms (Supreme Court, Senate) and the division of powers are redefined. It is worth recalling that four constitutional conferences on aboriginal demands have taken place in Quebec's absence, and they all failed miserably.

As we know all too well, the Meech Lake agreement now belongs to history. It has entered the pantheon of those innumerable reform projects that have never been implemented. However, one important dimension of the agreement has been passed over in silence. More than ten years have passed since Brian Mulroney's famous speech in Sept-Iles in August 1984, when he promised to bring Quebec back into the great Canadian family with honour and enthusiasm. After the September 1984 election, the federal government, the official opposition, and the governments of the English-Canadian provinces redoubled their efforts to satisfy Quebec's demands. All these political actors recognized, directly or indirectly, the existence of a fundamental problem undermining the Canadian constitutional fabric – a fact that could only enhance the credibility of the questions that surfaced in Quebec about the legitimacy of the constitution. It should be remembered that the Meech Lake Accord was the finest effort in a decade to redress the injustice done to Quebec and to have done with the question of the legitimacy of institutions. The crucial significance of this question was evinced in the report that members of the Constitutional Committee of the Quebec Liberal Party, gathered around Jean Allaire, presented at their party conference in March 1991:

In Quebec, Confederation has always been perceived as a solemn pact between two nations, a pact that could not be changed without the consent of the two parties. Circumstances have made Quebec the "national state of French-Canadians," so it is easy to imagine the frustration felt by Quebeckers one morning in 1981 when they learned that their Constitution, the fundamental law of their country, would be amended without their agreement. Even more serious, an amending process was being institutionalized that would enable future amendments, again without the agreement of Quebec. Furthermore, this result contradicted a solemn promise of the Prime Minister of Canada. In a way, the Meech Lake Accord recognized the illegitimacy of a Constitution that failed to include Quebec.[21]

For Locke to apply in the context of Canada and Quebec, the validity of a basic postulate must be accepted, namely, the existence of a predominantly French-speaking people in the territory of Quebec, who puts their trust in a representative body, the National Assembly, as well as in a government that bears the responsibility of executive power in accordance with convention. Since Quebec belongs to a federation – Canada – the people of Quebec also put their trust in the Canadian Parliament and government. The Québécois regard themselves as a people, and act accordingly.[22] The May 1980 referendum was nothing other than the manifestation of the existence of a people called upon to give or refuse their assent to the transformation of their constitutional status.[23]

In a federal system, powers and responsibilities are divided between the federal government and those of the federated states. Any change in the division of powers entails a transformation of the constitution, altering the balance between the different legislative bodies and governments. John Locke would have been very clear on this issue. If there really is a people in Quebec, it is imperative that it be called on to consent to any readjustment of powers between the federal government and the federated states, between Canada and Quebec. Julian Franklin, a Locke specialist, goes even further. In his view, Locke made a fundamental distinction between ordinary power and constituent power. Locke made into a basic principle the idea that even a democratically elected representative body cannot alter the constitution of a society without first gaining the consent of the community as a whole.[24] Yet this is exactly what transpired between 1980 and 1982. The constitution was altered, and the legislative powers of the National Assembly of Quebec were reduced, notably with respect to issues of language – without the consent of the National Assembly or the Government of Quebec. The federal government, even though its members could with justification claim a portion of the Quebec people's trust, had no specific mandate to act as it did. Nor did it attempt to obtain that consent after the fact.

Those who were on the front line in 1981–82, starting with René Lévesque, virulently denounced this fundamental flaw – the lack of consent from the Quebec people. Claude Morin expressed particular bitterness in the recollections he published under the evocative title *Lendemains piégés*. In this book, he recalled that a predominantly anglophone government in Ottawa, supported by nine anglophone provinces, went to London to ask the British authorities, inter alia, to reduce the powers of the only francophone government in North America.[25] At that time, the Parti québécois government could have been more recalcitrant. It could have held a referendum, or it could have resigned and gone to the people in an election campaign. In their vacillation, the Péquiste leaders revealed the depth of demoralization and inertia that pervaded the Quebec government in the aftermath of May 1980, as the recession battered the province.

The disapproval did not come exclusively from the PQ or even Quebecers. Donald Smiley, one of the most acclaimed observers of

Canadian federalism, wrote that Quebec had been fooled and betrayed, that Prime Minister Trudeau's promises had not been honoured.[26] This is the Lockean language of abuse of power, of breach of trust. For Donald Smiley, it was clear that the conventions of the Canadian constitution had not been respected. Conscious of the role played by duality in the history of Canadian federalism, Smiley seemed representative of the English-Canadian intelligentsia's attitude towards the new constitution in the months that followed its proclamation. However, by the end of the decade, the situation was completely reversed. In just a few years, the symmetrical and anti-dualist logic of the Constitution Act, 1982, and the Charter of Rights and Freedoms had reshaped English Canada's political culture and intellectual élite. I shall consider this in more detail in the final chapters of this book.

In *Two Treatises of Government*, Locke wrote that a government is dissolved, the people consequently have the right to resist, and the supreme authority devolves on them "if either [the Prince's or Magistrate's] illegal Acts have extended to the Majority of the people; or if the Mischief and Oppression has light only on some few, but in such Cases, as the Precedent, and Consequences seem to threaten all."[27] Section 23 of the Charter of Rights and Freedoms reduces the National Assembly's powers with respect to the language of education. Given the evolution of Quebec nationalism (and without prejudice to the wisdom or fairness of Quebec's language laws), it seems reasonable to claim that this is one of those cases where the "Consequences seem to threaten all." Whatever the PQ government's responsibility may be in this affair, the same no doubt applies to the adoption of an amending formula that allows for constitutional change without the consent of either the Quebec government or the Quebec people. According to Locke, a government – and all the more so, a people – may not surrender its power in such matters.

In chapter 1 I clearly established that Prime Minister Trudeau knowingly delivered an ambiguous speech during the referendum campaign of May 1980. Admittedly, there will always be doubts about this in the minds of many citizens and observers. But in a period that is so extraordinarily significant in the history of the Quebec people, such ambiguity fully warrants the use of Locke's notion of the trust between those who govern and those who are governed. The respected political analyst Alan Cairns has invoked these doubts to challenge the criticism levelled at Trudeau's behaviour on the constitutional stage during the early part of the decade.[28] The methodology of the history of political ideas does not provide absolute certainties on such questions. Thus, if one really wishes to do battle with Trudeau and his supporters on the issue of trust, one has to search for an irrefutable argument somewhere other than the referendum saga. One motif that keeps resurfacing seems to be the modification of the legislative power that is conferred on the National Assembly by the people of Quebec – the diminution of the assembly's powers against its will and without popular consultation. Once more, Locke gives us food for thought:

For that being in effect the Legislative whose Rules and Laws are put in execution, and required to be obeyed; when other Laws are set up, and other Rules pretended, and inforced, than what the Legislative, constituted by the Society, have enacted, 'tis plain, that the Legislative is changed. Whoever introduces new Laws, not being thereunto authorized by the fundamental Appointment of the Society, or subverts the old, disowns and overturns the Power by which they were made and so sets up a new Legislative.[29]

Changes to the constitution without prior consent from (or later ratification by) the people of Quebec, an intervention in the areas of education and language (regarded as particularly important to Quebec), and modification of the National Assembly's powers – according to Locke's principles, all this should lead to the dissolution of government and the people's reappropriation of this authority, which they can only delegate. Within the parameters of a political system dominated by the principle of the renewal of trust, the people briefly return their legislative power to the rulers, who in turn must treat it with the greatest care. This legislative power is supreme and sacred.[30] Those who alter it in one way or another, as was the case in 1981–82, "take away this decisive power, which no Body can have but by the appointment and consent of the People."[31] At this point, it is important to stress that the former Quebec cabinet minister Gil Rémillard, one of the people most intimately involved in the process of constitutional revision, proposed a very Lockean reading of events. In 1980 Mr Rémillard, who was then professor of law at Laval University, had just completed a book on federalism, hoping that a renewal of the Canadian constitution would recognize the specifity of the Quebec people, of the Quebec nation.[32] Mr Rémillard subsequently deplored the lack of popular consultation during the patriation episode of 1981–82. According to him, the people's consent should have been sought before sending a resolution to the Parliament in Westminster. That would have prevented – the expression is my own – the spectre of illegitimacy from hovering over the whole affair:

However, even though such a judgment must be qualified, the political implications are clear, since the people of Quebec, a sovereign people, were not consulted about patriation, any more than other Canadians were. It is indeed difficult to understand how a democratic country like Canada could amend its constitution so substantially without going to the people, especially as none of the governments involved, whether federal or provincial, had a specific mandate from the voters to carry out such constitutional amendments.[33]

Mr Rémillard's emphasis on popular sovereignty, on the necessity of the citizens' consent in changing the fundamental law of a society, shows his affinity with John Locke's political thought. Without explicitly referring to the *Second Treatise of Government*, Rémillard entered even further into its spirit in a text he wrote in 1983. There he outlined four possible ways in which, in his view, the deadlock could have been broken in 1982. The first three were a federal-provincial conference in which a satisfactory compromise for Quebec would be agreed on; a special election in Quebec, granting the government a mandate to negotiate constitutional reform; and the election, in Ottawa, of a party favourable to the idea of a new round of discussions in which the interests of Quebec would be further recognized.

The fourth is more immediately surprising in the historical context of Canada and Quebec: recourse to civil disobedience, as authorized by Thomas Aquinas in cases where the authorities use their power unjustly.[34] Such disobedience would have been legitimate, given what had just transpired on the constitutional front and the way things had unfolded. Here one can sense Locke's shadow looming forth. The right to resist and the affirmation of the principle of popular sovereignty are the culmination of a critical analysis heavily influenced by neo-Thomism. As Quentin Skinner has shown, the Spanish Jesuit Mariana played a decisive role in the genesis of political radicalism at the dawn of the modern era.[35]

Not only does Locke's political theory coincide with the Thomistic tradition in its recognition of a people's right of resistance; it also does so in recommending extremely cautious use of that right and in interpreting it very realistically. Here again, Locke can give us a better understanding of what has occurred in Quebec since 1982. While acknowledging that there were valid reasons for a dissolution of the government in 1982, and consequently for a devolution of the constituent authority on the people of Quebec, it must be conceded that the latter remained equally passive. They merely received the blow. Rather than exercising their "right" of political resistance, the people let themselves be mobilized by social and economic struggles. (The reader may recall the depth of the recession and the extent of the conflicts that shook Quebec in 1982–83.) Locke knew, having devoted considerable energy to the question over many years, that leading a people onto the road of resistance is no easy task: "To this, I Answer: Quite the contrary. People are not so easily got out of their old Forms, as some are apt to suggest. They are hardly to be prevailed with to amend the acknolwedg'd Faults, in the Frame they have been accustom'd to. And if there be any Original defects, or adventitious ones introduced by time, or corruption; 'tis not an easie thing to get them changed, even when all the World sees there is an opportunity for it."[36] The *Second Treatise of Government* goes on to say that the people harbour a deep aversion towards the idea of changing a political system; they are more disposed to suffer than to resist. They do not rise up for a trifle; only generalized calamity or oppression will spur them on. The people of Quebec clearly did not believe during the 1980s that the situation had degenerated to such a point in Canada. Whether justified or not, their trust in the government had still not been exhausted.

What of the situation today, several years after the rejection of the Meech Lake Accord? The three other possibilites mentioned by Gil Rémillard at the beginning of the decade suggest ways of understanding this. The first possibility to crystallize was that of a federal election enabling the people of Quebec to participate in the election of a party favouring constitutional reform. This is what transpired in September 1984. A large majority of Quebecers supported the Conservative Party, led by Brian Mulroney, who campaigned in Quebec on the theme of national reconciliation. He promised to bring Quebec back into the Canadian constitutional fold with honour and enthusiasm. December 1985 brought about a weakened version of the second possibility raised by Rémillard. Rather than having a special election to grant a specific mandate for constitutional negotiation, the people of Quebec carried Robert Bourassa's Liberal Party to power in a regular provincial election. Bourassa's party was clearly linked to the quest for renewed federalism. Its program listed the conditions to be satisfied before Quebec could feel comfortable within the institutions of Canadian federalism. As a Liberal candidate in the 1985 election, Gil Rémillard was associated with the elaboration of the list of conditions that a Liberal government would put forward. After 1985, he played an even more direct role in the realization of the third possibility he had mentioned: a federal-provincial conference leading to a compromise that would satisfy everyone, but primarily Quebec. This possibility became a reality in the spring of 1987 when the prime minister and the provincial premiers signed the Meech Lake Accord.[37]

On two occasions, Brian Mulroney and the provincial premiers achieved unanimous agreement: at the end of April 1987 at Meech Lake, and at the beginning of June 1987 at the Langevin Building in Ottawa. The interpretive clause of the accord, which recognized Quebec as a distinct society within Canada, was an important victory for Quebec and for the duality thesis. On this matter, I share Christian Dufour's interpretation.[38] In the following chapter, I shall explain its significance in the context of the intellectual history of Canada and Quebec, by comparing André Laurendeau's vision of federalism and that of F.R. Scott. I shall lay my cards on the table: the failure of the Meech Lake Accord is tantamount to the categorical expunging of André Laurendeau's vision from the symbolic order of the Canadian federal compromise. Henceforth, the system appears incapable of openly accepting the specificity of Quebec, of welcoming the principle of duality into its institutions. But I must not get ahead of myself. For the time being, it is sufficient to recall that in the federal election of November 1988 and in the provincial election of September 1989, the Quebec population gave its majority support to the political parties and leaders who had launched the Meech Lake Accord.

Ratification of the agreement before the deadline of 23 June 1990 would clearly not have solved all the problems of Canadian federalism. The incredible marathon session of June 1990 in Ottawa, while Quebec and Canada stood with baited breath for a whole week, contained additional elements – compromises that raised all sorts of questions: the relation between the distinct society clause and the Charter of Rights and Freedoms, the scope of a possible Canada clause, and the consequences of the participants' willingness to engage in Senate reform. Pierre Fournier is correct in writing that the last round would have watered down Quebec's gains (if Quebec had gained anything, that is).[39] The last round would not have secured constitutional peace for a thousand years. Yet it would at least have given the advocates of federalism a new lease on life by granting duality a new basis of support.

Let us return to the text of the Meech Lake Accord itself. In its final form, to give but one example, the distinct society clause did not offer Quebec any guarantee. The clause was a supplementary interpretative provision that the judicial system could have used when confronted with constitutional questions. The courts would gradually have produced a definition of the nature of Quebec as a distinct society. Other measures in the Meech Lake Accord established linguistic duality as a fundamental feature of Canada, recognized the equality between provinces, and specified that the distinct society clause could not be used to reduce the powers of federal or provincial governments and legislative assemblies. This shows just how much this agreement required Quebec to act on faith. Until June 1990, it might have seemed that the Canadian constitutional crisis was going to be resolved by this vote of confidence that the Government of Quebec was preparing to give to federalism. What had been taken away in 1982 was to be restored; the gulf of institutional legitimacy was to be filled. Those federalists who also defined themselves as Quebec nationalists – from Claude Ryan to Arthur Tremblay, through Solange Chaput-Rolland and Léon Dion – who had felt betrayed by Prime Minister Trudeau between 1980 and 1982, were to have their confidence in federalism restored. But we now know that these great hopes were dashed.

The collapse of the accord jeopardized Canada's very existence. Among the observers who have lucidly recognized this possibility, two have borrowed Locke's vocabulary. Peter Leslie has recalled that the constitutional accord of 1982, obtained without the consent of Quebec, is an affront to the principles of democracy. The violation of this principle generates an immense potential for political instability, according to Leslie.[40] Similarly, Ed Broadbent, who at the time was leader of the New Democratic Party, warned Canadians in one of his last speeches before his party's leadership conference that the rejection of the Meech Lake Accord could have disastrous and irremediable consequences. Broadbent brought up the darkest episodes of our history. He stressed that the Québécois had become a minority as a result of the Conquest of 1760, that the rights of francophones had been violated everywhere in Canada, and that over the last twenty years the Québécois had had to endure the imposition of the War Measures Act, the anguish of the referendum campaign, and Mr Trudeau's constitutional coup.[41] The New Democratic leader could have cited John Locke: "Over those then, that joined with him in the War and over those of the subdued Countrey that opposed him not, and the Posterity even of those that did, the Conqueror, even in a just War, hath, by his Conquest, no right of Dominion: They are free from any subjection to him, and if their former Government be dissolved, they are at liberty to begin and erect another to themselves."[42]

For the people of Quebec, the impact of Locke's words is clear. They have never been consulted on constitutional issues at any time in their history since the Conquest of 1760. They were not consulted in 1774, nor were they in 1791 – though I recognize that this statement has to be qualified somewhat, because, at the time, the leaders of the

"Canadiens" wanted a reform of the kind embodied by the Quebec Act of 1774, just as they subsequently wanted, and then made use of, the constitutional reform of 1791. But the essential point is that the people were never consulted. In 1840 the relations between Lower and Upper Canada were reorganized in an obvious attempt to ensure the political subordination of the francophone population. Again, in 1867, as Gil Rémillard has written, the leaders of the period had little sympathy for the principle of popular sovereignty.[43] Neither francophone nor anglophone Canadians were consulted. The Fathers of Confederation were much closer to Burke, with his conservatism and respect for traditions, than to Locke. The founders of Canada wanted a constitution that was faithful to the English model, one capable of maintaining "peace, order, and good government." They chose to proceed much as the moderates had done during the Glorious Revolution, against Locke's principles. As for the Constitution Act, 1982, I have already denounced its formal flaws on the level of consent. Similarly, no referendum took place in Quebec on the Meech Lake Accord. But on two occasions a majority of the people of Quebec have voted for a political party that was clearly identified with Quebec's integration in the Canadian constitutional framework, on the condition that a very specific list of demands be satisfied. This is what was thought to have been accomplished by the Meech Lake Accord.

Drawing inspiration from Locke, I would like to suggest that ratification of the accord could have helped Canada's political institutions achieve that legitimacy which until now has always eluded them. If the accord had obtained the assent of the people of Quebec and the rest of Canada, its legitimacy would have been further reinforced. The death of the agreement on 23 June 1990 substantially sapped the Quebec people's trust in Canadian federalism. Robert Bourassa's strategy of procrastination succeeded in the end in buying some time for the status quo. However, if my reading is correct, the Canadian political system has a fatal weakness at its core.

A return to the political thought of John Locke, as expressed in *Two Treatises of Government*, helps us understand the depth of the reservations based on the principle of popular sovereignty and the right of resistance in countries within the British constitutional tradition. Canada and Quebec are among the societies that share that heritage. The failure to seek the people's consent in modifying the constitution needs to be considered in the light of that tradition, within which the Glorious Revolution occupies an important place.

Locke's principles make possible a radical interpretation of our prevailing judicial and political situation. Between the 1980 referendum and the proclamation of the Constitution Act, 1982, the Quebec people's trust in their elected federal representatives was breached. This amounted to nothing less than a theoretical dissolution of the government. The rejection of the Meech Lake Accord deepened that breach. This does not mean that the death of the agreement brought together all the conditions necessary to convince the Quebec people of the need for change. Before turning its back on federalism once and for all, the people of Quebec will demand proof of the existence of a long list of "Abuses, Prevarications and Artifices."[44] I write this book because I believe that there has been sufficient abuse and artifice since 1980 to dissipate the federalist beliefs of a large number of Quebecers. Today, just a few years after the bicentenary of Quebec's parliamentary tradition, I shall one last time cite an abuse that seems especially decisive to me: the fact that the very principle of Quebec's legislative autonomy was held up to ridicule by the Constitution Act, 1982.

Locke would remind us that nothing obliges a people to change its political system. It is the people's task to consider the extent and immediacy of danger caused by an abuse of power, by the vitiation of trust. As members of a sovereign people, individuals are no more obliged to resist or even participate in political life. There is, however, a political obligation from which they may not exempt themselves: the obligation to judge for themselves, in their soul and their conscience, whether the government is still worthy of the trust that was placed in it.[45] The final decision belongs to the sovereign people, but it is imperative that each individual's political understanding remain alert. In Locke's view, there is nothing more dangerous for human property – understood as the right to life, multifaceted freedom, and the possession of material goods – than definitive, blind, and unconditional consent to political authority. This belief applies to Quebec's situation within Canadian federalism.

On the level of political philosophy, John Locke is the key figure of this study. The next chapter will be devoted to André Laurendeau and F.R. Scott, two beacons in the intellectual history of Quebec and English Canada. From the point of view of intellectual history, Laurendeau by himself is the centrepiece of my work. For it was his Canadian dream that foundered in Quebec on 23 June 1990.

CHAPTER THREE

The Meech Lake Accord:
The Search for a Compromise between
André Laurendeau and F.R. Scott

Over the last twenty years, political science in Quebec has deployed a whole array of methods to analyse the various political and constitutional crises that have shaken Canadian and Quebec society. Systems theory, policy analysis, political economy, the political history of institutions and events – each has been exploited in turn.[1] Approaches developed in the general framework of constitutional law should no doubt be added to this list.[2] Amidst these flourishing methodologies, it would seem that the history of political ideas, the historically contextualized study of political thought, has played a rather minor role.

If the history of political ideas has been somewhat neglected, this is even truer of one of its subfields, comparative intellectual history, especially the kind that seeks to create a parallel between Quebec and English Canada. The study recently published by Brooks and Gagnon is a real pioneering achievement in this area.[3] To adopt Léon Dion's point of view, it is as though the francophones had wanted to distance the English, the "other," from their subjectivity, the better to "represent the English to themselves as that 'other' who enables them clearly to grasp their own identity."[4] Sociologists of knowledge tell us that at the end of the 1960s, Québec political science had passed through the different stages of institutional maturity.[5]

In order to perfect this process in the 1990s, a decade after the 1980 referendum, we have to take English-Canadian society seriously, especially its intellectual history. From the standpoint of the history of ideas, English-Canadian society has much in common with our own. The relationship between the two societies constitutes an important part of their respective ways of life. From these premises, I intend to engage in an exercise of comparative intellectual history that will focus on the paths of André Laurendeau and F.R. Scott. An analysis of the respective routes which these two intellectuals pursued, coupled with an interpretation of their philosophical and political heritage, will surely shed new and original light on the political debates that prevailed over the Meech Lake Accord. The history of political ideas serves to elucidate the various stances and conflicting interpretations by placing them within the narrative framework of a country's or a society's history. Today's debates are sometimes merely reformulations of ideological and political confrontations that took place in the past. If, on a hypothetical level, one can understand that a certain debate continually recurs in our history, that the issues underlying it have never been resolved, this may well mean that on a certain number of fundamental levels the deeply entrenched realities of the country are not conducive to the emergence of consensus. Something like this occurred in Quebec and in Canada with the Meech Lake Accord. If the debate was so lively, it was because it hit a raw nerve, the most fragile elements of a symbolic order in which Canada and Quebec – to the extent that the latter is part of Canada – are rooted. Like their dialogue and their political visions, the trajectories of André Laurendeau and F.R. Scott serve to illustrate that aspect of a political crisis which could soon see its resolution. The dialogue between Laurendeau and Scott dealt with the very subject of this book: the meaning of duality and its results, a certain Canadian dream and its eventual fate.

I will not, therefore, offer an analysis of the complex balance between the different parts of the Meech Lake Accord.[6] I will tackle only the symbolic dimension of the whole affair, which in my view is the most important. My argument will be presented in five stages. First I will explain the place that Laurendeau and Scott currently occupy in the intellectual life of Quebec and English Canada. I will then offer a comparative analysis of their respective paths, of the high points of their careers. Next, I will study their major encounter, namely, the salient moments of their dialogue within the Royal Commission on Bilingualism and Biculturalism. This will culminate in an effort to interpret their political and philosophical heritage, and in a brief discussion of their heirs. Finally, I will interpret the Meech Lake Accord as a fairly balanced compromise between Scott's and Laurendeau's visions. By way of conclusion, I shall attempt to grasp the symbolic (but no less real) meaning of the failure of the Meech Lake Accord.

LAURENDEAU, SCOTT, AND US

The first died in 1968, the other in 1985, yet both men remain remarkably present among us. Conferences were devoted to André Laurendeau in 1988 and 1989, and four books about him have been published over the past five years. The renewed interest in him relates primarily to the re-examination of our educational system twenty-five years after the great reforms of the Quiet Revolution were launched. A certain nationalist resurgence is not without bearing on Laurendeau's position in this debate. He believed that educators should, above all, transmit a feeling of belonging to a given environment. He encouraged young people to experience the exalting feeling of building a province and giving expression to a nation. He also saw himself as the expounder of our North American condition: "We are a minority, and that is uncomfortable. We always will be one in North America. We might as well accept it. We are not great in number, but we ought to become so through excellence. They say that this would be asking an entire people to become heroic. Not at all. It is asking those placed in a difficult position, which they have not chosen, to rise a little above themselves."[7]

During the conference held at the André-Laurendeau Cégep in the autumn of 1988, Fernand Dumont, Charles Taylor, and Denis Monière accurately pinpointed the reasons for which Laurendeau has been a reference point in our debates on education and political life. Dumont noted that Laurendeau did not foresake rootedness in order to reach universality: "Authentic thought never elevated itself to great questions without shouldering the contingencies which brought it to deep reflection."[8] Laurendeau's thought both embraced masters abroad, such as Emmanuel Mounier, and at home, such as Henri Bourassa and Lionel Groulx. Charles Taylor went on to point out that Laurendeau accepted the tradition of the situation of Quebec intellectuals without giving in to the "thoughtless hegemony of forms of thought that claim to be universal."[9] Dumont and Taylor agreed that Laurendeau's experience of the universality of particularism was instructive for today's Quebec. At the same conference, Denis Monière showed the links between nationalism and education in Laurendeau's thought, which faithfully echoed that of his mentor, Lionel Groulx. Monière's analysis reveals how startlingly topical Laurendeau's dilemma remains: "Laurendeau remained convinced that Canada was an impossible country, at least as it was at the time. Yet he also believed that the fragmentation of Canada which the separation of Quebec would bring about would be even more disastrous for French Canadians than staying within Confederation."[10]

These different themes took centre stage again several months later, at a March 1989 symposium on Laurendeau, part of a series of conferences at the University of Quebec on the political leaders of contemporary Quebec. As it still does today, the failure of the Meech Lake Accord coloured every aspect of the political context. To those who doubt Laurendeau's relevance to a study of Meech Lake from the point of view of intellectual history, Denis Monière provides the following response: "We may thus conclude that Laurendeau's thinking still influences the debate on Quebec's political future and that it inspired Quebec's constitutional stance during negotiation of the Meech Lake Accord."[11]

The choice of Laurendeau stems from his ideas. It almost becomes inevitable in the atmosphere of crisis that characterizes this period in politics. As co-chairman and instigator of the Royal Commission on Bilingualism and Biculturalism, Laurendeau experienced a similar crisis twenty-five years ago. Reading the log he kept throughout those tumultuous years reminds us that the crisis of his day is still, in many respects, our crisis. As Paul-André Comeau points out in his preface to Laurendeau's diary (which is finally available to a wider audience), that was when he succeeded in "sketching out a notion of 'distinct society,' of a complete society embodied within the territory of Quebec."[12] Consequently, there is a renewed presence of Laurendeau among us in our discussions of education and in our political battles. But to grasp the extent to which Laurendeau can continue to contribute to our political education, to that of contemporary Quebec, one must in my opinion introduce another figure – F.R. Scott.

Political scientists and critics in Quebec greeted with complete silence the publication in 1986 and 1987 of a series of writings that clearly bring out the considerable influence that F.R. Scott had on politics and literature in Canada and Quebec throughout his life. Two of these books seem to me to be especially important: Doug Owram's study, *The Government Generation: Canadian Intellectuals and the State 1900–1945*, and Sandra Djwa's biography, *The Politics of the Imagination: A Life of F.R. Scott*.[13] Owram identifies Scott as one of the principal (political) leaders of a new generation of nationalist intellectuals in English Canada in the 1930s. These intellectuals were determined to reduce Canada's dependency on the British Empire, and they sided with the federal government in the power struggles that wracked Canadian federalism. Owram, a professor of history at the University of Alberta in Edmonton, demonstrates most convincingly that there was an alliance between nationalism and the welfare state in English Canada approximately thirty years before a similar pact emerged in Quebec during the Quiet Revolution.[14] Sandra Djwa's biography, which is admirable in all respects, regards Scott as the intellectual sponsor of a vision of Canada that was triumphantly objectified in the Constitution Act, 1982 – the vision of a patriated constitution and of a charter of rights and freedoms enshrined in Canada's fundamental law. I am anticipating my conclusion slightly by pointing out that

Djwa sees Pierre Elliott Trudeau as the indubitable heir of F.R. Scott's philosophical legacy in Canadian political life.[15] Historian Michiel Horn has complemented these two books, and provided an introduction to Scott's life, by publishing some of Scott's most representative articles on law, nationalism, federalism, and Canadian intellectuals.[16]

Why F.R. Scott? Quite simply because, while Laurendeau deserves to be considered a leading figure of Quebec neonationalism, updating the thought of his predecessors without rejecting it, Scott can be construed as one of the leaders of Canadian nationalism – both the Canadian nationalism that dominated the 1930s and that which has been current during the post-referendum period. Laurendeau is the intellectual torn between French-*Canadian* and Québécois nationalism – the Quebec patriot capable of loyalty to Canada. Scott the English-Canadian intellectual is also an Anglo-Quebecer. Of that whole generation of the 1930s, which included Brooke Claxton, Eugene Forsey, and Frank Underhill, it was Scott who devoted the most effort to understanding French Canada and Quebec, to informing his anglophone compatriots of the reality and complexity of the other side of the Canadian duality. Among the nationalist intellectuals of twentieth-century Quebec and Canada, André Laurendeau and Frank Scott were the representatives of openness to the "other." That is what makes the dialogue between them singularly instructive and politically significant.

SIMILAR PROGRESSIONS

To be sure, Laurendeau's and Scott's trajectories were not perfectly symmetrical. One was born in 1912, the other in 1899. They belonged to different societies and different environments that went about integrating new generations quite differently. However, their paths converged in numerous and important ways. First, their versatility was impressive. While both were intellectuals involved in the political debates of their society, they were also artists, two figures endowed with a remarkable aesthetic sensibility. Denis Monière tells us that Laurendeau's childhood was "bathed in the cult of music and works of the mind."[17] We know that he tried his hand as a novelist and playwright. Moreover, his refined character and taste were universally recognized. In this respect, Scott was his equal. In the early 1980s, he received the Governor General's Award for poetry. Furthermore, he translated the works of Saint-Denys Garneau and Anne Hébert, making them accessible to a larger public.[18]

Both Laurendeau and Scott were committed intellectuals who advocated a certain nationalism as early as the 1930s. In their case, however, nationalism was coupled with internationalism. Scott expanded his horizons at Oxford during the 1920s, discovering British radical reformism – the socialism of the Fabian movement. Laurendeau also "returned from Europe." Halfway through the 1930s, he spent time in France and embraced the *personaliste* outlook which enabled him to produce a synthesis between Catholicism and modernism. In view of their shared openness to internationalism, their sensitivity to social problems, and their residence in Montreal, our two figures were fated to meet at the end of the 1930s, on the eve of the Second World War.

Laurendeau's itinerary is more familiar to us than Scott's. We know that he was eager to breathe new life into French-Canadian nationalism and was one of the founders of the Jeune-Canada movement in his early twenties. In the midst of economic crisis, Laurendeau, Pierre Dansereau, and others attacked the trusts and challenged the federal government for appointing unilingual anglophones to management positions in Montreal. In Europe, Laurendeau developed the notion of "a complex nationalism which dialectically affirms the importance of rootedness as a mode of partaking of universality."[19] During the latter part of the decade, his nationalism found a vehicle in *L'Action nationale*, of which he had just been made editor and through which he opened nationalism up to social questions. The periodical had a pedagogical mission. It sought "to train minds, to lead public opinion ... to be the conscience of the nationalist movement."[20]

What of Scott during the same period? In this respect as in others, there is no pure symmetry between the Jeune-Canada movement and the League for Social Reconstruction (LSR), but one can claim that the latter was for Scott what the former was for Laurendeau. Created in 1932, the LSR gathered intellectuals who were both social reformers and Canadian nationalists.[21] Scott was one of its founders and one of the main editors of its manifesto. Impelled by crisis to rally and act together, the members of the LSR hungered for social justice and sought to influence their fellow citizens' minds. Their intentions were didactic. It was the objective of Scott, Underhill, and J.S. Woodsworth "to educate the public about socialist principles and goals through lectures and pamphlets."[22] Scott became the leader of the LSR in 1935, and the following year the LSR took over the *Canadian Forum*, which had been founded in 1920. The magazine was to become a means of acting on public opinion. Its role was similar to that which *L'Action nationale* had for Laurendeau and French-Canadian intellectuals. In 1936 Scott published a long article in the *Canadian Forum* on the French-Canadian nationalism inspired by Lionel Groulx. While

quite critical of the latter, Scott acknowledged that it was certainly
not English generosity that caused the politics of assimilation promoted by Lord Durham to fail. The following excerpt illustrates why
Scott was the ideal person for a dialogue with someone such as
Laurendeau:

It is well for the English to understand this struggle, and particularly to
realize that the British institutions for which the French Canadian is expected
to be so grateful by no means appear to him to be models of fairness and
freedom. He knows that in 1760 his civil law was taken from him, to be
restored by the Quebec Act of 1774 through fear of revolution in the Americas; he knows of his struggle for political freedom up to 1837, when he was
driven to violence to force concessions; he knows that the Act of Union of
1841 took away the official use of his language ... he knows that Manitoba
entered Confederation promising equal rights to the French language, and
later took them away ... Above all he knows that the British connection has
meant and will probably mean again that he will be expected to leave the
peaceful shores of the St. Lawrence and travel to some distant country in
which he is not interested, to fight people with whom he has no quarrel, for
the sake of an Empire in which he does not believe.[23]

For a French-Canadian nationalist in the 1930s, it was possible to
envisage a fruitful discussion with someone such as Scott. Of course,
that did not preclude numerous differences. Scott and the members
of the LSR were easily tempted to construe certain instances of
French-Canadian nationalism as racist and fascist. They were dis-
couraged by the simple-minded antisocialism and anticommunism
that raged in Quebec. In addition, when they listed their grievances
against the workings of Canadian federalism, their reasons were very
different from those of Laurendeau and his kind. Scott and the LSR
advocated greater centralization and wanted the federal government's powers strengthened. In their view, only the federal government had the capacity and desire to resort to the kind of socio-
economic planning that might resolve the crisis. The LSR's manifesto
is very clear on this matter.[24] Michiel Horn provides a good summary
of the educational dimension of the LSR's activity: "The LSR was for
a time a conscience to a country that so far has found neither social
justice nor itself."[25] The LSR's nationalism rested on two pillars:
obtaining genuine independence for Canada, and making the federal
state stronger in order to achieve social and economic objectives. To
this extent, its educational mission could conflict with movements
that inspired André Laurendeau's allegiance. The advent of the
Second World War caused Laurendeau and Scott to meet, yet it also

presaged aggravated conflict, polarization of the English-Canadian democratic left, and French-Canadian nationalism.

Laurendeau and Scott crossed paths for the first time in 1938–39. Laurendeau's primary goal was to build bridges to English Canada, which he did not know, and to make contact with representative figures from the other society.[26] Scott, for his part, wished to avoid a replay of the conscription crisis of 1918. He feared the fragmentation of Canada, which would inevitably follow from it. Scott's pacifism and neutrality were germane to Laurendeau's apprehensiveness about another conflict in which French Canadians would be called on to die to protect the interests of the British Empire.

The exchange between progressive elements of English Canada (such as Scott) and nationalists in French Canada (such as Laurendeau) lasted some two years. Its crowning achievement was a text written in the spring of 1939, "Toward a Canadian Policy in the Event of War/Pour une politique canadienne en cas de guerre prochaine." The intention was to send this anticonscription manifesto to the federal government, but events began to unfold rapidly.[27] War was declared at the beginning of September 1939, the English-Canadian left ended up rallying around the war effort, and the text written in the spring was not sent or even published. Laurendeau became one of the leaders of the opposition to conscription in Quebec. In 1942 Scott was elected "national" president of the Co-operative Commonwealth Federation (CCF) at a conference which saw the party endorse the principle of a plebiscite on the issue of conscription. It is worth noting that Scott was a dissenter within his own party on this issue. He met with Laurendeau and some of his friends once more in the weeks following the plebiscite of April 1942. He subsequently published an article in the *Canadian Forum*, warning of the political consequences of imposing conscription on Quebec and explaining to his anglophone compatriots that the French Canadians' vote was a vote against colonialism and imperialism.[28] The article caused a storm of controversy, and Scott was violently taken to task in English Canada.

Scott's position in the debate on conscription confirms how worthwhile dialogue between himself and Laurendeau could be. By the same token, however, his overall attitude towards the war just as clearly established that the two men did not conceive of Canadian federalism identically. To consider this more fully, one must reflect on the concrete forms of political activism that Laurendeau and Scott engaged in at that time.

Scott's work with the LSR in the early 1930s swiftly led him to campaign actively for the creation of a left-wing political party in

Canada. He was one of the authors of the Regina Manifesto, which in 1933 truly marked the ideological and political birth of the CCF. During those years of crisis, Scott and his friends widely proclaimed their revolt against the injustices of capitalism, against the orthodoxy of laisser-faire. Their solutions tended towards state interventionism and social planning, in perfect conformity with the work of the LSR.[29] At a time when several provincial governments in Canada were locked into conservatism and inertia, Scott and the left inclined towards the federal government. There was enormous disappointment when the Privy Council in London ruled that the Bennett government's social reforms were unconstitutional. This reinforced the alliance between nationalists and supporters of the welfare state. For his part, Scott began to wish for the abolition of the process of appealing to the Privy Council. More generally, one of the main objectives of his political activity, beginning in 1935, was to create a conducive context for the redistribution of power between the federal government and the provinces, with a view to granting Ottawa the kind of centralized system of fiscal control and social services deemed necessary for the nation's very survival.[30] Scott was among the group of English-Canadian intellectual nationalists who proclaimed the urgency of what was to become a royal commission on the relations between the dominion and the provinces (the Rowell-Sirois Commission). Short of being a member of the commission, Scott granted it all the political and intellectual support he could muster.

The federal government's emergency powers enabled it to apply the centralizing recommendations of the Rowell-Sirois Commission's final report (published in 1940) without revising the constitution.[31] Scott did not oppose this. As a socialist, he knew that planning was necessary. At most, he voiced the wish that the state's actions would not exceed the bounds of democracy. Such was the thrust of his activity during the years when he was president of the CCF, from 1942 to 1950. Scott made valiant attempts to establish the CCF in Quebec, but as he himself wrote in 1947, it was not easy to promote a party in Quebec that was dominated by Anglo-Saxons and, moreover, was linked to communism, centralization, and imperialism.[32]

Laurendeau's intellectual activity, like Scott's, led inexorably to political activism. While he was determined to modernize French-Canadian nationalism, Laurendeau was far from rejecting all its attitudes. Like Scott and the French-Canadian nationalists of the past, he would have preferred to see a neutral Canada in 1939. But unlike Scott, he saw centralization as a danger to the unity of the country.[33] Laurendeau was one of the great leaders of the anticonscriptionist movement that galvanized French Canada in 1942. As a founding member of the League for the Defence of Canada, he was associated with a new political party, the Bloc populaire, immediately thereafter.

It is interesting to note that French Canada's traditional historiography and Laurendeau's personal ideas, as expressed twenty years later within the Commission on Bilingualism and Biculturalism, were brought together in the ideology of the Bloc populaire. The latter regarded Canada as a nation built on the possibility of dialogue between two distinct nations, between two politically equal founding peoples.[34] The spirit of duality is no new phenomenon in the institutions and among the intelligentsia of French Canada and Quebec. While the Bloc populaire did not trumpet its roots within the socialist movement, it nonetheless came close to the CCF in accepting the principle of greater state intervention in social affairs. However, for Laurendeau and for the Bloc, this intervention had to respect the division of powers laid down in the British North America Act; it must not endanger provincial autonomy or threaten Quebec's sovereignty in its areas of jurisdiction. In this respect, the conflict between the visions of Laurendeau and Scott remained absolute. Laurendeau was successively general secretary of the Bloc populaire, leader of its provincial wing, and member of the Quebec legislature from 1944 to 1948. In a Quebec dominated by Maurice Duplessis and the Union nationale, the Bloc was far from achieving the success Laurendeau had expected. Four members after the 1944 elections was quite a meagre result. Feeling that his own activity within the party was leading nowhere, Laurendeau resigned to take on other challenges.

At the end of the 1940s and at the beginning of the 1950s, Laurendeau and Scott both felt the need to readjust their professional lives. They wished to withdraw somewhat from the frenzied pace of political life and to cultivate the inner man. For Scott, this urge was principally expressed through poetry; for Laurendeau, it emerged through journalism. For both men, the 1950s were an important rehearsal for the main act of the drama that brought their paths together: the Commision on Bilingualism and Biculturalism. Gradually, as the decade unfolded, Laurendeau and Scott were confirmed in their roles as *éminences grises* – as intellectual leaders, of Quebec and English-speaking Canada, respectively. Laurendeau won acclaim as editor-in-chief and editorialist of *Le Devoir*, while Scott made his mark as a law professor at McGill University and as an attorney in famous civil-liberties cases. During these years, each strove in his own way at truly pedagogical tasks.

Scott's audience consisted of students at McGill, as well as people (such as Pierre Elliott Trudeau) who were seduced by the quality of his intellectual approach to the study of Canadian constitutional law. In his teaching at McGill, Scott rejected the thesis of the pact between two founding peoples. He argued in favour of a strong central government that was not only capable of acting on the socio-economic stage, but was also unique in its ability to protect minorities adequately. While Scott was open to duality, he had enormous reservations about its political dimension. From this time on, confrontation with Laurendeau became inevitable. Slowly, Scott convinced his students of the importance of reflecting on the various modes of patriating the Canadian constitution, of the urgency of including within it a charter of rights. His courses reflected a true vision of Canadian federalism, which had been patiently constructed over thirty years.[35] Besides Trudeau, Donald Johnston and Michael Pitfield were among Scott's attentive listeners at that time.

Laurendeau's audience was that of *Le Devoir*, French Canada's enlightened voice of public opinion. In texts that were always well crafted, Laurendeau disseminated his ideas on the necessity of modernizing Quebec institutions, on the need for civil and religious authorities to accept urbanization and industrialization, and on their consequences for society's further development. To put it plainly, Laurendeau saw the antistatism and ruralism of the traditional élites as anachronistic. As a journalist, his pedagogy was founded on the principles of respect for human beings and the human intellect, and on the demand for social progress. These values roughly corresponded to those espoused by Professor Scott at McGill.[36]

Both figures were ranked among the principal adversaries of Duplessiste authoritarianism. In the legal guerrilla war that Scott led against the "padlock law," as well as against Duplessis's arbitrary actions towards Jehovah's Witnesses, particularly in the Roncarelli affair, he resolutely promoted respect for human beings and their intellect. Quebec historians who study the historical roots of the Quiet Revolution discourse at great length on the positive role played by such bodies as Radio-Canada, *Cité-libre*, the social science faculty at Laval University, *Le Devoir*, the unions, and the Institut canadien des Affaires publiques, as well as by the individuals who were prime movers within them. Frank Scott's courage and perseverance in winning respect for fundamental rights such as freedom of religion, freedom of thought, and freedom of speech and association have been insufficiently stressed. Let us be frank. Along with Jean Marchand, Scott was one of Quebec's real heroes in the anti-Duplessis struggle of the 1950s. In *Le Devoir*, Laurendeau incensed Duplessis by criticizing his attitude in the Roncarelli affair and by vituperatively denouncing his antidemocratic stance and autocratic tendencies.[37]

But while Laurendeau and Scott saw eye to eye on the core values of liberal humanism, they remained divided on one of Laurendeau's favourite subjects, provincial autonomy: Quebec's demands regarding the division of powers.

In the 1950s the vision of Canadian federalism that we now associate with André Laurendeau crystallized for good. Whereas the sources of Scott's outlook were philosophical and legal, Laurendeau's rested on historical and sociological foundations. Laurendeau saw social modernization as a precondition for the development of the French-Canadian nation. He was the man who joined the nationalist discourse of self-preservation with that of development, of catching up economically. The slogan of provincial autonomy, which was cherished by Duplessis and the traditional nationalists, aroused unfeigned enthusiasm in him. This autonomy that he so cherished fuelled his opposition to the federal government's desire to intervene in the spheres of education and culture at the time of the Massey Commission. But he refused to limit this autonomy to passive resistance. He wished to see it in the context of a more global project of reasserting the role of the state in Quebec.

Such a project would have been impossible in a federal system committed to reducing provincial power. That is why Laurendeau gradually sharpened his concept of decentralized federalism, visualizing one in which the provinces would maintain full sovereignty in their own areas of jurisdiction.[38] In 1949 he opposed abolition of the process of appealing to the Judicial Committee of the Privy Council, fearing that the Supreme Court, whose members were (and to this day remain) unilaterally appointed by the federal government, would thwart decentralization. He endorsed the theory of the pact between two founding peoples, which had been handed down from generation to generation by a school of French-Canadian historians, and of which the Tremblay Commission had provided a definitive statement in the 1950s.[39] Laurendeau's dualist sense of federalism was no more original than Scott's distrust of that dualism. What was maturing in Laurendeau's mind was the sociological reality of two majorities in Canada: French Canada, as principally manifested in the actions of the Quebec provincial state; and English Canada, expressed primarily in the activity of the central state. Quebec needed a special status because it was nothing less than the national state of French Canadians.[40] The essential point lies both in Laurendeau's demands and in those claims that Quebec will never be able to relinquish, short of repudiating itself.

As the Quiet Revolution dawned, Laurendeau and Scott could feel proud of how far they had travelled in their personal lives. Their

accomplishments had been numerous and diverse. They had proven
themselves as militant activists and leaders of public opinion within
their respective communities. Each had developed a complex, refined
political thought. In *Ces choses qui nous arrivent*, Fernand Dumont
aptly said of Laurendeau, "He embodied what is best in us."[41] The
remark applies to both men. As Quebec began to emerge from its
isolation and to modernize itself more rapidly, a confrontation with
English Canada became inevitable. The dialogue that took place
between Laurendeau and Scott in the Royal Commission on Bilingualism and Biculturalism was one of the noblest illustrations in
Canada during the 1960s of an effort, at long last, to bring together
two peoples who had been living together without recognizing each
other as political partners. When shall we see a conference at the
University of Quebec on F.R. Scott's political activism?

THE GRAND ADVENTURE OF THE ROYAL COMMISSION ON BILINGUALISM AND BICULTURALISM

A Short History of the Commission

The Royal Commission on Bilingualism and Biculturalism was set
up in July 1963 by Lester B. Pearson's Liberal government. Its mandate was to inquire into and report on the actual state of bilingualism
and biculturalism in Canada, to provide recommendations so that
the Canadian confederation could develop according to the principle
of equality between the two peoples that had founded it, while also
taking into consideration the contribution of other ethnic groups.
Apart from the two co-chairs, André Laurendeau and Davidson Dunton, the commission consisted of the following people: Father Clé-
ment Cormier, Mr Royce Frith, Mr Jean-Louis Gagnon, Mrs Gertrude
Laing, Mr Jean Marchand, Mr Jaroslaw B. Rudnyckyj, Mr Frank Scott,
and Mr Paul Wyczyinski. Mr Paul Lacoste and Mr Neil Morrison
fulfilled the function of assistant secretaries. Mr Michael Oliver was
research director, and Mr Léon Dion was research adviser. At Laurendeau's death, in June 1968, Jean-Louis Gagnon became co-chair.
When Jean Marchand joined the Liberal Party in September 1965,
Paul Lacoste succeeded him as a member of the commission. And
Mr André Raynauld succeeded Jean-Louis Gagnon as a member in
1968.

The commission published a preliminary report in the spring of
1965, declaring that Canada was going through the deepest crisis of
its history. In December 1967 there appeared a general introduction

(the blue pages, written by Laurendeau), as well as book 1, on official languages. Book 2, on education, was published in May 1968. Given his ailing condition, André Laurendeau did not sign it, but he had contributed to preparing and writing it. Book 3, on the world of work, appeared in September 1969; it was followed the next month by book 4, on the cultural contribution of other ethnic groups. In February 1970, books 5 and 6, on the federal capital and on voluntary associations, were published simultaneously. In 1971 the commission halted its activities without being able to make any recommendations on the great constitutional questions. That same year, Pierre Elliott Trudeau's federal government saw a law on multiculturalism through Parliament.

The Background

For ten years, the Royal Commission on Bilingualism and Biculturalism was at the centre of political life in Canada and Quebec. In a January 1962 editorial in Le Devoir, Laurendeau had ardently called for the creation of such a commission. Almost a decade later, in 1971, when the commission had not as yet completed the last part of its program, namely a series of overall recommendations on politico-constitutional questions, Scott was among a majority wishing to see the commission end.

The first years of the commission were characterized by Laurendeau's uncontested leadership. First, he was its instigator. Having chosen renewed federalism over separatism, which was gaining more and more followers in Quebec during the Quiet Revolution, he impressed all the members of the commission with his integrity and determination. This sense of determination was based on a heightened feeling of indignation about the lot of French Canadians in the country's history. He thought that in many places and on many occasions, "our people has had its back broken."[42] Laurendeau was also driven by a thirst for justice, by the quest for genuine equality between the peoples who had given birth to Canada. One can legitimately criticize Laurendeau for having neglected the contribution of the native people and other cultural groups. Without doubt, his vision has to be brought up to date by those who seek inspiration from his legacy in today's Quebec. The gist of Laurendeau's message was that the spirit of duality must be significantly empowered in Canada so that Quebec could have a stake in Confederation.

In spite of Canada's history, Laurendeau remained fundamentally optimistic. The situation could be altered. While he distinguished himself during the early phases of the commission, he later receded

as Scott slowly but surely took over. To the extent that the commission
adopted his methods if not his ideas, Scott was a dominant force from
1965–66 until the end, though he exerted significant influence from
the beginning. The shift in power was undoubtedly facilitated by
Laurendeau's illness and his death in June 1968. Let us examine this
more closely, without of course launching into a real history of the
commission – a task that remains to be accomplished.

For five years, André Laurendeau co-chaired the commission with
Davidson Dunton. It had been created by the Liberal prime minister
Lester B. Pearson in July 1963. Scott, who was then dean of the Law
Faculty at McGill, was one of the anglophone commissioners. Laurendeau and Scott plunged into the thick of it, despite reservations
in their respective communities. In Quebec, which was in the full
swing of social and political radicalization, many of Laurendeau's
friends suggested that he should not waste his time in Ottawa. As
for Scott, his socialist leanings had for some time cast him as a black
sheep in the eyes of the Montreal anglophone establishment. His
representativeness was questioned, all the more so because all the
anglophone commissioners were obviously bilingual as well as being
francophiles to some extent, and this clearly did not reflect the reality
of English Canada. In spite of their doubts, the commissioners
allowed themselves to be enrolled in the monumental enterprise of
studying the relations between the principal languages and cultural
communities in Canada a century after its foundation.

Would they have accepted Pearson's invitation if they had known
what it was to cost them in time and energy, at the expense of their
health and the requirements of private life? It is no doubt preferable
that we do not answer this question for them. In a preliminary way,
it has to be said that they carried out their task remarkably well. They
criss-crossed the whole of Canada countless times, met again and
again with politicians, opinion makers, ordinary citizens, researchers,
and the commission's staff, as well as among themselves. To my
mind, the commission is a remarkable symbol of dialogue – or, at the
very least, an effort to establish a dialogue – between French Canada
and English Canada. The relation between these two entities continues to be Canada's fundamental characteristic. Moreover, I am convinced that this is what historians here and abroad will speak of
tomorrow when they narrate the saga of Canada's twentieth century.
Contrary to what Wilfrid Laurier said, the twentieth century has not
been Canada's century; it has been the century of duality in Canada.
The example of Laurendeau and Scott is all the more gripping in that
their differences remained deep, yet this never prevented their relations from being marked by respect and admiration.

The creation of the commission was a great victory for Laurendeau. One could say the same of the commission's mandate: "To inquire into and report upon the existing state of bilingualism and biculturalism in Canada and to recommend what steps should be taken to develop the Canadian Confederation on the basis of an equal partnership between the founding races, taking into account the contribution made by the other ethnic groups to the cultural enrichment of Canada and the measures that should be taken to safeguard that contribution."[43] The definition of the mandate constituted a victory for Laurendeau in that it gave substance to the thesis that Canada was founded by two peoples; the spirit of duality was present in the commission's very mandate. This categorically contradicted the interpretation that Scott conveyed in his teaching at McGill, whereas the idea of equality between the two founding peoples essentially summed up the meaning of Laurendeau's political and intellectual activism. Lastly, the reference to biculturalism thwarted an instrumental conception of reforms in matters of bilingualism. The government and political institutions of Canada could not simply content themselves with providing expanded services in correct French. They had to reflect the culture of the French-speaking people in its entirety. Even though the mandate did not explicitly include the study of federal-provincial relations, Laurendeau took the lead from the start in advocating a broad interpretation. The commission, he believed, could not avoid confronting the constitutional aspect of the problem. Scott opposed this reading. Apart from himself, expertise in this matter was not widespread within the commission, and he argued that if the federal government had wanted this question broached, it would have said so clearly and would have nominated the commission's members accordingly.

In the commission's early stages, this difference of opinion was not significant. The first necessity was for Canadians to become more aware of the magnitude of the problem and the gravity of the situation. Everybody on the commission was in agreement on the educational dimension of the undertaking: it was important to pursue the political education of Canadians. According to the same logic, as I shall explain later, one might think that the failure of the Meech Lake Accord meant that a majority of the citizens of Canada had failed the final exam.

During the twenty-three regional sessions of the spring of 1964, Laurendeau, Scott, and the others were perhaps at their pedagogical best. The two chairmen and the commissioners, who were divided into groups, put questions to their English- and French-speaking fellow citizens. They asked them whether the two peoples could live together, whether they wanted to, and, if so, under what conditions. The experience was traumatic for everyone. Ignorance, indifference, and prejudice were very deeply anchored in people's hearts and minds. Some sessions in Quebec developed into a nightmare for Laurendeau, who was taken to task by nationalists who wanted independence. Considerably shaken by the regional meetings, the members of the commission decided to publish a preliminary report, in which they diagnosed the most important crisis in the history of Canada and in which they did not mince words. The report was immensely successful. Because of it, the commission positioned itself at the centre of the Canadian political stage. But after the publication of this report in the spring of 1965, things began to go wrong for Laurendeau.

Once the malady had been identified, it was of course necessary to find an appropriate remedy, but the first imperative was to decide how to go about finding a cure. The differences between Laurendeau and Scott were as fundamental as they were irreducible, both in content and form, and with respect to the how's and why's. To think seriously about the diverse areas of its responsibility – language, communications, labour, education, and ethnic groups – the commission had to choose between two modes of organization. Before broaching the question comprehensively in a final volume, it could allow itself to be ruled by the pace and logic of its research team, gathering facts and acting in an empirical fashion, publishing the results of its work, and making specific recommendations progressively as research was being completed. It could also manage its relationship to the research in a vertical rather than horizontal fashion, analysing different aspects of the problem in the light of an interpretive synthesis. Scott favoured the first method, Laurendeau the second.[44] Discussions on the issue were lively and lasted for more than a year. They had already begun in the spring of 1965, when the serenity of public hearings contrasted with the tension of regional meetings. In hindsight, one can see that this relative serenity masked the battle that raged behind the scenes. The commissioners did not manage to create a consensus on the general framework of an interpretive synthesis. Discussions stumbled on the meaning to be attributed to the commission's mandate, and they stalled over the necessity of making recommendations in matters of constitutional reform, as well as on the nature of such suggestions.

It should be noted that the two opposing factions in these discussions were represented by Scott and Paul Lacoste, who had succeeded Jean Marchand as commissioner and who advocated a decentralized federalism built on a new division of powers. As co-chair, Laurendeau found himself in an awkward position in this debate. The commission renounced for the time being the idea of an interpretive synthesis. By doing so, in order to pursue its work it endorsed the first method mentioned above: an empirical method and a horizontal conception of relations with its research team. It was a great victory for Scott. In pulling it off, he confirmed his position as the intellectual leader of English Canada within the commission. His biographer does not err when she writes:

Despite his English-Quebec credentials, Scott was perhaps the essential English Canadian in the subsequent debates. He did speak for that solid core of English Canada that could not conceive of Confederation as other than an historical union between separate colonies in British North America, a union that made certain provisions for the continuance of the French language and religion. His willingness to concede only up to a certain point language rights for Quebec, yes, but language rights for the minority English in Quebec also – augmented by his socialist belief in the necessity of a strong central government ... made him a formidable opponent to Quebec's demands for increasing autonomy.[45]

The commission began to publish the results of its work in the fall of 1967. It was the year of Expo '67, General de Gaulle's visit, French Canada's Estates-General, René Lévesque's departure from the Liberal Party, and the publication of his *Option-Québec*. It was centennial year, and relations between Quebec and Ottawa were at boiling point. In early December, the commission published a first volume on official languages. The book opened with what is conventionally called Laurendeau's political testament – the "General Introduction," the famous "blue pages." Short of being able to highlight the substance of his vision in terms of content and methodological approach, Laurendeau retained enough prestige in the commission to be granted the task of writing an introduction that clarified the meaning of the key terms of the mandate: equality between the two founding peoples, institutional bilingualism, biculturalism, equal opportunity, and the political dimension of this equality. The "General Introduction" unquestionably represents one of the finest pieces in the political and ideological arsenal of duality. It established the principles that have governed the political action of Léon Dion, Solange Chaput-Rolland, Gil Rémillard, Claude Ryan, and Arthur Tremblay.

If Laurendeau had lived beyond June 1968, he would have used this dualist interpretation in his discussions with Scott and the others concerning the composition of a final report, which the commission intended to produce. The compromise of 1965–66 was made with the design of concentrating on the facts and on each one of the specific aspects of the problem, even if it meant postponing till the end the attempt to achieve interpretive synthesis. Was such a synthesis still possible in 1968, when one of F.R. Scott's intellectual heirs, Pierre Elliott Trudeau, was poised to grasp the reins of power in Canadian politics? As co-chair of research and special adviser to the commission, Léon Dion did not think so, and he refused to succeed Laurendeau as co-chair.[46] If Laurendeau had survived, would he have managed to produce the synthesis himself? Claude Ryan does not believe so: "He was in some sense saved by death from a failure that was shaping up as increasingly probable and was subsequently confirmed."[47] (It should be noted that Ryan made this comment in March 1989, when it was still reasonably possible to hope that ratification of the Meech Lake Accord would achieve a posthumous victory for Laurendeau, avenging a defeat that had also been Ryan's.)

The exchanges between Laurendeau and Scott at the commission continued right up to Laurendeau's last moments of health and lucidity. But whatever the quality of their personal relations and their respective rectitude in dialogue, the two men stood far apart on the essential question. They could not arrive at a compromise. The work of the commission ended in failure, in an inability or refusal to produce the final volume on political and constitutional questions. Scott believed that it would not be wise to consider it; that work should be left to other channels of political life. In the end, the timeless factors of politics in Canada and Quebec prevailed over individual wishes in this great encounter between two utterly exceptional men within the commission.

Things did not stop there, however. Laurendeau's and Scott's heirs took up the work of the commission where the two men had left off. After 1968, two branches of Quebec nationalism could with legitimacy draw their inspiration from Laurendeau. The first noted the commission's failure to obtain convincing results in terms of political equality and increased powers for Quebec; it held that equality would henceforth have to be sought in Quebec's total sovereignty. I am of course referring to the line of thought represented by René Lévesque and the Parti québécois. This was the element that experienced a major defeat in the referendum of May 1980. The other body of opinion, surely the most important for me in this chapter and this book, never ceased to believe in the possibility of realizing Laurendeau's ideal: a renewal of Canadian federalism that was conducive to Quebec nationalism. The torch of a decentralized federalism, reconstructed on a more egalitarian basis, was taken up again by the Task Force on Canadian Unity between 1977 and 1979, by the Quebec

Liberal Party's beige paper in the winter of 1980, and by that party's political program during the referendum campaign. As we shall see, it was this branch of Quebec nationalism that temporarily triumphed at Meech Lake in 1987, especially in the clause recognizing Quebec's distinct character.

When all is said and done, Scott was more fortunate than Laurendeau. The principal aspects of his vision of federalism – a strong central government protecting the rights of minorities, and patriation of the constitution, together with a charter of fundamental freedoms – ended up in the program of Pierre Elliott Trudeau's government and the federal Liberal Party between 1968 and 1984. I will go even further and claim that with the Constitution Act, 1982, Scott's vision became the official concept of Canada. As we have seen, Quebec was excluded from the patriation process, a process that was to have provided one more opportunity, perhaps the last, for those who were in search of an honourable compromise between the ideas of Scott and Laurendeau.

Before commenting on André Laurendeau's heirs, I should like to say a final word on the last weeks of his life. They were agonizing. As usual, he lacked sleep. The commission's routine was not his own. In March 1964, he wrote: "Our nights are too short. We have early risers and night owls; also work must begin ... at hours that are too unreasonable, given that I go to bed at my usual hours: another cause of fatigue."[48] In the spring of 1968 the commission was preparing to launch book 2, on education, which Laurendeau was never to sign. He continued to work hard while complaining of violent headaches, and on 15 May 1968 he collapsed in his office. Thereafter, he only had brief moments of lucidity. On the morning following his death, Claude Ryan wrote a beautiful editorial in *Le Devoir*:

Even in his darkest moments, there was never any question in his mind of going backwards. One felt that he was becoming, thanks to this inquiry, more Canadian. Having had the opportunity to be more intimately acquainted with the diverse character of this country, he understood and loved its manifestations even more. But he never, at any time, gave the impression that this experience would shake his Québécois convictions. We were eager to know what synthesis he would arrive at in the end.[49]

Pierre Elliott Trudeau also delivered a fine tribute to his friend Laurendeau, as he was to do years later for Jean Marchand and René Lévesque. With Gérard Pelletier, these men constituted some of the finest examples of intellectual friendship this country has seen. However, I grant the reader the task of evaluating the relevance of

Trudeau's interpretation of Laurendeau's work at the commission: "It is this work that exhausted him, but not before he had shown Canada the path of its future."[50]

THE MEECH LAKE ACCORD AND THE PATIENT QUEST FOR A COMPROMISE

The patriation of the constitution in 1982 consummated Canada's long process of becoming autonomous, a process that F.R. Scott had been associated with since the early 1930s. In his eyes, the Charter of Rights and Freedoms at last enshrined in the constitution the basic freedoms, democratic rights, and legal guarantees that are necessary for the development of all Canadian citizens as individuals. It also protected minority language rights and erected barriers against all sorts of discriminatory practices, just as it acknowledged the right of women to equality and the prerogatives of native peoples and multicultural groups. In addition, it drew on the great ideals of distributive justice by ensuring that wealth would be shared among the regions. For Scott as for Trudeau, it represented a gigantic step forward towards the realization of a just society.[51]

For a Laurendeau, or those inspired by his thinking, the Charter and constitution of 1982, harbour profoundly unjust elements. Not only has Quebec still not signed these documents, but it had no part in conceiving them. Furthermore, the reform of 1982 completely ignored some of the most important aspects of the vision of federalism developed by Laurendeau, for example, cultural and political duality: the principle of two distinct societies and two majorities. I shall go even further and say that the reform of 1982, in its very principle, is a veritable war machine unleashed on the spirit of political and national duality (a point I shall come back to later). Yet Laurendeau's political testament was quite clear on this score. The texts speak for themselves. As he stated in the blue pages, the problem of cultural duality is "even deeper" than that of bilingualism.[52] Like the commission's 1965 *Preliminary Report*, his introduction specifies that the two dominant cultures "in Canada are embodied in distinct societies."[53]

Laurendeau emphasized duality in his writing at the very moment that his ideas began to carry less weight within the commission. In this context, certain passages in the introduction are utterly prophetic. Laurendeau points out that the commission's mandate calls for a broad interpretation, because the question of bilingualism, in spite of its great importance, is not a sufficient condition for t.. "complete preservation of a culture."[54] The notion of distinct societies is fundamental because a culture can only be fully experienced within the society in which it is embodied.[55] Where, if not in Quebec, is the francophone culture in Canada primarily embodied? This inexorable reality makes Quebec a province different from any other in Canada. Fully ratifying the principle of equal opportunity between the cultures, as called for in Laurendeau's introduction, means shifting one's thinking to the political relations between the communities, between the distinct societies. Each of them will need a certain degree of self-determination: "We have in mind the power of decision of each group and its freedom to act, not only in its cultural life but in all aspects of its collective life."[56] This leads us to the heart of Laurendeau's thinking, to the point where the introduction begins to state the question of dominant cultures and distinct societies in terms of territoriality and of two majorities:

A politically dominant majority easily takes its advantage for granted and does not take into account the difficulties of the minority, especially when that minority is treated with a degree of liberality, or at least an appearance of liberality, in cultural matters. But as soon as the minority is aware of its collective life as a whole, it may very well aspire to the mastery of its own existence and begin to look beyond cultural liberties. It raises the question of its political status. It feels that its future and the progress of its culture are not entirely secure, that they are perhaps limited, within a political structure dominated by a majority composed of the other group. Consequently, it moves in the direction of greater constitutional autonomy. Ideally, the minority desires the same autonomy for the whole of the community to which it belongs; but where it cannot attain this objective, it may decide to concentrate on the more limited political unit in which it is incontestably the majority group.[57]

The documents of 1982 simply reject this greater constitutional autonomy for Quebec, the only political context in which the French-language community happens to be dominant in Canada. Far from giving more power to Quebec, the events of 1980–82 clawed some back – in the area of language and on the amending formula. In order to reintegrate Laurendeau's vision into the Canadian constitutional panorama, it was necessary to take up this idea of increased autonomy for Quebec once more. To everyone's surprise, that is exactly what transpired at Meech Lake in the spring of 1987.

By stipulating that any interpretation of the country's constitution must henceforth accord with the acknowledgment that Quebec forms a distinct society within Canada, the Meech Lake Accord drew on Laurendeau's vocabulary and on his "General Introduction."[58]

Responsibility for protecting and promoting Quebec's distinct character were to fall to the National Assembly (the text of the agreement
refers to the *legislature*, a not insignificant difference in terms of
political semantics) and Government of Quebec. For the purposes of
this book, one thing is clear: inasmuch as Laurendeau's spirit was
present in the Meech Lake Accord, it was in the part dealing with
the new guidelines for interpreting the constitution. The distinct
society clause and the new role attributed to Quebec of promoting
that distinctiveness are scarcely negligible. They conferred a special
status on Quebec, at least potentially. In grey areas of the division of
powers, where there are overlapping jurisdictions, the courts could
have invoked the distinct society clause to rule in Quebec's favour.
No other province would have enjoyed such treatment. When the
time came to interpret section 1 of the Charter, the one that allows
restrictions of rights and freedoms "subject only to such reasonable
limits prescribed by law as can be demonstrably justified in a free
and democratic society," it would again have been possible for the
courts and Quebec (for Quebec alone here, too) to resort to the
distinct society clause.[59]

By recognizing the existence of reasonable limits to rights and
freedoms, the Charter implicitly acknowledges a collective right that
is valid throughout the Canadian political community. Canada is a
liberal society advocating the necessity and value of individual
rights, but it does not renounce the idea of a common good that could
prevail over individual rights and prerogatives in certain circumstances. The interpretation of this article of the Charter would also
have had to accord with the distinct society clause. Canada's common
good, the principle that defines the limits within which rights and
freedoms may be exercised, would consequently not always have
been identical with Quebec's common good. Quebec would have had
a special status from this point of view, to the extent that the balance
between individual and collective rights would have differed on its
territory from that which applied in the rest of the country. My
interpretation of this is reinforced by a provision of the Meech Lake
Accord that explicitly excluded certain articles of the Charter – in
particular, those pertaining to the rights of native peoples and to the
value of multiculturalism – from the sphere in which the distinct
society clause would be applied.[60] All the rest of the Charter, and
hence also the article that states the principle of reasonable limits to
rights and freedoms, would have had to be viewed through the prism
of Quebec's distinct society.

How could this section of the Meech Lake Accord be seen as
anything other than the work of Laurendeau's heirs? He believed in

equality, in equal opportunity. But for him, this was not synonymous with homogeneity, symmetry, or perfect concordance in the treatment allotted to individuals and collectivities. In the terminology of his "General Introduction" to the commission's first volume, Laurendeau subscribed to the principle of "a real equality of opportunity," seen in the light of historical realities, of geographical and political factors defining a society's situation.[61]

No politician or philosopher can determine the conditions of equal opportunity in advance, in the abstract. If they wish to achieve social justice, they must use judgment and prudence, subjecting their thought and actions to the specific requirements of the situation. Since Aristotle, the precepts of justice have always been defined on the basis of a similar process. Laurendeau would have reminded us that in granting special status to Quebec – in acknowledging through the distinct society clause that the ideal of the common good was embodied in an original manner in Quebec – the Meech Lake Accord was only making concrete the principle of real equal opportunities between distinct societies and between Canada's cultures. For Quebec's predominantly francophone political community, as well as for the individuals living within it, the distinct society clause was more than the crutch that former Prime Minister Pierre Elliott Trudeau doggedly calls it.[62] It satisfied the demands of practical reason in that it was not blind to the power relations between political and cultural communities on the North American continent.

I have placed strong emphasis on the meaning that must be attributed to the distinct society clause, but in my mind the Meech Lake Accord was clearly not a victory, pure and simple, for those who draw inspiration from André Laurendeau. Had it been accepted, the accord would have become only one part of the Canadian constitution, alongside texts such as the 1982 Charter and the Constitution Act, 1867 (and, for that matter, alongside a host of customs and conventions). What pleased F.R. Scott in the 1982 patriation process, especially the enshrining of individual rights into the Charter, was not intrinsically subordinate to what would have satisfied André Laurendeau in the Meech Lake Accord, namely, the distinct-society clause. The two would have co-existed in a relationship of compromise, since the courts would have had to decide the order of priority in the cas d'espèce. Some legal experts believe that this compromise leaned toward Scott's vision. To quote but one example, Henri Brun reports that the Supreme Court requires that any restriction of rights and freedoms under section 1 of the Charter must be shown to be not just reasonable but necessary.[63] Such a tendency, if confirmed, would have reduced even further the chances of the distinct society

clause having any real effect. Whatever the case may be, a multitude
of factors combined to endorse the view that the Meech Lake compromise favoured Scott's vision more than Laurendeau's.

Although the text of the agreement established limits to the federal
government's spending power, it accepted, for the first time, the full
legal validity of federal government intervention in areas of provincial jurisdiction. Federal encroachment on provincial turf had accel-
erated as a result of the Second World War, with the support of
intellectuals such as Scott. It had continued quite vigorously in the
areas of education and social affairs. As several observers in English
Canada have remarked, the Meech Lake compromise provided an
unhoped-for opportunity to bring Quebec back into the Canadian
constitutional fold practically at a discount. When Laurendeau
alluded to a possible special status for Quebec during the second half
of the 1960s, he no doubt had in mind much more than a clause, a
simple interpretive rule, recognizing the distinctive character of Quebec. Quebec's essential demand at that time was decentralized federalism, with a new division of powers that would make it fully able
to shoulder its responsibilities as the national homeland of French
Canadians and the seat of their culture. Quebec's complaints also
included the federal government's emergency powers, its powers of
reservation and disallowance, and its residual and declaratory power.
While Scott was with the LSR and later the CCF, he put a lot of energy
into vindicating all these aspects of federal power. He was not opposing a new division of powers; he was opposing one that already
existed and, in his eyes, threatened the country with balkanization.
In drawing up its list of conditions that was to lead to the Meech
Lake Accord, Quebec had abandoned all the other demands that it
had voiced in the 1960s. Scott's vision was clearly far from having
been overcome.

Quebec's specificity within Canada deserves to be recognized. It is
legitimate. It colours the interpretation of the whole of the Canadian
constitution, and that may in time have political consequences
worthy of the name. This is what I discerned in the distinct society
clause, and this is what makes me claim that the Meech Lake Accord
opened the door to André Laurendeau's vision. But in considering
the agreement more closely, one soon notices that the door was ajar
more than open. The final version of the accord's preamble (that of
3 June) included the stipulation that provincial equality be recognized in the constitution. This principle is obviously incompatible
with the idea of special status for Quebec. The courts would have
had to take it into account, and they could not have ignored it
completely when deciding on an interpretation of the distinct society

clause. Dismissing this principle out of hand would have been even more difficult for the courts by virtue of the fact that another item had been added to the initial text of the accord. The section that affirmed the distinct character of Quebec scarcely reduced the powers, rights, or privileges of the legislatures and governments of the other provinces or those of the federal government and Parliament. In sum, the signatories of the accord did not wish to modify the balance of power between the levels of government. The accord did not give Quebec what it had so wanted at the end of the 1960s, namely, a redefinition of sections 91 and 92 of the British North America Act. The essence of the Canadian political system, which the late Donald Smiley referred to as "quasi-federal," was thus preserved. In this respect, F.R. Scott's heirs could breathe a sigh of relief.

So far, I have deliberately abstracted the distinct society clause from its precise legal context within the interpretive rule. The time has come to consider this context in its totality:

2. (1) "The Constitution of Canada shall be interpreted in a manner consistent with

(a) the recognition that the existence of French-speaking Canadians, centred in Quebec but also present elsewhere in Canada, and English-speaking Canadians, concentrated outside Quebec but also present in Quebec, constitutes a fundamental characteristic of Canada; and

(b) the recognition that Quebec constitutes within Canada a distinct society."[64]

Quebec was recognized as a distinct society in the same interpretive rule that affirmed, in its first subsection, that linguistic duality was a fundamental characteristic of Canada. The distinct character of Quebec did not have the status of a fundamental characteristic. This was tempered by the fact that Quebec was granted the role of protecting and promoting the distinct society, whereas the federal Parliament and the legislatures of the other provinces were granted only the role of protecting linguistic duality. The distinct society clause was not necessarily, logically, or explicitly subordinated to duality. On this matter, François Rocher and Gérard Boismenu were wrong in their interpretation.[65] However, it is true that in deciding which of these two aspects should be awarded priority in actual cases, the courts would also have taken into consideration the preamble affirming the principle of equality between the provinces, and also the safeguard clause specifying that the division of powers remained intact. It is no doubt fair to say that when seen against the backdrop of the sum of these provisions, the distinct society clause seems more vulnerable and more aleatory in its application than it did at first sight. Linguistic duality occupies an implicitly more favourable position than the clause defining Quebec as a special entity. But one cannot compel the texts to say anything further on the matter.

The difference between Laurendeau and Scott is echoed in this fragile balance between linguistic duality and distinct society. For Laurendeau, dominant cultures were embodied in distinct societies. Quebec could not, therefore, be totally satisfied with a reform that guaranteed institutional bilingualism and granted linguistic rights to individuals. Yet this is as far as things went in Canada. Bilingualism was dissociated from biculturalism. The Official Languages Act of 1969 and the Charter of Rights and Freedoms of 1982 almost completely ignored the collective and political aspects of linguistic questions. The wording of the clause that made duality a fundamental characteristic of Canada in the Meech Lake Accord was very instructive in this respect. It made no mention of culture. As with the distinct society, linguistic duality had no effect on the section of the Charter of Rights and Freedoms that concerned the promotion and development of the multicultural heritage of Canadians. Moreover, the new law on multiculturalism goes so far as to render the latter a fundamental characteristic of Canada, and it imposes the role of promoting this characteristic on the federal government.

As well as ignoring culture, the final text omitted all reference to the two majorities, the two political communities. The duality that was recognized referred strictly to language. Although the text mentioned the existence of French-speaking individuals, concentrated in Quebec but present elsewhere in the country, one could not tell from reading it that they are the majority in Quebec, where they form a political community. An important dimension of Laurendeau's thought is missing from the chosen formulation. The Meech Lake Accord incorporated an inadequate concept of duality. This becomes particularly evident when one compares the definitive text of the linguistic duality clause with the earlier version that won unanimous approval at the end of April 1987:

(1) The Constitution of Canada shall be interpreted in a manner consistent with

(a) the recognition that the existence of French-speaking Canada, centred in but not limited to Quebec, and English-speaking Canada, concentrated outside Quebec but also present in Quebec, constitutes a fundamental characteristic of Canada.[66]

For those who recognize themselves in Laurendeau's thought, this first version had the merit of subscribing to the principle of the duality of communities, but without specifying the majority or minority status of these communities in Quebec and in the rest of the country. While this may be an insignificant detail, the final text spoke of a fundamental characteristic "of Canada" rather than of a "Canadian federation." Some may have wished to avoid the idea of a federation defined as a pact between two founding peoples, between two political communities, in a spirit of "equal partnership" – to use an expression current at the time of the Laurendeau-Dunton Commission.

Whatever the case, it seems to me that the interpretive rule was not an unequivocal victory for Laurendeau's ideas. The safeguard clause establishes the status quo on the level of the division of powers. In its first formulation, the linguistic duality clause made reference to a French-Canadian collectivity concentrated in Quebec, and this could have lent more weight to the distinct society clause. But this was no longer the case in the final version of the text. If a fundamental characteristic of Canada – and the only one mentioned in a text bearing constitutional authority – consists of the duality of idioms and of individuals who possess linguistic rights, the chances are that this characteristic will conflict with the collective aspect of the distinct character granted to Quebec, with the actions that Quebec will undertake to promote the language and culture of the French-speaking community that is the majority in its territory.

To win the people of Quebec over to the benefits of the Canadian federal system, the Meech Lake Accord had to achieve a compromise between the vision of federalism developed by F.R. Scott and that set forth by André Laurendeau. It is clear to me that this compromise withered, to Quebec's detriment, as the accord went through successive drafts. The text that emerged from the deliberations at the Langevin Building did not bear the stamp of political duality as the original documents signed at Meech Lake had done. Nonetheless, the recognition of Quebec as a distinct society, even narrowly defined, was an important concession to Quebec nationalism by those who, like Scott, believed in the dream of a Canadian national identity and who feared that this ideal would be weakened by too great an institutional and symbolic acceptance of Quebec specificity.

The atrophy of the necessary compromise between the nationalisms of Scott and Laurendeau continued until the last week in the life of the Meech Lake Accord. During the marathon session of 3–9 June 1990, the Quebec government jettisoned a lot of ballast to protect the essence of the agreement. It accepted that a letter from experts would specify the relationship between the distinct society clause and the Charter of Rights and Freedoms. Robert Bourassa's government also agreed to commit itself to Senate reform on the basis of parameters that came dangerously close to symmetry between the different provinces. Finally the government opened the door to debate on a Canada clause, which would have sweetened the distinct society by adding a number of fundamental characteristics in the country's constitution. No one will ever know what would actually have happened had the constitutional deals of 1987 and 1990 been ratified. It is difficult, however, to believe that political duality was reinforced by the June 1990 marathon in Ottawa.

One of Laurendeau's heirs and one of the most ardent defenders of the Meech Lake Accord, Claude Ryan, recently wrote that Laurendeau had wanted "first and foremost to serve the people of Quebec, which he never hesitated to call a 'nation,' and that his main insight had been to see that Quebec formed a national community, and not simply a province like the others in the Canada."[67] Michael Oliver, who was director of research for the Royal Commission on Bilingualism and Biculturalism, detects a similar insight in Scott's thinking:

For Scott has always been, and has become more and more deeply, a Canadian nationalist. His feeling for the entire land, expressed so completely in the poems he wrote on the long boat and barge trip down the Mackenzie with Pierre Trudeau, is not just a fleeting emotion, but a constant part of his make-up.

In a note I received from him recently, Frank refers to "my darling country." The phrase startled me, and moved me deeply. It is the kind of unabashed patriotism which occurs so often in Quebec writings.[68]

By enabling Laurendeau's and Scott's visions to coexist in the country's constitution – that "common house" – even if, as we have seen, the two partners did not occupy equal or symmetrical positions, the Meech Lake Accord built a bridge between two nationalisms. In Quebec, as in English Canada, the new balance would not have won unanimous consent from nationalists, but important factions from each nationalist camp would have found something in it for themselves, at least for a time. They would have had the impression that the future was open, that collaboration was henceforth an option, even while pursuing their struggle to impose their respective visions. However, definitive approval of the accord would not have solved all the problems, all the potential conflicts, between views such as those of Laurendeau and Scott. In *La Presse* on 30 May 1987, Claude Ryan was already discussing the following round of negotiations, on the division of powers. But at the very least, confidence would have been restored in a climate of "dialogue turned toward the challenges of the future."[69] The consequences of the other possibility – failure of the accord, which was what in fact happened on 23 June 1990 – have yet to be considered in the light of the comparison between Laurendeau and Scott.

CONCLUSION

The dialogue between Laurendeau and Scott was interrupted in the spring of 1968 by Laurendeau's death. It took their heirs twenty years to reopen it. During these two decades, these heirs worked on their own, often relentlessly, to impose their own vision. Those in Ottawa who adopted Scott's conception were able to benefit from the political divisions among the forces in Quebec that shared Laurendeau's legacy, the proponents of independence and those of nationalist neofederalism. With the exception of some more or less fleeting polemics, the real intellectual exchanges between the different camps were restricted to their simplest form. The political arena monopolized all the available energy. Both camps tirelessly vied with each other to convince public opinion rather than each other.

The Meech Lake Accord created a favourable opportunity for the renewal of dialogue, for the first real dialogue between Laurendeau's heirs and Scott's. If I am right, it effected an objective compromise between two great visions, those of the constitution and the institutions. Moreover, since three years were set aside for ratification of the deal, intellectuals had ample time to achieve, at their level, the compromise sanctioned by the politicians. But nothing of the sort occurred. Today's intellectuals were no more fortunate than their predecessors, Laurendeau and Scott, in their efforts to resolve their differences, or at the very least to find a compromise, a philosophically satisfactory ground of agreement. Between the spring of 1987 and the summer of 1990, Scott's heirs – Pierre Elliott Trudeau, Ramsay Cook, Michael Behiels, Donald Johnston, and Eugene Forsey – fought with all their might to bring about the failure of Meech Lake.[70] Let there be no mistake: they and their ideological fellow travellers influenced a certain number of politicians in English Canada, generating momentum against ratification of the deal. In later chapters, I shall have the opportunity to examine the ins and outs of the intellectual and ideological opposition to the accord. Here I shall simply state that if my reading is correct, if the Meech Lake Accord constituted a compromise between Laurendeau and Scott, and if the deal opened up only a limited space for Laurendeau's outlook, when all is said and done, the meaning of the accord's rejection could not be clearer. Scott's heirs have simply said to Claude Ryan, Arthur Tremblay, and their allies that there is no place in the Canadian constitutional structure for André Laurendeau's ideas, for his political dualism and his nationalism, for the two majorities, and for Quebec as a distinct society.

Visions such as Laurendeau's and Scott's have been present in the Canadian constitution since 1867.[71] Ambiguity and misunderstandings have prevailed since the country's birth. The 1982 constitution dispelled that ambiguity somewhat. In the debate on the Meech Lake deal, Scott's heirs have shown that they want to cast off this burden once and for all. They have had enough of the constantly recurring confrontations and compromises among divergent visions. They seek transparency, a constitution as clear as crystal.[72] It seems as if they have been exhausted by more than a century of conflict. On listening to Scott's heirs, one is tempted to adapt an expression made famous by Hubert Aquin and speak of English Canada's political fatigue rather than of the cultural fatigue of French Canada.

"Promises" were made to Quebec in 1980. They were not respected. The Canadian constitution was patriated and modified without Quebec's consent – and, indeed, to Quebec's detriment. So far as many of us are concerned, this constitution was and remains illegitimate. A project aiming to solve this problem in a spirit of openness towards Quebec, represented by André Laurendeau's vision and the distinct society clause, failed in 1990. All these facts have placed Quebec in a remarkably grave situation. Léon Dion ranks among the Quebec intellectuals best equipped to understand the scope of the dilemmas we face. A study of his political and intellectual itinerary will perhaps provide us with an ounce of wisdom.

CHAPTER FOUR

The Addresses to the Nation of Johann Gottlieb Fichte and Léon Dion

In reading the addresses to the nation of Johann Gottlieb Fichte and Léon Dion, one is prompted to trace a parallel between Germany in the late eighteenth and nineteenth centuries on the one hand and contemporary Quebec on the other.[1] Germany two centuries ago was politically fragmented. It was subject to unrelenting pressures from the French language and culture, which were soon followed by the regiments of Napoleon's army. That language and those soldiers paraded under the banner of universalism. While today's Quebec is not politically broken up, it is profoundly divided. It endures a daily battering from the English language and the invasive model of the Canadian reality, a mirror of American culture. In the minds of many, even among us, this language and culture exhaust the meaning of modernity.

Yesterday's Germany and today's Quebec share a profound uncertainty about the future. A few years ago, in *La petite noirceur*, Jean Larose sketched some of the similarities between the two societies:

There are, for that matter, many analogies between modern Quebec and Romantic Germany, where Pan-Germanic nationalism was gestating: the prophetic function ascribed to the artistic genius; an envious and jealous admiration, sometimes transmuted into hatred, for France; a call for the restoration of what is "purely and properly" national; the vision of a messianic role for the nation in the regeneration of a world that has lost touch with real life. In the case of Germany I am thinking of Novalis who wrote *Christendom or Europe*; in the case of Quebec I have in mind what André Beaudet in May 1980 called the "sovereign utopia" of Paul Chamberland, who had proposed to establish a land of welcome and global convergence in Quebec.[2]

I do not view the parallel between Germany and Quebec in the same way Larose does. In my view, nationalism can in both cases avoid the pitfalls of organicist Romanticism (which is perilous for individual liberties) and resentment of the "other." Furthermore, the critique of one form of universalism cannot be equated with the refusal of any universalism. Like the Germany of yesterday and the Germany of today, Quebec has been called on to perform the difficult task of achieving a synthesis between the universal and the particular. This task is made all the more urgent by the breakdown of duality in the operations of Canadian federalism. I have thus chosen to examine more closely the paths of two intellectuals: Johann Gottlieb Fichte in Germany and Léon Dion in Quebec. Other comparisons would have been possible – for example, between the works of Gérard Bergeron and the spirit of the Enlightenment, between Fernand Dumont and Herder, between Gaston Miron and the writers linked to the *Sturm und Drang*. But the choice of Léon Dion is most compelling for my immediate purposes because he was and is the typical proponent of duality within the universe of social and political science in Quebec. His intellectual itinerary over the last twenty-five years thus takes on a symbolic value.

FICHTE AND DION

In the winter of 1807, Johann Gottlieb Fichte, one of the masters of German philosophical idealism, delivered a series of lectures in Berlin entitled *Reden an die deutsche Nation* (Addresses to the German Nation).[3] Fichte had temporarily put aside the conceptual acrobatics so typical of a disciple of Kant and a theorist of rational natural law. His lectures were aimed at a larger public than usual, inasmuch as he wished to respond to the disasters that had humbled the German states during the previous years: the Prussian defeat in Jena, the Brunswickian loss in Auerstedt, and the dissolution of the Holy Roman Empire, followed by the French occupation of Berlin and Prussia. These calamities had traumatized Fichte, and he had decided to speak and write in opposition to the German supporters of Napoleon. His intentions were clear: to propose new directions for German patriotism.

In the fall of 1987, Léon Dion, one of the pioneers of political science in Quebec and a theorist of liberal society, published a book entitled *A la recherche du Québec*, which was designed to be the first in a series of four volumes studying Quebec between 1945 and 2000.[4] As a professor of political science at Laval University for more than thirty-five years, Dion is also capable of conceptual acrobatics within the framework of systems analysis.

It is my contention that Dion's book represents an address to the Quebec nation. Its public is not limited to his usual political science audience. Dion emerged from comparative silence as a sixty-five-year-old university professor in order to respond to the catastrophes that had shaped Quebec in the 1980s. He was still working on his book in the early fall of 1987. At that time, Quebec was characterized by an atmosphere of postreferendum apathy and moroseness, which was reflected in the apparent decline of nationalism, the rapid collapse of the Parti québécois, a collective withdrawal into private life, and an artistic production that oscillated between blasé hedonism and postmodern amoralism, between meaningless laughter and self-deprecating comedy.5 With the exception of the new enthusiasm of the business community, the forces that a short time earlier had been responsible for the dynamism and vitality of Quebec seemed asleep somewhere between comfort and indifference.6 These circumstances inspired Léon Dion to take up the pen once again and involve himself in ideological debates. He would oppose the prophets of the extinction of Quebec nationalism. He would also propose some new orientations to what, by personal preference, he calls Quebec patriotism.7

Starting from Fichte's *Reden an die deutsche Nation* and Dion's *A la recherche du Québec*, can we establish Léon Dion's place in twentieth-century Québécois and Canadian intellectual history, and discuss modern Quebec nationalism as well as the current impasse in Canadian politics? As we saw in the chapter on Laurendeau and Scott, a large number of people in Canada reject duality and believe that a single national community exists in this country. As Kenneth McRoberts has noted, they hold that "the federal state is the legitimate expression of a national will."8 Although Dion writes primarily for a Québécois audience, his book conveys an urgent message to those who are currently involved in the resurgence and transformation of Canadian nationalism in English-speaking Canada. Some years have elapsed since Dion's vibrant appeal. Since the failure of the Meech Lake Accord, we know that this appeal was not heard. What political lessons can we draw from this? But before answering this question, let us explore the parallel between Dion and Fichte.

INTELLECTUAL INVOLVEMENT AND NATIONAL IDENTITY IN TIMES OF CRISIS

The German states of the early nineteenth century, occupied by French troops and searching for unity, bore a resemblance to contemporary Quebec, traversed as it is by a demographic crisis and dissatisfied with its political fate in Canada. Debates in both places centred on questions of identity and had a tendency to gravitate towards immoderation and hypertrophy. Fichte intervened with his *Addresses*

at a time when intellectuals in the German states were inflamed by
Napoleon's victories and by the collapse of Prussian military might.
The Protestant theologian Schleiermacher criticized the poor quality
of political life in the German states and deplored the absence of the
kind of energy that real citizenship gives to human beings. Others,
such as Arndt, proclaimed the need for a national and popular state
that would be united by the links between language, culture, and
thought.[9] Those influenced by Herder and the Romantics emphasized
the need for the cultural and political autonomy of Germany, in order
to facilitate the expression of its popular genius. Intellectuals such as
Novalis and Friedrich Schlegel, who belonged to the Jena Romantics
alluded to by Jean Larose, advocated the politics of traditionalism
and ultraconservatism. But others, including Fichte, favoured more
radical and republican options. The sheer quality and intensity of the
discussion, caused by the collective understanding of the urgency of
the situation, was remarkable. Something similar to this can be
adduced with regard to contemporary Quebec.

Léon Dion's addresses to the Quebec nation belong to an impressive group of books published in recent years on such topics as the
fate of culture, the balance sheet of nationalism, and the evolution of
Canadian and Québécois identity from tradition to modernity. Daniel
Latouche's *Le bazar*, Christian Dufour's *Le défi québécois*, and Daniel
Jacques's *Les humanités passagères* especially spring to mind.[10] While
it is legitimate to speak of a silence of the intellectuals in Quebec, one
must hasten to add that the silence did not last very long. My
thoughts on duality clearly belong to the same ideological and political context as those writings. I have often drawn inspiration from
them, though sometimes I wished to dissociate myself from them.

The quest for collective identity has been accompanied by anxiety
throughout Quebec history. Referring to a number of historians and
poets, Dion argues that Québécois writers are haunted by the possibility of a tragic destiny.[11] If there is a constant in their intellectual
development, it is their fundamental uncertainty. Like Fichte, Dion
is convinced of the urgency of the situation for his national community. Things are bad when collective consciousness and historical
memory are characterized primarily by a number of major defeats:
the Conquest, the failure of the 1837–38 Rebellions, the French school
crises in Ontario and elsewhere, the conscription crises, and of course
the failure in the 1980 referendum. In itself, the death of the Meech
Lake Accord constitutes another failure for Quebec, which sought to
be recognized as a distinct society and was rebuffed. This is the
failure of the Canadian dream that was cherished by a large part of
Quebec, including many intellectuals, including André Laurendeau

and Léon Dion. We had not yet come to that pass in 1987. In addition to the setbacks already listed, Dion's sense of urgency was brought on by Québécois hesitations about the value of language and culture and by a dramatic decline in both the birth rate and the fertility rate. In view of all this, it was normal to entertain doubts about the capacity and desire of a people for survival.[12]

Léon Dion is not a prophet of doom. He remains moderately optimistic about the chances for the Quebec nation in North America. Like Fichte, he wrote his book in order to rekindle the flame of hope, to make clarifications on issues of identity, and to raise the level of pride about that identity so that he could then present a series of suggestions that would be likely to contribute to the well-being of Quebec as a whole. There is no disguising that this is an ambitious book. Father Lévesque, the founder of the Faculty of Social Science at Laval University, used to say, tongue in cheek, that his former student, Léon Dion, sometimes seemed to think he was the father or saviour of the nation. I am convinced that the ambition that prompted Dion to write the book was not wasted. The book is a remarkable teaching tool in Quebec studies. It will withstand the test of time.

DIFFERENCES BETWEEN DION AND FICHTE

As a philosopher, Fichte was at the zenith of the German metaphysical and speculative tradition. He inaugurated transcendental and subjective idealism, which was transcendental solipsism in the eyes of more critical observers. The ego in his system posits itself, its "other," and the whole reality of the world. Although Dion has been a keen student of nineteenth-century German thought, he does not belong to the same tradition as Fichte. He is a neoliberal, typical of the twentieth century in the English-speaking world.[13] In particular, he has embraced systems analysis, as developed in American political science, which ascribes primary importance to interest groups, pluralism, tolerance, and functional equilibrium.[14] John Meisel of Queen's University, a longtime friend, has recently remarked on the heterogeneity of Dion's thought, on his refusal to accept monocausal explanations. Meisel believes that there is a symbiosis between Dion and Quebec. His remarks are useful in pegging down Dion's outlook:

This emphasis on something more or other than reason, or more than what is narrowly rational or political, is also echoed in less explicit aspects of Léon Dion's writings. His aesthetic sensibility shows up unexpectedly ... One of the characteristics of Dion's personality is an exceptionally open mind. That tolerance is obvious in his receptiveness to reformist ideas, and in the visible understanding he has displayed for the problems of young people ...

At the heart of his beliefs, there is humanism. We have already spoken of one of his points of view, concerning the importance of love. Another has to do with equality. He is an eloquent proponent of equality.[15]

As a liberal and a defender of individual rights, Dion is in basic agreement with the theses expressed by Fichte in 1792–93. During these years, the German thinker argued for a substantial limit on the sphere of state intervention in the life of individual human beings.[16] However, Dion dissociated himself from some of the viewpoints developed by Fichte a decade later in the *Reden an die deutsche Nation*, when Fichte became a partisan of state socialism. He advocated strong interventionism by the state in order to obtain full public control of culture.[17] Dion does not have much sympathy for Fichte's vision of the German people.[18] Fichte thought that the German people was the absolute nation, the one most suited to the actualization of liberty and progress. From such a vision of the German nation flowed a messianism that would not always be limited by the humanistic and universalistic foundations of Fichte's thought.

On the issue of national ontology, Dion is closer to Herder than to Fichte. The Quebec nation does not need to base itself on some hyperbolic definition that would see it as an absolute people endowed with a mission to reformulate the idealism of the triumphalist church of Laflèche, Bourget, and Paquet. Its historical existence, as Herder would put it, is simply a concrete manifestation of the plurality and diversity of humankind. Its disappearance would impoverish humankind. Like the great majority of contemporary intellectuals, Léon Dion has learned to distrust certain forms of nationalism, particularly the German nationalism of the twentieth century (his doctoral dissertation was a study of the political ideology of national socialism). Nevertheless, Dion has not become a doctrinaire antinationalist. He establishes a sharp distinction between a healthy patriotism and the kind of exacerbated nationalism that is articulated around a hatred of the "other."[19]

Certainly, as early as 1797, Fichte accepted the Romantic idea of the state, stressing its independent organic existence.[20] This vision could lead to a modification of the relationship between the individual and the state. In Fichte's thought, however, it was expressed in harmony with the fundamental parameters of his political situation: he belonged to the camp of the reformists, the anti-Napoleonic German republicans who were opposed to all forms of obscurantism and despotism.[21] If one can find his name in the mouth of right-wing student brotherhoods in post-1918 Germany, or even in the texts of some neo-Nazi ideologues after 1945, one can also encounter it with greater legitimacy in the tracts of the 1848 liberal and nationalist movement, in those of the republican politicians of Weimar, and in the meetings of liberal and republican youth associations after the defeat of the Third Reich. Fichte and Dion belong to two entirely different times and worlds, yet there are remarkable similarities in their individual trajectories and their political formulations.

DIMENSIONS OF CONVERGENCE BETWEEN FICHTE AND DION

Speaking up on the major issues of the day, Fichte and Dion were both aware of the importance of their position in their respective national and intellectual communities. Their situation allowed them to intervene as *éminences grises*, as spiritual advisers in troubled times. It is an enviable role and one that does not come without responsibilities.

Both men knew that in order to triumph over what is perceived as a gloomy present, a nation must conceive plausible projections towards the future that are built on the best elements received from the past.[22] A striking similarity is the personal evolution followed by the two thinkers. Both gradually abandoned their remoteness, their lack of identification with the fate of their respective national communities. But they did not immediately come by an acute sense of civic duty. As a result of either the postulates of universalistic cosmopolitanism or those of the natural law tradition, Dion and Fichte ultimately gave up their lack of involvement and embraced without mediation the cause of the communities in question.

There is also a parallel between the young Fichte, in search of himself, who paid a visit to Kant in Königsberg in 1792, and the young Dion of the early 1950s, who wrote to André Laurendeau in order to exorcise his vision of an insipid and boring Quebec under Duplessis. Dion's relationship to Laurendeau did not remain merely that of a disciple to his master. It evolved over the years. At the time of the Royal Commission on Bilingualism and Biculturalism, Laurendeau considered Dion his peer, someone from whom he often sought advice – for example, on the nature of his opposition to F.R. Scott. For Fichte and Dion, it is the personal and collective experiences of negativity, of suffering, that explain the metamorphoses between the formulations of 1792 and 1807, for the one, and the conceptions of the 1950s and those of 1987, for the other. Historical events and occurrences induced in them what Charles Taylor – a professor of

political science and philosophy at McGill University, and one of
Quebec's most famous academics – calls processes of enabling transition, and thereby provided Fichte and Dion with what they came
to regard as a more adequate understanding of their thought and
identity.[23] Taylor's concepts are an actualization of the philosophical
tradition of Hegelian phenomenology, which in turn is derived from
the German literary genre of the *Bildungsroman*. This is the language
in which I shall attempt to synthesize the Québécois experience of
duality over the past decade.

Léon Dion recalls in his 1987 book that he became a Quebec patriot
gradually. A real national affiliation with Quebec manifested itself
only with the victory of Jean Lesage's Liberal Party in 1960. It took
five more years and the debates within the Royal Commission on
Bilingualism and Biculturalism (the Laurendeau-Dunton Commission) for him to realize that his rootedness in Quebec took precedence
over his persistent loyalty to Canada.[24] The defeats, crises, and dis-
graces of the twenty years since then have consolidated his attachment to Quebec, especially the October Crisis, the referendum, and
the constitutional isolation of 1982. Writing after these sometimes
tragic historical developments, Dion emphasizes that his identification with Quebec and its destiny has never been greater. His feelings
have been magnified by the vulnerability of Quebec that he perceives
with such acuity.

Dion came "to broach the issue of Canada from a Québécois outlook" through contact with Laurendeau during the writing of the
preliminary report of the Royal Commission on Bilingualism and
Biculturalism: "It was the only logical way for me to make sense of
the affirmation of Quebec's specificity as one of the "two peoples,"
or "two societies," that make up Canada. From that affirmation, there
followed the statement of the two principles of equality and duality,
which were by the way expressed so truly and completely in the blue
pages that the latter remain to this day the basis for any constitutional
reform acceptable to Quebec."[25]

Léon Dion has demonstrated great perseverance in his fight for
political duality since 1965. As he himself puts it, it was the leitmotiv
of his involvement in the Task Force on National Unity (Pepin-
Robarts Commission) between 1977 and 1979, and it remained so
right up to the debates over the Meech Lake Accord. It is thus
unfortunate that he refused the strategic post as director of research
for the Royal Commission on Bilingualism and Biculturalism in 1963.
He would have been in a better position to wield influence in the
discussions evoked in chapter 3. When will a genuine analytical and
critical history of the Laurendeau-Dunton Commission be written?

Duality suffered such setbacks between 1965 and 1968 that Dion refused to succeed Laurendeau as co-chairman: "I did not allow myself to be swayed in spite of the sorrow I read in the face of Davidson Dunton, whom I respected deeply. My reasons were twofold. He knew the first well: I could not leave Laval University, my first and only home. The second reason shook him, however. I told him that I knew ahead of time that I would not be able to succeed where Laurendeau, in my opinion, had already failed."[26] Like Fichte, Dion's political thought matured progressively. The outcome was a dualist concept of Canadian federalism, in which allegiance to Quebec remained the priority. This, incidentally, is the creed of conditional federalists, whose ranks included the majority of Quebecers until 1990.

One of the most significant aspects of the parallel between the two men is their understanding of patriotism. For both, it meant the possibility of realizing the universal ends or goals of humankind, which are never negated, within one's own patria.[27] Fichte reconciled the German neohumanism of the late eighteenth century and its strong universalizing tendencies with what constituted the specificity of Germany, namely, its cultural and linguistic traditions. Dion too was inspired by the humanism of Schiller and Beethoven, which revealed, he said, that "a human being is solid and authentic only when he can consider his fellow man, no matter who that person may be, as his equal."[28] From this ideal of equality, Dion drew conclusions regarding the relationships between peoples and nations. This vision of equality is at the very heart of his understanding of the fundamental reality of our country: the relationship between Quebec, which is predominantly French, and the rest of Canada, in which English is dominant. If he shares the universalistic ideals of German neohumanism, Dion proposes a vision of it that is neither abstract nor disembodied. Unlike Pierre Trudeau, he believes that these values can be reconciled with the advocacy of a Quebec patriotism and nationalism. It is such a synthesis that led him to write that the survival and *épanouissement* of a French language and culture in Quebec, in North America, requires that the best products of the system of education have access to the universal in all fields of activity: philosophy, science, business, politics, arts, and letters: "We will have failed miserably if Quebec is not able, at the turn of the twenty-first century, to boast of at least a hundred eminent, world-famous figures, who will project the culture and the whole of Quebec society into the universal, each in their own way."[29]

Dion confirms here at a very sophisticated conceptual level the lesson taught by Charles Taylor with regard to the Herderian and post-Romantic origins of cultural and linguistic nationalism. To put Dion's position in terms of Taylor's argument, such a nationalism requires room for linguistic expression at all levels of social action. It must lead to the kind of realization associated with modernity, and it must obtain self-satisfaction and self-certainty through recognition.[30] In the case of Quebec, if it reached a high level of expression in the French language, which constitutes its identity, and if it showed the kind of creativity that caused it to be recognized by "others," without which the quest for identity would lead to a dead-end, then the nation would gain access to the universal while maintaining its integrity and originality. By insisting on the role of élite personalities for the health of a people and a culture, Dion recapitulated the intuitions of Fichte. The latter argued about the necessity of forming a diversified intellectual élite precisely to facilitate "the leap into the universal" and "the production of geniuses for the edification of the people."[31]

A "diversified intellectual élite" is unthinkable without an excellent system of education. On the issue of the centrality of education, it is not surprising to observe a strong affinity between Fichte and Dion. Both thinkers occupied prestigious positions in the academic institutions of their countries: in Jena and Berlin in the case of Fichte, and at Laval and various other universities as a visiting professor in the case of Dion. Both contributed substantially to the analysis, reform, and administration of the educational systems of their respective nations. Fichte was rector of the University of Berlin between 1810 and 1812. Dion was head of the Department of Political Science at Laval, and he wrote at length about the political context of the educational reforms of the 1960s in Quebec.[32] Later, in the 1970s, he was involved in the reform of graduate studies and research in the humanities and social sciences in Canada, and he presided over a commission on the reform of Laval University.

Both Dion and Fichte insisted on the role of civics as a pillar of any education system. It was one of the major dimensions of the programs of reform they had in mind for their nations. Dion, in particular, deplores the excessively radical thrust of the reforms of the 1960s, which omitted from the much-expanded public school sector not only the defects but also the good qualities of the education provided by the classical colleges. He also criticizes the shallowness of the Québécois *vis-à-vis* their own history, targeting not only lack of knowledge but their lack of appreciation. On this score, he sees eye to eye with Charles Taylor, who views the desire to break with the past and to wipe the slate clean as a threat to Quebec. Taylor has pointed out that Laurendeau is held in such esteem today because he was a reformer who nevertheless "always felt he was in continuity with the situation experienced by those who preceded him."[33]

Like Fichte, Léon Dion displays a great familiarity with the literary masters of his linguistic and cultural tradition. Believing as he does in the intimacy of the dialectics between the world of imagination and that of reality, he sees in literary masterpieces a foreshadowing of the possibilities of existence for his national community. Literary definitions tell members of a nation what they have become and what they could become. Dion appeals to the creativity of Québécois writers; he makes them aware of their role in the current national predicament.

Education and artistic creativity are important affairs in their own right, but they are not enough for someone who wishes to formulate a comprehensive program of national regeneration. Léon Dion's addresses to the nation have not ended with the publication of his book of reflections on the issue of identity. They will continue to borrow explicitly from Fichte as they survey Quebec's destiny from the antecedents of the Quiet Revolution to the uncertainties of the twenty-first Century. Fichte included a living religion, a strong economy, and an autonomous state among the requirements for the well-being of a community based on language and culture. Dion states that the same elements will be incorporated in his future works.[34]

Given the different intellectual standpoints that characterize the evolution of the two men, and given their definitions of patriotism and their programs for the future of their respective nations, it has been well worth drawing the above parallels between Johann Gottlieb Fichte and Léon Dion. But as I have shown in this particular case, comparisons are not only about resemblances. They are also about dissimilarities. I would therefore like to deepen my analysis by exploring the differences between Dion and Fichte. This will give me a better purchase on Dion's message to English Canadians in general, and English-Canadian intellectuals in particular, at the time when the fate of the Meech Lake Accord still hung in the balance. Dion's book was published in the fall of 1987. I shall therefore try to take into account what has happened since.

A FUNDAMENTAL DIFFERENCE BETWEEN FICHTE AND DION AND ITS MEANING FOR ENGLISH-SPEAKING CANADA

In 1807 Fichte had become dissatisfied with the virtues of humanitarianism – with compromise and dialogue, openness and generosity

– in the relationships between states, nations, and peoples. The Prussian debacle in Jena was a turning point for him. After that shattering German defeat, he was more attracted to Machiavellian realism and the defence of the state, and he proclaimed the need for a strong and powerful German state.[35] Dion notes in his book that for both Fichte and Hegel, a nation without a state represented an incomplete society. We should also remember that in the *Philosophy of Right*, Hegel argued that wars between states were a necessity for the formation, the *Bildung*, of the citizens.[36] It was a crucial stage in their apprenticeship towards the universal.

Léon Dion's judgment differs from the one expressed by Fichte in that he has not yet renounced the virtues of dialogue, compromise, and openness in the relationship between French-speaking Quebec and English-speaking Canada. His book concludes with a passionate plea for a constitutional reform that would recognize the equality between what he chooses to call "our two different societies," our "two distinct peoples."[37] He continues to believe that the most economical solution to Quebec's identity puzzle would be a major reshuffling of Canadian federalism. He often reiterates his loyalty to the Canada, which is for him a country rather than a nation. It is with pleasure that he recognizes his debt to English-Canadian intellectuals such as C.B. Macpherson, John Meisel, and Frank Scott; he acknowledges the enriching experiences that he has gained through these individuals.

Without any hesitation, he also recognizes that the Québécois are partly responsible for the lamentable state of linguistic and cultural relationships in Canada; he thinks that they have frequently turned down generous offers of dialogue. He points out that artists and intellectuals – those responsible for the imagination and creativity of English-speaking Canada – have been much more open to Quebec than the politicians who represent them. Dion is particularly proud of the evolution of interpersonal relations and institutions within the Canadian and Québécois political science community, where duality and sovereignty association have become a way of life. If a Canadian dream is crumbling, it is not on the whole the political scientists' fault!

In general, according to Dion, English-speaking academics and intellectuals have spent much more energy studying Quebec than their French-speaking counterparts have channelled towards the analysis of the rest of Canada. How is it possible to explain this? From the Quebec side of the dynamics between "self" and "other" in Canada, there is a profound mistrust rooted in collective consciousness. This mistrust obviously arose as a result of the Conquest and because of immigration and centralization policies, the exodus of French Canadians, and all the events that have so often poisoned the atmosphere during the past century. Quebec has responded by expelling the English-Canadian "other" from the Québécois national imagination and by expressing a deep indifference to the intellectual, cultural, and literary production of English Canada.[38]

In the community of Québécois intellectuals, Léon Dion is one of those who have been most successful in going beyond this mistrust and indifference. He has invested an important part of his physical and intellectual resources in an effort to rebuild political bridges between French-speaking Quebec and English-speaking Canada. One only has to mention his contributions to the Royal Commission on Bilingualism and Biculturalism in the 1960s, the Task Force on Canadian Unity in the 1970s, and his efforts within the Canadian social science community. He can understand why anglophones have hesitations about the two-nations thesis. He knows that the dualist vision of the country is not easy to get across and that it is illusory to hope it will end up monopolizing the Canadian symbolic universe. Yet he perseveres in trying to convince his anglophone compatriots of the dangers inherent in the absence of a symbolic and meaningful recognition of the originality of Quebec. He has remained to this day a convinced federalist. As a Quebec patriot, he has never compromised his liberal philosophy. His entire political thought, as he himself points out, is marked with the seal of moderation. As an intellectual, he seems keenly aware of the responsibilities of his vocation. In the preface to *La prochaine révolution*, he wrote that it was always possible to see behind Robespierre the shadow of Saint-Just.[39] For terror to take hold and become ingrained, there must be people to justify it ideologically. Dion is not at all tempted by such a task.

In this context, the message transmitted by Léon Dion to the Quebec public, to the independentists, and to his friends the moderate federalists, takes the shape of some prophetic warnings. It is this message that in my opinion has great relevance for English-speaking Canadians, for their intellectuals, and their political leaders. At the present time in Canada, it is illusory to believe that there is consensus about the vision of the political community or about national identity.[40] Similarly, it was wrong in 1987 to associate the results of the referendum and the troubles within the Parti québécois with the agony of Quebec nationalism. Dion has spendt considerable energy outlining the various dimensions of the Québécois identity: attachment to the land, the *grandeurs* and *misères* of the French language and culture, and the weight of history in the collective consciousness. Like Fichte, he finds the highest, the most noble formulations of national identity in the literary heritage. His voyages through the layers of the Québécois imagination have led him to affirm the constant, permanent reality of Quebec nationalism and to find with Laurendeau the deep origins of nationalist demands in a sense of injured dignity.[41] Dion must surely have been glad when Father Lévesque, who was no stranger to the rise of a certain antinationalism, wrote in the latter part of his life that even though the people of Quebec might not agree on the means, they would nevertheless unite around nationalism.[42]

The refusal of any Quebec government, whatever its political stripe, to sign the Constitution Act, 1982, is a manifestation of what Laurendeau and Dion termed the hurt dignity of the Quebec people.[43] Reflecting on the eventual judicial interpretation of the distinct society clause in the Meech Lake Accord, Dion was conscious of a certain danger. The clause could have become an "empty shell,"[44] since the fragile balance between different principles offered Quebec no guarantees. If that had happened – if the distinct society clause had failed to guarantee to French-speaking Quebec the protections necessary to safeguard its language and culture in the peculiar conditions of North America – Léon Dion would have been forced to make a momentous decision: "If my hopes were disappointed, like many others, I would not hesitate to take the road finally towards independence, if the proof was made that there is no constitutional security for the French language in Canadian federalism. I really wish to trust but I refuse to be duped."[45]

Léon Dion would not happily give up his convictions after forty years of being committed to federalism, but this would not prevent him from doing so fervently if necessary. Contrary to a certain orthodoxy that has seduced many among us, Dion does not believe in the absolute necessity of a correspondence between nation and state. One cannot find in his writings a linear philosophy of history stating that either Canada's existence or Quebec's independence is essential. The telos for him, as a Quebec patriot, is the protection and blossoming of the French language and culture. In 1987 he still thought this goal could be achieved within the framework of the Canadian federal state, but he was ready to consider the alternative of a Quebec state if all the avenues of renewal for Canadian federalism were blocked. Léon Dion's judgment of the current political situation in Quebec and Canada could best be summed up by the following formula, which paraphrases Prime Minister W.L. Mackenzie King's famous words: not necessarily independence, but independence if necessary.

Inspired by the ideas of Fichte and by the position Fichte occupied in the intellectual life of Germany in his time, Léon Dion returned in

A la recherche du Québec to some of the sources that constituted his philosophical education during his student days at Laval and in Europe. The systems approach he learned from American political science remains omnipresent in his work, but the pillars that support the whole come from elsewhere. They originate from the tensions, the anxieties about identity, and the tradition of profound reflection that characterized Germany in the early part of the nineteenth century. Fichte's *Addresses* were, on the whole, unsuccessful in the years following their publication, but in the century that followed, Germany had the resources to live up to Fichte's ideals, to lose itself in the abyss of nazism, and to rise once more from its ashes. Léon Dion no doubt felt in 1987 that Quebec's situation, given its size and precarious situation in North America, was even more urgent than that of Fichte's Germany.

THE MEECH LAKE ACCORD AND THE DUALIST DREAM

Several years have elapsed since the publication of Léon Dion's book, and we now know that his message was not heard by his compatriots in the English-Canadian provinces – not by the intelligentsia or by the political leaders. Quebec was duped once again in the Meech Lake saga, and the Canadian dream of Léon Dion and many other heirs of André Laurendeau suffered a harsh blow. In the memorandum that Vincent Lemieux presented to the Commission on the Political and Constitutional Future of Quebec, he wrote: "While in 1980 a majority of Québécois said no to the party that proposed a break away from Canada, in 1990 this same Canada said no to the party that proposed that Quebec not break from Canada. In other words, after a majority of us demonstrated that we wished to remain Canadians, Canada rejected us. One must not underestimate the symbolic power of this gesture of ingratitude and imagine that it will pass."[46]

The failure of the Meech Lake Accord has profoundly dismayed the supporters of duality. As Léon Dion had the opportunity to recall in the autumn of 1988, during the conference marking the fiftieth anniversary of the Social Science Faculty at Laval University, the deal provided no guarantee to Quebec. To see it as an important stage on the way to the solution of Quebec's main problems required a strong dose of faith.[47] The deal was merely one timid measure in the grand project of an asymmetrical restructuring of Canadian federalism. Dion considered Quebec's demands so modest that he recommended that the Quebec government stand firm in the autumn of 1989 and not accept any modifications. He opposed the idea of a parallel accord in the wake of Frank McKenna's proposals. He even went so far as to implore Premier Bourassa not to go to the last-ditch conference in Ottawa in June 1990.

The full nobility of dualist federalism comes across in the writings of Léon Dion, as in those of André Laurendeau before him. It was a grand dream, and its torch was not carried in vain. Can such a dream still be kept alive in today's Quebec and Canada? Can the Canadian constitution be reformed in a way that is conducive to duality and the interests of Quebec? In the wake of the Meech Lake Accord, the people of Quebec were invited to reflect on this question through the medium of an expanded parliamentary committee on the political and constitutional future of our society, co-chaired by Michel Bélanger and Jean Campeau. The worst thing at the moment, in my view, is that the Constitution Act, 1982, in addition to being illegitimate for Quebec, is graven in stone. Any effort to make it legitimate is likely to come up against insurmountable obstacles in practice. Eugene Forsey stressed in the spring of 1987 that it was remarkably difficult either to add important things to the constitutional arrangements of 1982 or to remove important elements.[48] The achievement of the Meech Lake Accord – and this cannot be repeated often enough – was nothing short of miraculous. But the 1987 pact faced a second obstacle: the process of political ratification.

According to the amendment formula provided for in section 39 of the Constitution Act, 1982, a unanimous agreement aimed at modifying the constitution must be solid enough to last three long years. The agreement must survive changes in government as well as reorganizations of the leadership and party systems at the federal and provincial levels. It must also be proof against incessant criticism from all the intellectuals and intermediary groups who are dissatisfied with the new reform. In a country such Canada, the criticisms will always be legion, and the press, by its very nature, will tend to reinforce these reservations. The 1982 reform was the result of fifty years of debate. Any tampering with this fragile compromise necessarily aroused the strongest passions. The conception of the Meech Lake Accord demanded enormous political skill from all the participants. Its ratification called for simultaneous virtuosity of the rarest order from all the people involved, together with a generous helping of good luck.

The significance of this second obstacle becomes fully apparent when one recalls that the initial political circumstances were very auspicious for the Meech Lake Accord. Robert Bourassa and Brian Mulroney led very popular majority governments. Quebec had excellent relations with the government of Ontario, and relations were also very good between Ottawa and the Conservative governments of the majority of English-Canadian provinces. Economic growth was stable, and moderation coloured the tone of Quebec's demands. Despite all this, the Meech Lake Accord ultimately collapsed. Healthy realism obliges Quebec to assume what might happen if it ever subjects a new, improved set of demands to the mechanisms provided for by the amending formula of 1982 and its process of political ratification. Meanwhile, in 1992, against all odds, the partners in the federation once again reached unanimity – this time on the Charlottetown Accord – only to see the citizens of Quebec as well as the rest of Canada reject what their leaders had approved. The status quo seems to have reached congelation.

Although it is illegitimate in Quebec, the edifice of 1982 appears well equipped legally and politically to withstand any project of renewal. One could compare it to a medieval fortress. The fortress sits enthroned on an almost inaccessible peak. That is the amending formula. It is surrounded by a defence system of low walls and moats. That is the political ratification process. The ramparts and the people who live in the fortress represent the third obstacle. It is an obstacle of this kind that has transformed the Constitution Act, 1982, into an impregnable citadel. The instruments of this last and most powerful line of resistance operate according to a transparent logic, the logic of the new Canadian nationalism. The most lucid promoter of this logic is the very man who conceived it: Pierre Elliott Trudeau. In the debate over the Meech Lake Accord, Mr Trudeau made no secret of his intentions:

The Canadian nation is composed of citizens who belong to minorities of many kinds: linguistic, ethnic, racial, religious, regional and so on. Throughout the negotiations leading to the Charter in 1982, our government kept in mind that Canadian history has consisted of a difficult advance toward a national unity that is still fragile and is often threatened by intolerance ... I have been talking about the Charter as the culmination of a political endeavour whose purpose was to strengthen Canadian unity through the pursuit of a Just Society based on freedom and equality.[49]

The Constitution Act, 1982, and especially the Charter of Rights and Freedoms, must be viewed within the context of a grand endeavour to build the Canadian nation. There is pluralism in the bilingual and multicultural aspects of this nationalism, but there is also a deep aspiration towards homogeneity, which Quebecers would be wrong to underestimate or neglect. The Charter of Rights and Freedoms harbours a complex balance of individual and collective rights.[50] From this point of view, it unites liberalism and communitarianism. If the basic freedoms and political rights are individual, the articles defining the rights of native and multicultural groups make room for the values of collectivities. It is worth anticipating, in the space of a few paragraphs, the guiding threads of a future chapter on Canadian political culture.

The 1982 constitution and the Charter work to redefine the individual identity of Canadian citizens. According to Alan Cairns, one of the leading experts on this issue, the Charter is in the process of shaping a new political culture for English Canada.[51] Through the intervention of the Charter, more and more Canadians base their allegiance to Canada on the institutions of the central government that have granted them, and that protect, a whole panoply of rights. According to Cairns, the Charter is an intrinsically centralizing and nonfederal document that homogenizes provincial legislation and erodes the social differences between each set of laws.[52]

It seems to me that the deep aspiration towards homogeneity conveyed by the Charter has grave implications for any realization of the federalist and dualist dream, for any project aimed at promoting a distinct society in Quebec. In the final analysis, the Meech Lake Accord foundered because the distinct society clause collided head-on with the Charter. Could it have been otherwise? Its pluralist façade and its appeals to liberalism may well make us forget the Charter's essential nature. It is a very nationalistic political instrument, designed to create a homogeneous Canadian community in which individuals and groups share the same set of fundamental values. By its very nature, the Charter is incompatible with a concept such as that of distinct society, and with any idea of particular status for Quebec. It does not allow for asymmetry in the treatment of individuals or provinces. Every province must have an identical status. The federal government – which, outside Quebec, people always speak of as the "national" government – is the only authorized voice of Canadian national sovereignty.[53] All individuals, whatever their linguistic or cultural origins, must consider themselves Canadians "first and foremost."

The Charter of Rights and Freedoms does not reject the principle of collective rights out of hand. Its categories include several similar rights. However, it opposes the idea that the people of Quebec, given their situation in America, should have different collective rights from other Canadians. That is why I viewed the Meech Lake Accord as a confrontation between nationalisms. The *raison d'être* of the reservations regarding the distinct society clause, and of the wish to assure the supremacy of the Charter, was to be sought elsewhere than in liberal philosophy. In reality, liberalism has only served as a pretext. The distinct society clause was quite simply incompatible with a reductionist concept of Canadian nationalism.

During his testimony before the Bélanger-Campeau Commission, Léon Dion did not fail to underscore the dangers to Quebec of the 1982 constitution and Charter of Rights and Freedoms:

Quebec must at long last obtain an absolute right of veto over any amendment to the Canadian Constitution. I had not hitherto seen one of the consequences that flows from these Quebec demands. In the final analysis, what I am rejecting is the 1982 revision of the Constitution in its entirety. English Canada ascribes great importance to the Charter of Rights enshrined by that revision. The Charter suits it well. We should not propose to amend it in various ways; we should reject it root and branch. We have had our own Charter of Rights for years. It suits us. We should strengthen its legal validity. Each person and group would thus appeal to a single Charter of Rights. Everybody would be better off for it.[54]

The problem of legitimacy that plagues the Constitution Act, 1982, is singularly exacerbated by the proliferation of obstacles blocking any attempt at reform coming from Quebec. The rigidity of the amending formula, the process of political ratification, and the new Canadian nationalism all lend a Sisyphean aspect to Quebec's initiatives. Nor should we forget the presence of a fourth obstacle on the side of this impregnable fortress: time. The passage of time will not improve things for Quebec. The longer the Charter of Rights and Freedoms goes on refashioning the Canadian identity along the lines of provincial homogeneity and the symmetry of individual rights, the greater will be the distrust of concepts such as distinct society or dualist and asymmetrical federalism.

Like André Laurendeau, Léon Dion devoted much energy, for many decades, to realizing Quebec's Canadian and dualist dream. He ran into the same foes as Laurendeau. Mr Dion describes how the members of the Royal Commission on Bilingualism and Biculturalism wrote to Prime Minister Trudeau twenty years ago to inform him of their inability to go on, as the commission came to an end without having been able to develop any political and constitutional recommendations. Léon Dion concludes: "This letter filled the prime minister with joy."[55] Trudeau defeated the supporters of duality in the late 1960s, and they later felt duped by the way he hijacked the 1980 referendum. Looking back in the autumn of 1988, Léon Dion was harsh in his judgment: "The defeat in the referendum, as well as the failure to mount sufficient opposition to prevent the patriation of the constitution without Quebec's consent, have reduced those who contest the legitimacy of the Canadian state to virtual impotence, at least for the present."[56]

English Canada's repudiation of the Meech Lake Accord radically altered the situation described by Dion. It virtually extinguished the last hope of a dualist reconstruction of Canadian federalism, and it increases exponentially the legitimation crisis that is rocking the system to its very foundations. To shed further light on the situation, we must once again discuss that devil of a man who "haunts us still," Pierre Elliott Trudeau.[57] Let us begin with his pivotal role in the saga of the Meech Lake Accord.

CHAPTER FIVE

Trudeau and the Meech Lake Saga

The failure of the Meech Lake Accord marks a real turning point in the history of Quebec and Canada. It demonstrates that the dualist dream which Quebec intellectuals and politicians passed on from generation to generation is virtually impossible. In my opinion, the Meech Lake saga is one of the last chapters in the history of a federal system that began more than 125 years ago. While shrouded in a certain sadness, this history will at least have the merit of ending dramatically. Many remarkable episodes punctuated the incredible events played out against the background of a small lake in the Outaouais region of Quebec, and one forgets too readily that the signing of the constitutional document in April 1987 took most observers by surprise. The initial astonishment was followed by dismay and relief when the accord came close to failing during the marathon session in Ottawa's Langevin Building in early June 1987. Some weeks later, in the National Assembly, Robert Bourassa proclaimed that Quebec had just achieved one of its finest victories in two centuries.

After being ratified by Quebec's National Assembly on 23 June 1987, the Meech lake Accord was subjected to a three-year process of ratification in the federal parliament and in all the provincial legislatures. Each legislative assembly was invited to endorse the unanimous agreement that had brought the accord to life. This aspect of the ratification process proved to be the deal's Achilles' heel. While in retirement, Pierre Elliott Trudeau had lost none of his strategic sense, and he was quick to note the weakness of the ratification process. In taking advantage of it, he made use of a whole array of talents, thereby playing a key role in the dismantling of the accord. His role in the saga is one more brilliant chapter in his political career. It is particularly revealing, because it brings to light both his virtues and his foibles. Through this episode, Trudeau's fate became more than ever entangled with the destiny of twentieth-century Canada. That is what I shall try to demonstrate in this chapter.

Trudeau did not engineer any sudden dramatic reversal between May 1987 and June 1990. Rather, he undertook the patient labour of undermining the Meech Lake compromise. With a little luck on his side, his efforts were crowned with success. The sudden dramatic gestures came from other quarters, especially in the last few scenes of the play. First there was Lucien Bouchard's shocking resignation, which took place the day after the tenth anniversary of the May 1980 referendum. His resignation rendered the Charest Report null and void and blocked any effort to modify the deal by way of a parallel accord. Since the Charest Report bowdlerized the Meech Lake Accord even more, disappointment in Upper Canada's bureaucratic and media circles was acute. Then came that incredible week of last-ditch negotiations in Ottawa. After four long days, Premier Bourassa announced that Quebec was withdrawing from all negotiations sur-rounding the distinct society clause. At that point, exasperation in Quebec was at a boiling point. The next day, a deal was believed to be imminent, but that hope too was dashed. The talks lurched from one sudden development to another, until the evening of 9 June, when a ceremony was orchestrated to proclaim agreement on a con-stitutional side deal to the Meech Lake Accord. It was a sham. That night, Clyde Wells, one of Pierre Trudeau's political allies, reminded Robert Bourassa that the people of Quebec should also be "first and foremost Canadians." The real meaning of this warning will become clear to the reader at the end of this chapter.

The Meech Lake saga did not end on that warm evening of 9 June. There was still the last act, the most unbelievable of all. Elijah Harper, with the support of the native peoples of Canada, resorted to all sorts of dilatory measures in the Manitoba legislature. Meanwhile, in New-foundland, Clyde Wells intensified his procrastination. As the days went by, we had to acknowledge that we were all spectators, impo-tently witnessing the death throes of the Meech Lake deal. A last-minute effort by Lowell Murray and the federal government threw everybody into turmoil but in no way changed the course of history. On 23 June 1990, three years to the day after Robert Bourassa's triumphant speech at the National Assembly, the Meech Lake Accord died. The April 1987 compromise had been torn up. In my opinion, the Canadian and dualist dream of the Québécois also was shredded.

On the evening of 23 June 1990, in the solemnity of the National Assembly, Robert Bourassa declared with considerable gravity that Quebec was and would forever remain a distinct society, free and capable of taking charge of its own development. Meanwhile, in

Calgary, where the federal Liberal Party's leadership convention was preparing to crown Jean Chrétien, the enemies of the accord were jubilant. One after the other, Carstairs, Wells, Axworthy, Johnston, and Trudeau were seen on television congratulating one another. These were highly charged, unforgettable scenes. Finally, on 25 June, a huge crowd marched in the streets of Montreal, celebrating Saint Jean-Baptiste and chanting: "Meech Lake is dead, Quebec lives on!" The curtain had just fallen on the constitutional accord, on political duality, and, in a certain sense, on the Canadian federal system as conceived in 1867 and renewed in 1982.

The preceding paragraphs evoke the dramatic context that served as a background to our "Meech Lake" years.[1] To my knowledge, no one has as yet systematically analysed the part Pierre Elliott Trudeau played in derailing the 1987 deal. If one were to compare the life of the accord to a play, it would be an exaggeration to say that Trudeau played a leading role in any formal way. As a retired politician, he had to satisfy himself with spectacular though episodic appearances, which at first glance were far removed from the site of political decision making. Yet I shall aim to establish that behind the scenes, Mr Trudeau pulled all the strings of opposition to the deal. Moreover, I shall go even further and claim that within the context of a study of Mr Trudeau's political commitment, the Meech Lake saga takes on the form of a classic ancient tragedy. Alongside the great moments of this tragedy, the dramatic events evoked thus far begin to pale into mere anecdotes.

In recalling Mr Trudeau's major contributions throughout the Meech Lake campaign, I shall start with his famous article in *La Presse* in May 1987. This will be followed by a discussion of the political thought of the Renaissance, specifically that of Niccolò Machiavelli. In Machiavelli's thought I shall locate the key to illuminating Trudeau's political behaviour over the last decade, and by using concepts drawn from Machiavelli, as well as from Max Weber and Jean-Jacques Rousseau, I shall highlight certain lacunae in Trudeau's merciless critique of the Meech Lake Accord. I shall also try to prove that Trudeau did indeed exert a determining influence on the people who, in the final analysis, succeeded in bringing down the Meech Lake Accord. As is proper, I shall reserve my comments on the tragic apotheosis for the very end.

IN THE SHADOW OF MACHIAVELLI

During the referendum campaign, Pierre Elliott Trudeau was at the height of his power. The whole formidable federal machine was behind him. His interventions, as previously noted, were selective and were paced to produce maximum effect. His language was that of a statesman who wished to instil doubt in the minds of his fellow citizens from Quebec. In the Meech Lake odyssey, however, Trudeau's starting point seemed radically different. During his retirement, he could no longer count on the support of the federal state apparatus, and consequently, to get his message heard, he had to resort to a more scathing prose, a more polemical tone. In going to war against the Meech Lake Accord, Trudeau had to recapture the finest hours of the early *Cité libre*. Thus, in his joust with the deal, he deployed the lively style that had won him the reputation of the most brilliant apologist of antinationalism in Duplessis's Quebec.

Trudeau's contributions in the Meech Lake saga fall into four categories. In the first place, there is the brick he threw into the relatively calm waters of Meech Lake on 27 May 1987, in an article simultaneously published by *La Presse* and the *Toronto Star*: "Say Goodbye to the Dream of One Canada." Trudeau promoted blind courage in the face of the realities of North America, claiming that the new generation needed no crutches. Secondly, he indulged in lauding Canadian nationalism. Here one must include the texts prepared for his appearances before the joint parliamentary committee on the Meech Lake Accord in August 1987, and before the Senate in March 1988. The titles of these documents were wholly unequivocal: "There Must Be a Sense of Belonging" and "We, the People of Canada." To rally the troops of English Canada, Donald Johnston and Trudeau gathered all these texts and published them in the fall of 1988, right in the middle of the federal election campaign. The title of the book, *With a Bang, Not a Whimper*, restated the conclusion of Trudeau's presentation before the Senate. If Canada was doomed to disappear, it should be "with a bang, not a whimper."

Trudeau understood quite early on that his clarion calls against the deal had to be aimed at provinces such as New Brunswick and Manitoba that were reluctant to have their legislative assemblies ratify the deal. The battle would be won or lost not in Ottawa but in the provinces of English Canada. For all that, the former prime minister did not remain inactive in Quebec. This brings us to a third category of contributions to the debate. As we saw in chapter 1, Trudeau strongly denied Marcel Adam's insinuations in *La Presse* in the spring of 1989 and undertook to rewrite the history of the referendum. The exchange between Trudeau, Adam, and Claude Morin sent a message to English Canada. It reminded those who had not yet ratified the Meech Lake Accord that Trudeau was convinced that he had indeed delivered the goods in May 1980 and that there was no reason to believe that a previously duped Quebec deserved compensation. A French edition of *With a Bang, Not a Whimper*, entitled *Lac Meech: Trudeau parle* ... (which included the various polemical pieces on the 1980 referendum, the transcripts of Trudeau's major appearances before Parliament, and his initial reaction to the signing of the deal) was launched at the end of October 1989, ten days before a first ministers' conference that was to deal mainly with constitutional issues.

Finally, in March 1990, while the federal Liberal Party's leadership race was in full swing, Trudeau and Thomas Axworthy published a book assessing the performance of Liberal governments between 1968 and 1984. Its title evoked the mood and ideological direction of a whole epoch: *Towards a Just Society: The Trudeau Years*. As well as Trudeau and Axworthy, its authors included Marc Lalonde, Jim Coutts, Gérard Pelletier, Jean Chrétien, and historian Ramsay Cook, among others.

In historical studies as in films, Pierre Elliott Trudeau has often been compared to Machiavelli's Prince. The parallel seems apt. Let us flesh it out by starting with a juxtaposition of two passages, the first written by Trudeau, the second by the Florentine thinker:

In politics, the same applies. It means putting all your cards on the table and competing, so to speak, with your visor up. And trusting in chance as much as in skill.[2]

Still, rather than give up on our free will altogether, I think it may be true that Fortune governs half of our actions, but that even so she leaves the other half more or less in our power to control. I would compare her to one of those torrential streams which, when they overflow, flood the plains, rip up trees and tear down buildings, wash the land away here and deposit it there; everyone flees before them, everyone yields to their onslaught, unable to stand up to them in any way.[3]

Trudeau claims that a political leader should rely as much on fortune as on skill, but not more. To do so is to apply one of Machiavelli's main tenets. Trudeau's career is a good illustration of the tension that Machiavelli discerned between fortune (luck) and virtue (skill). Indeed, Machiavelli's spectre hovers conspicuously over Trudeau. Ever since his entry into politics in 1965, Trudeau devoted himself intransigently and tirelessly to the realization of two fundamental objectives: the battle against Québécois nationalism and the inclusion of a charter of rights in a patriated Canadian constitution. To those who accused Trudeau of having been obsessed with such

designs, a disciple of Machiavelli would answer that if a prince wants
to succeed, he cannot proceed otherwise: "A prince, therefore, should
have no other object, no other thought, no other subject of study, than
war, its rules and disciplines."[4] As Michel Vastel so clearly saw,
Trudeau and his principal lieutenants, such as Marc Lalonde and
Michael Pitfield, were real hawks, not gentle doves. The McDonald
Commission's report on the RCMP and the recent revelations surrounding the Morin affair speak volumes. These politicians appeared
ready to brave anything in order to preserve national security and
national unity. They were faithful to Machiavelli, for they devoted all
their energy to their project; they knew how to deploy extreme
measures both rapidly and brutally, as in the October Crisis of 1970.
Generally, one can say that Trudeau was inspired by the Machiavellian concept of virtù:

You should consider then, that there are two ways of fighting, one with laws
and the other with force. The first is properly a human method, the second
belongs to beasts. But as the first method does not always suffice, you
sometimes have to turn to the second. Thus a prince must know how to make
good use of both the beast and the man ... Since a prince must know how
to use the character of beasts, he should pick for imitation the fox and the
lion. As the lion cannot protect himself from traps, and the fox cannot defend
himself from wolves, you have to be a fox in order to be wary of traps, and
a lion to overawe the wolves.[5]

Between 1965 and 1979, Mr Trudeau displayed enormous skill on
the antinationalist and constitutional fronts. In 1968 he checked Quebec's momentum during a constitutional conference in which his
rhetorical skill overwhelmed the elder Daniel Johnson. During the
October Crisis, he fought ferociously against FLQ terrorism. And in
Victoria in 1971, he was a hair's breadth from bringing about the
patriation of the constitution. In the years that followed, he increased
these types of initiatives, though without success. Then, after eleven
uninterrupted years in power, the Liberal government was defeated
in the May 1979 general election. Several months later, Pierre Trudeau
announced his resignation.

This happened just a few months before a referendum in which
Quebec might begin its march towards sovereignty. One could sense
the imminent triumph of Quebec nationalism against a Canadian
federalism fettered by its outmoded constitution. Trudeau's virtue –
his pervasively recognized skill – proved insufficient. Yet fortune, in
her magnanimity, was preparing to grant him one more chance. The
incompetent handling of a budget speech by Joe Clark's Conservative

government gave Trudeau one last opportunity to realize his most cherished dream. In the last paragraph of *The Prince*, believing that Italy faced a unique opportunity to free itself from foreign oppression, Machiavelli wrote: "The occasion must not be allowed to slip away; Italy has been waiting too long for a glimpse of her redeemer."[6] After such a long wait, Trudeau was not going to miss the opportunity that presented itself in 1980. He would remain at the head of the Liberal Party, win the 1980 February election, and use all his skills during the referendum campaign and the 1981 constitutional negotiations to destroy the PQ's project of sovereignty association, and to remove the obstacles to enshrining a charter of rights in a constitution that had finally been Canadianized.

In chapter 1, we observed the tricks and subterfuges that Trudeau the fox resorted to during the referendum campaign. He was never keener to accept Machiavelli's teachings than on that day when fortune granted him an unhoped-for opportunity: "In the actions of all men, and especially of princes who are not subject to a court of appeal, we must always look to the end."[7] After the referendum, Trudeau became a lion and launched his unilateral initiative on the constitutional front. However, there was a court of appeal in Canada, the Supreme Court, and it expressed doubts about the legitimacy of the whole affair. Trudeau once again listened to Machiavelli and once more became a fox: "I believe further that a prince will be fortunate who adjusts his behaviour to the temper of the times, and on the other hand will be unfortunate when his behaviour is not well attuned to the times."[8] Let us recall Trudeau the fox's feat of November 1981.

René Lévesque, Claude Morin, and numerous other Quebec intellectuals have made famous the night of 4–5 November 1981, which gave birth to a constitutional deal struck, in the absence of Quebec, between the federal government and the governments of the predominantly anglophone provinces. It was the famous night of the long knives, the night of an odious plot against Quebec that reduced the powers of the government representing the only predominantly francophone society in North America. People all too often forget that Trudeau made that night possible by completely outfoxing René Lévesque. On the morning of 4 November, the constitutional conference seemed to be heading towards another deadlock. Pierre Trudeau and his allies from Ontario and New Brunswick were in one camp, and the group of eight, formed by René Lévesque and the premiers of the remaining provinces, were in the other. Then came the dramatic turn of events: Trudeau addressed Lévesque during a public session ("You, the great democrat ...") and proposed a pan-Canadian referendum. Throwing caution to the winds, Lévesque rose to the bait and immediately acquiesced.

During the break, the journalists seized on the issue. Lévesque's allies, who did not want a referendum, felt they had been betrayed. When work resumed, Lévesque quickly understood that he had been had. Trudeau suddenly came up with a new referendum project, which was no longer in any way acceptable to Lévesque, who was therefore compelled to withdraw his consent. The manœuvre lasted only a few hours, but it was of pivotal importance. It offered the recalcitrant provinces of English Canada the pretext they were seeking to secure an agreement of their own with Trudeau. The night of the long knives would have been inconceivable without the morning trap. In Machiavelli's words, Trudeau displayed virtù once again.

To those who would question Trudeau's choice of action during the early 1980s, Machiavelli offers the following reply:

Wherefore the prudent organizer of a state whose intention it is to govern not in his own interest but for the common good, and not in the interest of his successors but for the sake of that fatherland which is common to all, should contrive to be alone in his authority. Nor will any reasonable man blame him for taking any action, however extraordinary, which may be of service in the organizing of a kingdom or the constituting of a republic.[9]

In truth, Pierre Elliott Trudeau's ambition was to give Canada a fresh start. As we shall see in the following chapters, the Constitution Act, 1982, and especially the Charter of Rights and Freedoms, introduced such important changes into Canada's institutions and political culture that it would not be an exaggeration to speak of the founding of a new political system. Mr Trudeau's allies went about it with wisdom and skill, having learned from Machiavelli that to succeed in such an undertaking, one "must needs retain at least the shadow of its ancient customs, so that institutions may not appear to its people to have been changed, though in point of fact the new institutions may be radically different from the old ones."[10]

In knowing when to use fortune and skill, Pierre Elliott Trudeau triumphed over his lifelong foes in 1980–82. The referendum on sovereignty association was defeated, and the constitution was patriated and was graced with the most magnificent of jewels, the Charter of Rights and Freedoms. When he gave up politics in 1984, Mr Trudeau was able to leave with the assurance that it would be difficult for any Canadian prime minister to raise himself to the heights that he, Trudeau, had reached. The hydra of separatism? Buried once and for all. The Parti québécois and its leader René Lévesque? Routed. Resting on a foundation as solid as the Charter of Rights and Freedoms, a veritable code of the "nation's" values, the Canadian political experience would be very long lasting.

From June 1984 to May 1987, Mr Trudeau refrained from any comment on public affairs in Canada. His mission had been accomplished. Returning to Montreal in perfect health, he devoted himself to his children's education. One imagines him readily rediscovering the company of the classics that he had enjoyed at the turn of the 1960s, when he was a professor at the University of Montreal. He could have found a hint of the coming Meech Lake saga in these lines from Machiavelli's *Discourses*: "Fortune arranges this quite nicely. For, when it wants a man to take the lead in doing great things, it chooses a man of high spirits and great virtue who will seize the occasion it offers him. And in like manner, when it wants a man to bring about a great disaster, it gives precedence to men who will help to promote it; and, if anyone gets in the way, it either kills him off or deprives him of all power of doing good."[11]

On 30 April 1987, Prime Minister Brian Mulroney and his ten provincial counterparts, including Robert Bourassa, signed a historic accord at Meech Lake which aimed to bring Quebec back into the Canadian constitutional fold with honour and enthusiasm. Pierre Elliott Trudeau immediately saw that the system into which he had breathed new life in 1982 was threatened by overwhelming change and even ruin. In his retirement, far from power, he may have felt for the twinkling of an eye that he lacked the means to do anything useful against this "disastrous" transformation of the order he had created. However, as a man determined to preserve the place in history that he had arrogantly seized, Trudeau resorted to deploying his rhetorical skill and influence on the political and ideological actors. Thus he sought to stem fortune's tumultuous tide, which threatened to sweep over the fortress he had erected in 1982.

TRUDEAU'S FIGHT AGAINST THE MEECH LAKE ACCORD

As a great polemicist, Pierre Elliott Trudeau used his most vituperative quill to express his profound disagreement with the constitutional direction that Canada would take if the Meech Lake Accord was ratified. On 27 May 1987 he published an article, in both *La Presse* and the *Toronto Star*, which bore the inflammatory title "Say Goodbye to the Dream of One Canada." Trudeau the founder spoke out against the balkanization of the country: "For those Canadians who dreamed of the Charter as a new beginning for Canada, where everyone would be on an equal footing and where citizenship would finally be founded on a set of commonly shared values, there is to be nothing left but tears."[12] Trudeau believed that fortune had been on the side of the Canadian government since 1982. Alas, no one had foreseen that the government would one day fall into the hands of a "coward," Brian Mulroney. From the moment he entered the debate, Mr Trudeau focused his criticism on the clause that would eventually bring down the Meech Lake Accord, namely, the one that recognized Quebec as a distinct society and defined the concomitant obligations of the National Assembly and the Government of Quebec to protect and promote this distinctness. Trudeau saw this clause as the return of the hydra of special status, granting Quebec powers denied the rest of Canada.

Let us now consider more closely the concept of courage contained in Mr Trudeau's attacks:

The *real* question to be asked is whether the French Canadians living in Quebec need a provincial government with more powers than the other provinces.

I believe it is insulting to us to claim that we do. The new generation of business executives, scientists, writers, filmmakers and artists of every description has no use for the siege mentality in which the elites of bygone days used to cower. The members of this new generation know that the true opportunities of the future extend well beyond the boundaries of Quebec, indeed even beyond the boundaries of Canada itself. They don't suffer from any inferiority complex, and they say good riddance to the times when we didn't dare to measure ourselves against "others" without fear and trembling. In short, they need no crutches.[13]

Mr Trudeau's vision lacks neither greatness nor nobility. It stipulates that the Québécois are quite strong, that they do not need crutches to rival their fellow Canadian citizens in any area whatsoever. However, Trudeau's idealism does not withstand the test of Quebec's rootedness in North America. His individualistic and symmetrical approach would be more credible if Canada and Quebec were in central Europe, surrounded by countries in which several languages of relatively equal power coexisted. For better or for worse, that is not our situation. We live in North America, and English is the continental (and also global) *lingua franca*. On the North American scale, English dominates French in a ratio of fifty to one; three to one on the Canadian scale. Quebec tries to maintain a distinct and modern identity in America, while its principal neighbour is an anglophone country, the United States, that is also the greatest cultural, economic, military, and technological power in human history. Mr Trudeau recoils into the splendid insularity that typifies university professors when he asks the Québécois to dispense with "crutches" such as language laws and the distinct society clause of the Meech Lake Accord. In so doing, he dismisses concrete reality.

Those who demand such legislative provisions have no wish to imprison our society and its citizens in a ghetto. They do not ask us to walk with crutches. It is more, I think, that they are lucidly accepting Quebec's particular situation in North America. In drawing upon Aristotle, one of the great masters of ancient Greek philosophy, I venture to suggest that the supporters of the distinct society clause display prudence and practical wisdom. In the best of all possible worlds, where all individuals and all national, cultural, and linguistic communities have equal power and share the same situation, no one would need special status. In the best of all possible worlds, justice and courage would be the same for all. Yet Aristotle teaches us that human beings never deliberate in the abstract in the best of all possible worlds. They have difficult moral choices to make and must consider the paths that appear before them according to the circumstances that mark their specific place of origin. In concrete reality, courage will not be the same for everyone. According to Aristotle, courage is a a moral virtue that consists of the kind of action that one undertakes when choosing the mean between the extreme poles of pusillanimity and recklessness. In asking the Québécois to abandon their safety net of language laws – guarantees such as those they would have obtained from the distinct society clause – Mr Trudeau is in fact asking them to be rash, to ignore reality and its dangers.

One can easily understand why Pierre Trudeau cavalierly dismissed any additional recourse to the state and the community by his fellow citizens. According to Christina McCall, he embodies the bicultural man par excellence; he is a sort of racial hermaphrodite. He came from a rich, bilingual family and was born in the most bicultural and bilingual of great Canadian cities. In the darkest moments of the Depression and the Second World War, he enjoyed a most exceptional education. I am convinced that this man could live ten or twenty years in Vancouver or Edmonton without losing any of his wealth of language and culture. Would it be wise to expect as much from people less fortunate than himself, in every sense of the word? I do not think so. When the state intervenes to protect the citizens' language and culture, as in the case of Quebec, it does not do so for the sake of the Pierre Elliott Trudeaus of our society. While one must applaud Mr Trudeau's personal courage, one can only denounce the appeal to rashness that lies hidden beneath his impassioned prose.

Criticism aside, one must recognize the seductive power of the pamphlet Mr Trudeau wrote in May 1987. He invoked the symmetrical and disembodied notion of equality in Canadian society conveyed by the Canadian Charter of Rights and Freedoms. He hoped that ordinary Canadians would listen to him. The future would prove him right. Let me skip over some of the mediations and recall that in the spring of 1990, at the decisive moment when the forces opposed to the Meech Lake Accord were gathering, Mr Trudeau based his final attack on the deal on the key values of his just society, values expressed in the Charter of Rights and Freedoms. Equality was one of the fundamental values uniting Canadians. The distinct society clause threatened the concept of justice conveyed by the Charter, since it presented a threat to national unity. When the Charter ceases to be common to all, the Canadian nation is weakened.[14]

In his second series of public interventions, Mr Trudeau presented himself quite simply as the high priest of Canadian nationalism. On 27 August 1987, he delivered a brief entitled "There Must Be a Sense of Belonging" to the Special Joint Committee of the Senate and the House of Commons. A further brief presented to a Senate committee on 30 March 1988, "We, the People of Canada," was a model of constitutional classicism.

Pierre Trudeau first sounded the alarm in May 1987. That autumn, he explained to the alerted troops the real reasons for the struggle he was asking them to undertake. The unity and the very survival of the country were at stake. It is worth recalling that these texts were compiled and published in the fall of 1988, during a federal election campaign in which John Turner was rousing Canada's nationalist forces against the free trade agreement with the United States. Having lost the battle against free trade, the Canadian nationalists became an ideal public for Mr Trudeau's harangues. This was reinforced by the fact that Robert Bourassa's government invoked "the loathsome" notwithstanding clause in December 1988 to exempt Quebec language laws from the Charter provisions on freedom of expression. Bourassa and Quebec were flouting the new founding myth of the Canadian nation. In the space of two months, Quebec had endorsed the free trade agreement and had held the sacrosanct Charter of Rights and Freedoms up to ridicule. This sufficed to incite anger with the distinct society clause and the Meech Lake Accord among Canadian nationalists. Pierre Trudeau's speeches acted as their guiding beacons.

BUILDING MOMENTUM AGAINST
THE MEECH LAKE ACCORD

Apart from Machiavelli, Jean-Jacques Rousseau is one of the thinkers who teaches us the most about the founding of republics, the building of political systems, and the individuals who are undaunted by such tasks. In *The Social Contract* Rousseau writes: "Those who dare to undertake the institution of a people must feel themselves capable, as it were, of changing human nature, of transforming each individual, who by himself is a perfect and solitary whole, into a part of a much greater whole, from which he in some measure receives his being and his life."[15] According to Rousseau, the legislator's work has less to do with political, civil, or criminal laws than with what "is inscribed in the hearts" of the citizens: "I speak of manners and morals, customs, and more than all, of opinions."[16] In other words, the legislator's task is to shape a political culture. In the following chapter, I shall explore the ins and outs of the political culture of Canadian nationalism that Pierre Elliott Trudeau and the Constitution Act, 1982, promoted. Here, it will suffice to show the link between Mr Trudeau's public interventions in 1987–88 and the rise of the opposition to the Meech Lake Accord in English Canada.

On 27 August 1987, Mr Trudeau appeared before the Special Joint Committee of the Senate and the House of Commons that was studying the constitutional amendments proposed at Meech Lake. During this appearance, he vigorously defended the idea of a Canadian national sense of belonging, an allegiance to the Canadian whole – the nation, the people, the country – which he deemed superior to loyalty felt to provincial roots. To his eyes, the suggested amendments bowdlerized the meaning of Canadian nationalism and the nation-state; the whole deal worked to corrode the national will and national patriotism, from the distinct society clause to the anticipated arrangements on immigration, as well as the selection mechanisms for institutions such as the Senate and the Supreme Court. The patriotic customs which the 1982 reform had sought to engrave in the hearts and minds of the people would be considerably weakened, he maintained. The essential focus of his opposition was the distinct society clause:

Finally, I come to what is perhaps the most important point of all: the one dealing with Quebec as a distinct society ... But let us also recognize right from the start that when we talk about a distinct society, and particularly when we enshrine that into the Constitution as an operative clause, we are, by definition, by the actual meaning of the terms, working towards or promoting a provincialist view of Canada. Not national patriotism, not the national spirit that Blake was talking about! ...

I think that if we want to have a federal and not a confederal country, we have to have a national government, a national parliament that will speak out for all Canadians.[17]

Throughout the summer and fall of 1987, Mr Trudeau's allies in the federal Liberal Party and the English-Canadian intelligentsia spoke out in ever greater numbers. Like Trudeau, they denounced the weakening of Canadian "national" institutions incurred by the Meech Lake Accord. In its editorial of 1 June 1987, the *Toronto Star* wrote: "No one spoke for Canada."[18] On 11 June, in the *Ottawa Citizen*, Liberal political scientist Robert Jackson stated, "Meech Lake Agreement will fracture Canadian federalism ... A reasonably strong central authority is needed to ensure that Canadians all enjoy the same rights and privileges."[19] In *Saturday Night*, in August 1987, Robert Fulford wrote that Canada as a nation had just capitulated: "The Meech Lake Agreement shows that Brian Mulroney and the provincial premiers agree about the nation's future – a loose collection of ten independent duchies."[20] Mr Trudeau's brief to the joint committee coincided with the publication by his first biographer, George Radwanski, of a series of articles in the *Toronto Star*: "Instead of a Pan-Canadianism that sees Canada in terms of 10 more or less equal provinces federated into a nation, Meech Lake proposes a dualism that redefines the country into a distinct Quebec on the one hand and the nine other provinces on the other. The whole thrust of the initiative originating in 1982 was to create a Canada in which all Canadians, Quebecers included, could feel at home from coast to coast."[21]

Mr Trudeau and his allies did not succeed in derailing the Meech Lake Accord in 1987. Despite their opposition, the ratification process was formally set in motion. Following Quebec's acceptance in June, the Saskatchewan legislature accepted the deal at the end of the summer. In Ottawa, subsequent to the joint committee's report, Parliament ended up voting in favour of the accord, though not without Trudeau's like-minded Liberal senators greatly complicating the operation. However, the joint committee's hearings revealed to Mr Trudeau that his work as promoter of a Canadian national community rested on very fertile ground. The representatives of a host of interest groups had appeared before the parliamentary committee to express virulent opposition to the deal. The feminist associations of English Canada, the multicultural groups, the official-language minorities, and the leaders of native peoples all claimed to have been excluded from the Meech Lake negotiations. In invoking the Charter and its promotion of equality, as well as the sovereignty of the people, these groups criticized the "conversations among élites," so typical of executive federalism.[22]

Slowly, the opposition began to organize on the political front as well. In the fall of 1987, when Liberal Frank McKenna became premier of New Brunswick, he declared that he was willing to ratify the Meech Lake deal in exchange for reinforced protection of official-language minorities. But McKenna's voice alone could not suffice. To remedy the situation, Mr Trudeau exploited his awareness of symbols and their important role in social and political life: "Apply the distinct-society clause to the Canadian Charter of Rights, for example. The crucial importance of the Charter meant that we all share a set of common values and that all Canadians are thence on an equal footing; whether they be Quebecers, Albertans, French, English, Jewish, Hindu, they all have the same rights. No one is special. All Canadians are equal, and that equality flows from the Charter."[23]

Over the years, particularly in English Canada, the Charter of Rights and Freedoms has become a sacred symbol. Bolstered by this fact, Mr Trudeau continued with ever-increasing success to criticize the violation of this national symbol at Meech Lake. On 26 April 1988, the Conservatives, led by Gary Filmon formed a minority government in Manitoba, and Mrs Sharon Carstairs, leader of the Liberal Party (which had gained from Jean Chrétien's support during the campaign) declared that she would not endorse the Meech Lake deal unless the distinct society clause was explicitly subordinated to the Charter of Rights and Freedoms.[24]

That spring, in an effort to galvanize the opposition, Mr Trudeau presented a brief to a Senate committee, drawing much public attention. His appeal, entitled "We, the People of Canada," was an all-out assault on duality, or dualism: "Dualism, by definition, is a division of people."[25] Had any readers of Machiavelli been present that day, they could have reminded the former prime minister that the Florentine thinker believed the opposite – that dualist visions, quarrels, and tumult between opposing "humours" contribute to the health and equilibrium of a republic.[26] The senators, however, had to be content with an apologetic version of Canadian history, culminating in the work of a prime minister – Mr Trudeau himself! – who had "brought in a Charter of Rights and Freedoms entrenched in the Constitution, and which was meant to create a body of values and beliefs that not only united all Canadians in feeling that they were one nation."[27]

Mr Trudeau's brief to the Senate committee has to be regarded as the gospel of those Canadians who refuse the principle of asymmetry in relations between the various governments and provinces. If the Meech Lake deal were to be ratified, he stated, there would be "a probability that the Constitution will be interpreted differently for Quebec than for the rest of Canada."[28] It would mean the end of equality, of national patriotism founded on the Charter, and ultimately of Canada itself. At the end of his analysis, Mr Trudeau invited the senators, the members of the provincial legislatures, and ordinary citizens to unite against the balkanization of Canada. He expressly congratulated Frank McKenna of New Brunswick and Sharon Carstairs of Manitoba. He knew he was running a risk in this battle, but he insisted that it was worth the effort: "But, then, Thucydides wrote that Themistocles' greatness lay in the fact that he realized Athens was not immortal. I think we have to realize that Canada is not immortal; but, if it is going to go, let it go with a bang rather than a whimper."[29]

In December 1988, Robert Bourassa "desecrated" the fundamental symbol of Canadian nationalism by making the Charter of Rights and Freedoms inapplicable to Quebec's language policy. This was all that Gary Filmon needed to put off ratification of the Meech Lake Accord in his province indefinitely. In the spring of 1989, the Manitoba government established a tripartite committee, which was mandated to hold public hearings and report to the legislature. As Pierre Fournier relates, the committee insisted that the Charter of Rights and Freedoms prevail over the distinct society clause and that a Canada clause be inserted in the constitution, specifying the existence of Canada as a federal state with a distinct national identity.[30] On 20 April 1989, Mr Clyde Wells, another of Pierre Trudeau's allies, became premier of Newfoundland. Opposed to the distinct society clause and to any particular status for Quebec, Mr Wells announced that the House of Assembly would withdraw support for the Meech Lake Accord. Like Pierre Trudeau, Clyde Wells is a ferocious supporter of the equality of citizens and provinces within a single Canadian nation. In the months leading to the definitive derailing of the Meech deal in June 1990, Mr Wells became a real media star in English Canada. Slowly but surely, the winds changed. Although originally greeted with some indifference, the Meech Lake Accord was eventually rejected not only by some provinces but by a good portion of the Canadian population outside Quebec. That is what André Blais and Jean Crête concluded at the end of a study of the evolution of public opinion in English Canada after the 1988 federal election: "There is no doubt that rejection of the Meech Lake Accord was what the majority of English Canada wished. The mobilization of opposition to the Accord can be explained essentially as a reaction to the distinct society clause."[31]

From May 1987 to June 1990, no one had so frequently and systematically assailed the distinct society clause as Pierre Elliott

Trudeau. In an earlier chapter, I tried to show how limited in scope the clause was. What did the former prime minister's intransigence actually conceal?

CONCLUSION

In the last stretch of his political career, fortune served Pierre Elliott Trudeau well. In the winter of 1980, it provided him with one last opportunity, which he exploited brilliantly with all the intellectual and physical resources at his disposal. Thanks to this combination of fortune and skill, he achieved his greatest victories: the February 1980 election, success in the referendum, and the final consummation of his constitutional initiative. After two decades of unceasing personal endeavour, all this assured him an enviable place in the history of contemporary Canada. When he retired in June 1984, Trudeau could boast about his stature as the most important political personality of twentieth-century Canada. This man marked our lives the way Churchill, de Gaulle, and Roosevelt marked the lives of the British, the French, and the Americans. When Trudeau quit politics, he could pride himself on having succeeded in what is, according to Machiavelli, the most difficult and perilous of political undertakings – the radical transformation of his country's constitution. To this extent, we must see him essentially as the new founder of Canada. At sixty-five years of age and at the height of his powers (thanks again to a combination of skill and fortune), he retired to Montreal to see to the education of his three sons.

Had the story ended in this manner, Pierre Trudeau's spirit would indubitably have survived a long time within Canada's constitutional and political structure. In the memory and gratitude of future generations, it would even have achieved immortality. Of all the political actors of our epoch, here and elsewhere, few would be so ambitious as to dream of a similar destiny. But as incredible as it may at first seem, Pierre Trudeau was not content with such a fate. His role in the Meech Lake debate clearly demonstrates that he aimed even higher. He was not content to win; he dreamed of total victory. He wanted to witness the definitive annihilation of his Québécois adversaries – nationalist sovereigntists as well as federalist dualists – in his own lifetime. In my opinion, he wanted to occupy the entire constitutional stage on his own. His speeches and articles in the Meech Lake saga are stamped with the seal of excess and insatiability. Because of Trudeau's Meech Lake performance, Canada and Quebec have come close to a tragic fate for one of the few times in their history.

Trudeau ultimately succumbed to a weakness that Machiavelli knew well: the inability of human beings to rein in their hopes. Even the most disciplined and the wisest of individuals, those who have repeatedly demonstrated sound judgment, sometimes yield, against their better nature, to the temptation of hubris and excess. Oh, they may often emerge unscathed, because they know how to be audacious, cunning, and merciless in action; fortune can continue to smile on them for a time, even in their excess. Yet those who choose the inebriation of action will pay a price. They may win, but if perchance they suffer defeat – if fortune abandons them – there is no end to their losses and distress. Trudeau fervently and unrestrainedly wished nothing less than absolute victory over duality. He knew how to take risks in opposing the Meech Lake Accord. In the short term, he won – once again – for the accord was derailed and the perfect unanimity of 1987 disappeared. But as I write these lines in August 1994, it is conceivable that Trudeau will soon lose everything: the Charter, the 1982 constitution, Quebec in his Canada, and perhaps even Canada itself. No one can be a soothsayer in a context as uncertain as ours.

Gérard Bergeron, a sage if there ever was one, thinks that the winds of history are not blowing in favour of Quebec independence; rather, there are some cold rains in store for us. Perhaps. As for myself, transferring the analysis onto Canada as a whole, I sense that this country will not succeed in overcoming the present crisis, which is too severe. As we saw in earlier chapters, some of the events leading up to the 1982 constitutional reform reduced the legitimacy of the Canadian federal system in Quebec to its most rudimentary form. Flowing from the 1982 reform, as we shall see, are a political culture and an institutional logic that are tainted because they are based on a negative, anti-Québécois ambition.

In his introduction to the French edition of Max Weber's *Politics as a Vocation*, Raymond Aron wrote: "At critical times, living systems produce persons who can save them."[32] To save Canadian federalism from the wrong Mr Trudeau has done Quebec and to heal it of the unhealthy excess that coloured his actions in the Meech Lake saga would take more than a great man or a courageous woman: it would take a character of divine stature. Such a character rarely comes in our midst. As a disciple of Machiavelli's realism, Max Weber believed that to dare to leap into the political arena, one has to be ready to envisage the foundering of all of one's dreams.[33] If Canada founders, largely because Pierre Trudeau in his last years failed to curb his passions, we shall find out whether the man with the rose really had politics as a vocation, in the Weberian sense of the word.

CHAPTER SIX

Canadian Political Culture and the Charter of Rights and Freedoms

He haunts us still. Six years after he resigned as prime minister, a quarter of a century after he first sought office, Pierre Elliott Trudeau and his ideas remain dominant in the northern attic of the continent, a standard against which other political actors, thinkers, theorists, and hopefuls – past and present – measure themselves and are measured.

Stephen Clarkson and Christina McCall

Trudeau's spectre still hovers over Quebec and Canada.[1] All those who involve themselves, either closely or peripherally, in the political and constitutional crisis that has raged since the death of the Meech Lake Accord will have to get used to his presence. For in these uncertain times of ours, one thing at least is sure: as long as he lives, Mr Trudeau will never remain silent on the question of the constitution and the status of Quebec. His remarks at the beginning of October 1991 on the distinct society and the spectre of the deportation of the English in a sovereign Quebec will at the very least have served to confirm this.

Mr Trudeau will continue to haunt us in this chapter. In it, I intend to foster a better understanding of the institutions – the Charter of Rights and Freedoms being first among them – that have governed the political life of Quebec since 1982. The adoption of the Charter is undoubtedly the most significant event in the evolution of Canadian political culture in the twentieth century. To grasp the scope of these institutions, I believe it is necessary to look at the intentions of their founders. One cannot comprehend the 1982 constitutional reform if one does not constantly keep in mind the objectives of Pierre Elliott Trudeau.

I shall begin by restating and developing one of the lessons learned in the preceding chapter: that during the 1980s, Mr Trudeau became reconciled with Canadian nationalism. I shall then show that English-Canadian political scientists explicitly acknowledge that the Charter of Rights and Freedoms, around which the 1982 constitutional reform revolves, is a crucial stage in a nationalist trend that has successfully imposed itself over the past decade. Thirdly, the triumph of that movement, along with the advantage of historical distance, should afford us a better appreciation of the dilemmas faced by Quebec's elected representatives, Liberals as well as Péquistes, in 1981–82, during the Canada round, as well as in the decisive times ahead. Finally, I shall consider whether the 1982 reform addressed the demands of popular sovereignty.

Before going any further, I would like to make some preliminary remarks about the constitution. We have been speaking about it for such a long time in Quebec that we tend to forget the seriousness and perils of such a project. To change a constitution is to alter the nature, the very being, of a political body. It is an extraordinarily difficult affair, one that is rarely graced with success. It is likely to destroy the best of those who have the nerve to undertake it. Reading such masters of political thought as Machiavelli and Rousseau, as we shall do in the first section of this chapter, will give us a better sense of the challenges and dangers inherent in any venture into the world of constitutional reform. Revising the constitution is arduous in itself, but the founding of a new system is even more difficult. Nonetheless, that is what transpired in Canada, as the Bélanger-Campeau Commission noted: "Far from revising the *Constitution Act, 1867*, the 1982 Act contains a new constitutional definition of Canada which has altered the spirit of the 1867 Act and the compromise established at that time."[2]

In 1982 Pierre Elliott Trudeau and his collaborators succeeded where the best and strongest of a political community most often fail. The meaning of this feat and the worth of those who achieved it need to be weighed at some length. Anyone who would challenge the 1982 Act will face a formidable foe in Mr Trudeau. He will not remain silent on this question, since he is the true founder of the political system under which we have lived since 1982. His place in history is linked to the fortunes of this system, which he will defend to the last with all the energy that he can muster.

TRUDEAU AND CANADIAN NATIONALISM

I should like to start this section by drawing the reader's attention to two quotations, the first by Thomas Axworthy, and the second by Pierre Elliott Trudeau:

A second criterion will be the contribution of the Charter towards the development of a sense of national community. The attachment of Canadians to a sense of national community, and to a belief in the strength of shared values, claims, obligations and opportunities, is a fundamental objective of a nation-building quest. The Charter was the Ark and the Covenant in the federal vision.[3]

And then we have the real country – that is, the unorganized coalition of Canadian individuals and groups scattered across the nation, for whom Canada is more than a collection of provinces to be governed through wheeling and dealing. To them, Canada is a true nation, whose ideal is compassion and justice and whose desire is to be governed democratically in freedom and equality.[4]

While the fight against nationalist ideology as a whole, and more specifically against Québécois nationalism, was the main business of Pierre Trudeau's intellectual and political life, the means he adopted to reach that particular target did not always conform to the general philosophical principles of his project. During the 1980s, after the Quebec referendum, Mr Trudeau came to terms once and for all with Canadian nationalism. Better still, he became its tireless promoter, its most effective advocate in this century. Christina McCall and Stephen Clarkson fall short of a critical analysis and lapse into apologetics when they make Trudeau into a champion of the federalist vision of Canada: "He still believed that what he was after in trying to patriate the Canadian constitution was a more fully realized democracy where 'the people' as an entity would assume responsibility for the nation's social contract and at the same time achieve greater individual liberty through his proposed Charter of Rights and Freedoms."[5]

Pierre Elliott Trudeau's relations to the question of nationalism are sufficiently complex to warrant an independent study. Michael Oliver has recently made a remarkable contribution to this subject.[6] In the following paragraphs, I shall restrict myself, in large part, to recalling the extent to which Trudeau seized the torch of Canadian nationalism in the last years of his active political life. But first, I shall endeavour to sketch an explanation of his commitment to this nationalism.

Pierre Trudeau was unquestionably the most brilliant antinationalist intellectual of the 1950s and 1960s in Quebec. For more than fifteen years, he spoke on every platform with eloquence and panache, denouncing the hypertrophy and idealism of the nationalist security system that was slowing the development of French-Canadian society.[7] Like others in the early 1960s, he was nonplussed by the rise of movements calling for independence, by terrorism, and by the decolonizing and inflammatory revolutionary discourse of the young intellectuals associated with the magazine *Parti pris*. Trudeau found their discourse wholly disconnected from Quebec society. It was in this period that he wrote some of his most virulent texts against Quebec nationalism in its various guises. Let us listen to what he had to say to the twenty-something generation in "The New Treason of the Intellectuals": "Nationalism, as an emotional stimulus directed at an entire community, can indeed let loose unforeseen powers. History is full of this, called variously chauvinism, racism, jingoism, and all manner of crusades, where right reasoning and thought are reduced to rudimentary proportions."[8]

According to Trudeau's last articles in *Cité libre*, every nationalism is by definition an expression of tribalism and primitivism, and is rooted in emotionalism and irrationality.[9] In his recent study, Michael Oliver observes that Trudeau's anger was directed as much at sociological nationalism (which holds a people together) as at judicial nationalism (which serves this function for a state). However, he was concerned most particularly with the kind of sociological nationalism that was practised in French Canada. According to Oliver, Trudeau "could be a harsh critic of English Canada's s nationalism [sociological nationalism] and its efforts to create a Canadian j nationalism [judicial nationalism] in its own image, yet he denounces French-Canadian nationalism with a passion rarely present in his statements on English Canada."[10]

In the 1960s, Trudeau believed that a federal state composed of several sociological nations should not, in theory, have to resort to emotionally charged nationalism to preserve its cohesion and unity. Reason should suffice. Oliver goes to the heart of the matter when he writes that Trudeau was far from even-handed in his condemnation of the two nationalisms; he was both exhaustive and merciless in his critique of the sociological variant but was taciturn about "how to defend oneself against the spokespersons of the existing state, who deploy language and affective symbols historically linked to s nationalism, in order to transfer feelings of loyalty from the s nation onto the j nation."[11] Fifteen years later, this silence was to turn into active promotion of Canadian nationalism.

During the constitutional round of 1980–82, the Charter of Rights and Freedoms was the principal stuff of a strategy aimed at binding the Canadian nation together. Over the years, Trudeau's rhetoric shifted in order to justify the enshrining of a fundamental declaration of rights and freedoms in the constitution. He subscribed to this idea in 1965, at a time when he seemed to feel the urgency of constitutional reform far less than the political and intellectual leaders of Quebec.[12] The project of a charter of rights did not become a real priority for him until he became federal minister of justice in 1967. Between the summer of 1967 and the notorious constitutional conference of February 1968 – the scene of the well-known confrontation between Trudeau and the elder Daniel Johnson – the federal government developed the strategy of creating a charter of rights as a bulwark against Quebec's desire for decentralization.[13] Quebec insisted that the division of powers be placed at the top of constitutional priorities, but the federal government replied that a charter of rights had to be discussed first. Dominique Clift has noted a significant gulf between Trudeau's statements in 1967–68, and 1981–82: "When he was Minister of Justice in 1967, Pierre Trudeau presented the Charter of Rights as an ideal line of defence against the arbitrary use and abuse of state power. In 1981, those same rights had become the instrument enabling the federal government to impose its authority on the provinces. Individual rights, which had been identified with justice, were now to be used to complete the task of nation-building."[14]

After having fought Quebec nationalism intellectually, Pierre Trudeau relentlessly combatted it on the political stage between 1965 and 1982. To achieve victory, he finally resolved to link the project of a charter of rights to the development of Canadian nationalism. As noted in the preceding chapter, one too often forgets that Trudeau came close to catastrophe in this undertaking. Let us recall once more the major developments of this gripping saga. In the spring of 1979, some three years after the Parti québécois victory and its prefiguration of intensified conflict, Trudeau and the Liberal Party experienced defeat during the federal elections. Some months later, Trudeau announced his intention to leave politics. Had his career ended then, he would have had to give up his two great ambitions: the patriation of the constitution and the defeat of Quebec nationalism. But fate, or fortune as Machiavelli prefers to call it, granted him one last chance. When the Clark government fell in the autumn, Trudeau remained at the head of the Liberal Party, and he became prime minister of Canada again with a majority government in 1980. When fortune grants a political figure one last opportunity to carry out his most cherished projects, he must know, as Machiavelli puts it, how to take advantage of it.[15] He must deploy every ounce of strength and all the means at his disposal. Trudeau's biographers, Stephen Clarkson and Christina McCall, show clearly that he was in such a state of mind in 1980: "The promises uppermost in Trudeau's mind were the ones he had made to himself thirty years before when he decided that his mission in life was to save Quebec from its parochial nationalists and bring it into the modern world. At the age of sixty, he was facing the climactic years of a long struggle and he was determined, in a way he had never been before, to win the victory that really mattered to him."[16]

It is worth repeating that Trudeau rose to the occasion that fortune had afforded him. He gave his all in the referendum battle, he did so again in the unilateral initiative of patriating the constitution, and he witnessed the realization of his dreams on 17 April 1982. That day, the Queen gave her assent to a new constitution for Canada, crowned by the Charter of Rights and Freedoms. Meanwhile, Quebec nationalists appeared to have been reduced to impotence. Strengthened by his victories, Trudeau withdrew from politics in 1984, and he remained silent on Canadian affairs until the announcement of an agreement at Meech Lake in April 1987.

Less than a month after the signing of the Meech Lake Accord, Mr Trudeau began to criticize it through and through in a series of texts and sundry interventions that did not cease until the accord's death in June 1990 – under well-known circumstances. Mr Trudeau's anti-Meech salvos illustrate how much the project of enshrining the Charter of Rights and Freedoms was intimately linked to the promotion of Canadian nationalism. The Meech Lake Accord, he averred, destroyed the dream of a single bilingual and multicultural Canada, sweeping away the project of a country in which, thanks to the Charter, "everyone would be on an equal footing and where citizenship would finally be founded on a set of commonly shared values."[17] On many occasions, he recalled that the spirit of 1982 favoured the development of a national sense of allegiance to Canada. In March 1988, Mr Trudeau explained before the Senate that the 1982 reform was aimed at nothing less than uniting all Canadians in feeling that they were one nation.[18] How should this be interpreted? It recalls Jean-Jacques Rousseau's *Social Contract*, in which the great legislator is described as having to feel capable of transforming human nature.[19] To unite Canadians (including, especially, the people of Quebec) by constitutional means would mean modifying the country's political culture, changing the political identity of the citizens, strengthening the allegiance of all to the Canadian nation, and consequently weakening the Québécois' national sense of belonging. It is because he had invested so much effort in finally securing the "constitutionalization" of all Canadian citizens in 1982 that Mr Trudeau so ferociously opposed the Meech Lake Accord, especially the distinct society clause that nodded symbolically in the direction of Quebec nationalism. He saw the clause as a return to the hydra of duality, a principle that was incompatible with the project of a great Canadian nation that united the country's citizens. The same man who resorted to Canadian nationalism after the referendum had written fifteen years earlier that "nationalism cannot provide the answer," that "in the advanced societies ... nationalism will have to be discarded as a rustic and clumsy tool."[20]

I have tried in this section to explain the origins of Pierre Elliott Trudeau's commitment to Canadian nationalism, which he explicitly recognized in the debate over the Meech Lake Accord. In the following section, we shall see that English-Canadian political scientists openly acknowledge the profoundly nationalist character of the Charter of Rights and Freedoms. But first, let us grant Michael Oliver the final word regarding the means Mr Trudeau used to triumph over Quebec nationalism:

He offered the people an attempt to make the Charter of Rights and Freedoms, and Canadians' right to be the masters of their own constitution, the expression of a national will. In the face of provincial intransigeance, Trudeau did all that he could to arouse a feeling of Canadianism more powerful than the provinces' particular wishes. It is hard not to form the impression that he was using j nationalism as a bond whose strength he hoped would be lasting in Canada.[21]

POLITICAL SCIENCE IN ENGLISH CANADA AND THE CHARTER OF RIGHTS AND FREEDOMS

To understand how Pierre Elliott Trudeau could become the greatest champion of Canadian nationalism in the twentieth century, one must first consider what distinguishes this nationalism from its French-Canadian and, subsequently, Quebec counterparts. In English Canada, the state created the nation. The opposite is true of French Canada. Admittedly, the provincial state has played a considerable part in crystallizing Quebec nationality since the beginning of the Quiet Revolution, but in the case of English Canada, the central state's contribution to nation building goes back to Confederation. The task of constructing a national identity had scarcely begun in the northernmost Victorian dominion in 1867. It was the central state – the federal government and its apparatuses – which undertook this task. Philip Resnick, one of English Canada's leading political analysts, has recently recalled the different stages of this enormous project of national construction in his book *The Masks of Proteus: Canadian Reflections on the State*. As he points out, from 1867 on, the central state had to invest colossal sums of money for more than a century before a sense of Canadian national identity became widely felt in the hearts and minds of our English-speaking fellow citizens.[22]

Building the Canadian nation has always been one of the main aims of the supporters of a strong central government in this country. This centripetal perspective was adopted by politicians of every political stripe: Macdonald, Borden, and Bennett among the Conservatives,

King and Saint-Laurent under the Liberal banner, and Woodsworth, Douglas, and Lewis in the CCF and the NDP. Intellectuals did not remain aloof from this movement. Thus, in the 1930s, when the Privy Council in London opposed Bennett's New Deal, many intellectuals redoubled their efforts to encourage the federal government to reform federalism, so that it would provide itself with the power to determine economic development and social policy.[23] In the eyes of men such as Eugene Forsey, Vincent Massey, F.R. Scott, and Frank Underhill, centralization was in the interest of the Canadian nation. This was the argument they defended in the debates surrounding the Rowell-Sirois Commission at the end of the 1930s. No new constitution was drawn up in 1939–40, but the Second World War gave Mackenzie King's Liberal government the opportunity to use its broad emergency powers to develop a Canadian welfare state and push ahead with nation building. Resnick sums up the different stages in the invention of a Canadian national tradition by the federal state:

The identification with Canada, as distinct from Britain, would come out of the slaughter of the First World War and again the Second and out of the shift, economically, culturally, and politically, between the 1920s and the 1940s, from the British to the American spheres. It would take sustenance from the greater international recognition that Canada as a state achieved through membership in the League of Nations, the Commonwealth, and the United Nations; from those nation-building activities associated with crown corporations such as the Canadian National Railways, the Canadian Broadcasting Corporation, and Trans-Canada Airlines; with the sense of national solidarity associated with social activities of the state – old-age pensions, unemployment insurance, and family allowances; and from the symbolism of post-1945 Canadian nationalism – the Canadian Citizenship Act (1947), abolition of appeals to the Privy Council (1949), naming of Canadians to the position of governor general (1952 and on), creation of the Canada Council (1957), the Bill of Rights (1960), adoption of a new Canadian flag (1965), Expo '67, and patriation of the Canadian constitution (1982).[24]

Such a list may seem pedantic at first sight. Nonetheless, it demonstrates the inextricable link between nation and central state in English Canada. In this context, any attempt to reduce the powers of the central state will likely prove unpopular. Quebec learned this to its detriment in the Meech Lake Saga. About a year before the collapse of the accord, Philip Resnick explained why English-Canadian public opinion had reservations about it:

What I am trying to drive home is that our sense of nation is in many ways rooted in the federal government you so disdain, that without that central state there really cannot be a Canadian (or English Canadian) nation. Over the century and a quarter since Confederation, our symbols of nationhood have been associated with it. From mounted police to railway projects to armed forces to national broadcasting, social programs, or the flag, the route for English Canadians has entailed use of that state. To weaken or dismantle it is to strike a blow at our identity.[25]

The Constitution Act, 1982, and especially the Charter of Rights and Freedoms that is enshrined within it, must therefore be seen in the light of this long tradition, in which the central state and its related institutions have shaped and invented the Canadian nation. In Trudeau's vision, as we saw above, the Charter was not only a legal device to be used in the quest for justice for individuals living in a liberal society; it was also a crucial step in building the Canadian nation. By making the system evolve in a centripetal fashion by reinforcing institutions such as the Supreme Court that are under federal jurisdiction, Mr Trudeau was catering to a typically English-Canadian nationalism. According to Resnick, that nationalism views the central state as the primary constitutive element of its identity. With the Constitution Act, 1982, the Québécois were invited to commune at the altar of a Canadian national spirit whose genealogy goes back to an English-Canadian nationalism. The fundamental objective of the authors of the 1982 constitution seems to have been to promote throughout Canada (including Quebec) a political culture capable of reinforcing in each citizen the feeling of belonging to a single Canadian nation.

In this section, I would like to show that Quebec intellectuals and academics associated with the nationalist movement were not the only ones to construe the 1982 Charter of Rights and Freedoms as an instrument of Canadian nationalism. The leading English-Canadian experts on the subject have been repeating it insistently for ten years. As early as 1983, Peter Russell saw the strengthening of national unity as one of the Charter's two principal political goals (the other being the protection of fundamental rights and freedoms).[26] At the time, Russell believed that the Charter made three great contributions to the work of nation building.

First, the Charter could operate as a unifying symbol.[27] In stating in a constitutional document the fundamental values shared by Canadians, it would act on the attitudes and beliefs of each Canadian and would foster a better understanding of the importance of fundamental freedoms and the institutions that protect them. The Canada clause played a similar role in the Charlottetown Accord of 1992. As Rainer Knopff and F.L. Morton, two of Russell's disciples, have recalled, there was a primarily symbolic function to enshrining policies on bilingualism and multiculturalism in the constitution. The status of these policies as fundamental elements of Canadian citizenship and identity was thereby reinforced.[28]

Secondly, the Charter would work towards the unification of the nation by homogenizing policies across the country. This is crystal clear in the area of language policy. In matters of bilingualism and access to minority language schools, Mr Trudeau's government held steadfastly to the principle of "national standards." Sections 16 to 23, which deal with these questions, are among the most specific in the whole document. Moreover, these sections are protected from the notwithstanding clause, which permits governments to exempt themselves temporarily from applying certain parts of the Charter. As is well known, the 1982 Charter directly challenged Quebec legislation by imposing national language standards.

In his 1983 article, Peter Russell did not think that the area of language exhausted the Charter's homogenizing potential. He noted another feature of it in an article guaranteeing mobility of manpower. Although this entailed some progress, Russell wrote that many obstacles still thwarted the development of a real Canadian economic union. Reading Russell's text helps us indirectly grasp the nationalist dimension of the Charlottetown Accord – for example, in the provisions regarding harmonization of economic policies. Such harmonization is not dictated by an exclusively economic rationality.

Beyond the symbolic dimension and the will to homogenize public policies, it was in the judicialization of the Canadian political system that Russell saw the Charter's third and main tendency in terms of nation building. His 1983 remarks are still relevant.

I think the Charter's nationalizing influence will be felt most through a process scarcely mentioned by its political sponsors – the process of judicial review ... Judicial decisions on the Charter will be unifying in that the very debates and controversies they produce will be national and on issues that transcend the regional cleavages which are usually a feature of national political controversy in Canada. Court cases on the Charter normally will not pit region against region or the provinces against the feds. Instead the principal protagonists will be interest groups and aggregations of individuals from all parts of Canada ... Although the controversy will be intense, it will be waged on a national level in the arena of national politics and on grounds that do not call into question the legitimacy of Canada as a national political community. It is in this sense that the Charter may well turn out to be a nation-building instrument.[29]

The 1982 Charter shifted the ground of conflict, drawing it out of provincial confines and inserting it in a pan-Canadian legal and political arena, where the Supreme Court, which is under the jurisdiction of the central state, is the court of final appeal. To enshrine this Charter, Pierre Elliott Trudeau had to overcome the opposition of several provincial governments. To bend them to his will, he appealed directly to the interest groups and individuals who were most concerned with the protection of individual rights. These groups made their presence felt during the hearings of the Special Joint Committee of the Senate and the House of Commons, in the winter of 1980–81, that gave rise to important modifications of the federal project.

In a certain sense, Canada's federal character was an obstacle to the enshrining of the Charter. The notwithstanding clause was a concession granted to the most ferocious defenders of parliamentary supremacy and executive federalism. However, they obtained only a meager consolation, a pyrrhic victory. Through the judicialization of the political system, the Charter works against Canada's federal nature, for the judicial power reflects the federal reality of our country most poorly. The Charter unquestionably achieves its best results on the level of centralization. The federal government unilaterally appoints judges to all the high courts of the country, including the Supreme Court. In their analyses of the jurisprudence emanating from the Charter, the leading experts, such as Peter Russell, Rainer Knopff, and F.L. Morton, have concluded that the Charter has succeeded in recentralizing the Canadian federation. There has definitely been a homogenization of public policies, and not only in the area of language. Uniform national standards have been imposed where previously regional diversity reigned supreme.[30] Note that this jurisprudence not only standardizes certain social practices; it also contributes to the convergence of common law and Quebec's civil code, which is central to Quebec's distinct society. Some ten years after the Charter's inception, Russell, Knopff, and Morton observed that the Supreme Court of Canada, which presides over the judicializing of politics, now plays a more important sociopolitical role than its American counterpart.[31]

The 1982 Charter's judicialization of the Canadian political system was carried out in the name of popular sovereignty. The federal government's project was presented as a "people's package," deriving its legitimacy from something more fundamental than the federal principles invoked by the recalcitrant provincial governments. Reference to the citizens' constitutional primacy and to universal human rights was used to circumvent the political system's federal character and to inspire greater allegiance to the Canadian national community.[32] As a result of the logic of 1982, federalism became blurred in a number of ways. It became secondary in the order of legitimation

principles. It also progressively receded as "national standards" were
spelled out. The Supreme Court's standardization of laws and provincial rules did not leave the critics indifferent. Some have accused
the court of not taking the diversity of provincial communities sufficiently into consideration.[33] According to Patrick Monahan, the criteria by which the Supreme Court has chosen to interpret section 1
of the Charter (which recognizes the existence of reasonable limits to
the exercise of rights in a free and democratic society), occluded the
communitarian values that nonetheless belong in this same Charter
and in the whole of Canadian society.[34]

In the debate over the Meech Lake Accord, many in English
Canada criticized the indefinite and imprecise character of the distinct society clause. Historian Ramsay Cook was one of these critics.[35]
People wondered what Quebec would do once it was armed with
this clause. In his study of the Charter, Michael Mandel responded
to Cook's arguments, pointing out that the ultimate imprecision is to
be found in the Charter rather than in the distinct society clause, and
that consequently the Supreme Court enjoys extraordinary interpretative latitude. Given the judicial power's centralization and the
Charter's place in the project of building the Canadian nation, this
latitude should give the Quebec legislators pause for thought:

The phrases are so vague and the notion of "reasonable limits" so inherently
flexible that, though the new clause [that of distinct society in the Meech
Lake Accord] might give the courts new arguments for conclusions they
might want, on other grounds, to reach, it can in no sense be said to limit or
even to guide them. While it is undoubtedly true that giving the courts such
wide scope is not wise, it is a little absurd to say that the danger of this
latitude is to the Charter (Cook, 1987), *because the Charter is itself the epitome
of unguided judicial power.* (My emphasis)[36]

In the Quebec debate over the Meech Lake Accord, it was not
unusual to hear people claim that the conflict between the supporters
of the distinct society clause and those of Charter supremacy was
actually a conflict between those who endorsed collective rights and
those who preferred the absolute guarantee of individual rights. In
my opinion, the Québécois did not renounce individual rights any
more than their Canadian counterparts rejected the principle of collective rights. In fact, the 1982 Charter of Rights and Freedoms must
be regarded as a manifesto of Canadian nationalism rather than a
symbol of the triumph of liberal individualism. In principle at least,
the Charter makes it possible to reconcile individual and collective
rights. The recognition of multiculturalism and the affirmation of the

ancestral rights of native peoples are good illustrations of the collective rights enshrined in the Charter.

There is no consensus among Canadian nationalists and experts on what place collective rights should occupy in the political culture and legal structure of the country. People such as David Elkins and Philip Resnick think it should be significant. Elkins writes that Canadians have learned to respect the "verdant variety of community-based ways of life" that is objectified in the Charter.[37] Others, such as David Bercuson and Barry Cooper, consider collective rights a philosophical aberration in a society that considers itself liberal and democratic. Bercuson and Cooper go so far as to recommend that Quebec be categorically expelled from Canada because its collectivist nationalism threatens Canada's liberal culture.[38] As we saw earlier, the Charter does not put an end to ideological polarization. The conflicts persist. However, since 1982, these conflicts have occurred primarily on the "national" stage, in the pan-Canadian political arena. Public opinion on the right and left appeals to the same national standard, namely, equal rights for all Canadians. When the principle of symmetrical equality regarding the rights and status of individual citizens (irrespective of their place of residence in the country) gradually becomes encrusted in the public mind, we are witnessing the triumph of Pierre Elliott Trudeau's nationalist project.

The work of Professor Alan Cairns of the University of British Columbia admirably accounts for Trudeau's success in strengthening the Canadian nation. According to Cairns, the Charter of Rights and Freedoms is undoubtedly an instrument of prime value in Trudeau's gigantic battle to consolidate a pan-Canadian national identity:

The Charter's message is not however indifferent to the distinction between provincial communities and the coast-to-coast pan-Canadian community. The Charter's message is a Canadian message. The rights it enshrines are Canadian rights. The community of citizen membership that it fosters is the overall Canadian community. It is the Canadianism of the Charter that explains the continuing lesser sympathy for, and the previous opposition to the Charter by provincial governments.[39]

Cairns convincingly demonstrates that the Meech Lake Accord violated the norms of equality among provinces and equality of citizenship that had been objectified in Canadian political culture following the 1982 reform.[40] He also succeeds in explaining the weakening of the Canadian tradition of executive federalism over the last decade. The Charter created a whole series of new constitutional players: women and their organizations, multicultural groups and visible minorities, native peoples, and official-language minorities. The interest groups that represent these players have in a sense colonized the constitution. The rights they obtained by way of the Charter are symbols of their new status in society, in the Canadian nation. One of the Charter's objectives was to diminish the sense of regional and territorial "belonging" experienced by the members of these groups and to promote among them an unmediated identification with the Canadian national community as a whole. Cairns invites those who question the realization of this objective to consider the role of these "Charter patriots" in opposing the distinct society clause in the debate over the Meech Lake Accord.[41]

As we shall see more fully in the following chapter, the Allaire and Bélanger-Campeau reports highlighted the importance in Quebec of a dualist interpretation of the history of Canadian federalism. This duality can be expressed in terms of founding peoples, nations, and distinct societies. The idea underlying this vision is that there are two majorities in Canada, one of which is established in Quebec. According to Cairns, the Charter of Rights and Freedoms succeeds in circumventing this notion of two majorities by promoting a political culture founded on constitutional minoritarianism. For various reasons, the power of these actors, and their ability to influence the later rounds of constitutional negotiations, can only grow. They henceforth possess rights, status within the system, and real constitutional identity. The social movements with which they are associated – new ethnicities, feminism, native resurgence – are passing through a period of growth throughout the world. Moreover, these groups have developed their own bureaucratic infrastructure, which can rely on experts, university curricula, and specialized journals, as well as on sympathetic treatment by the media. Immigration is gradually in the process of transforming Canada into a country that is ever more open to multiculturalism and racial pluralism. According to Cairns, these various minorities benefit from a contagion effect: each gain obtained by one encourages the others to follow suit, reinforcing the general system of constitutional minoritarianism.[42] Buttressed by their new rights, they will continue to fight relentlessly and passionately. As Cairns points out, they speak of "shame, pride, dignity, affront, inclusion and exclusion, humiliation and recognition."[43] None of this bodes well for the principle of two majorities.

One might think that constitutional minoritarianism illustrates the open-mindedness and respect for diversity that pervades twentieth-century Canadian federalism. The work of Alan Cairns reminds us that there are limits to this tolerance, to this respect for diversity. The Canadian nationalism that inspired the 1982 constitutional reform does not recognize Quebec as a distinct society or as an autonomous national community. As to the levelling tendency within this reform, Cairns's views coincide with the position of the Bélanger-Campeau Commission's report:

The Charter generates a roving normative Canadianism oblivious to provincial boundaries, and thus hostile to constitutional stratagems such as the Meech Lake "distinct society" that might vary the Charter's availability in one province. Federalist and even stronger dualist justifications for constitutional recognition of Quebec as a distinct society clashed with a Canadian Charter norm applied to Quebec by those who lived elsewhere. The Quebec rationale for an asymmetrical Charter confronted a homogenizing Charter-derived-rights-bearing Canadianism that applied not to the *Québécois* but to Canadians who happened to live in Québec.[44]

The last sentence of this passage deserves serious consideration. The homogenizing variety of Canadianism conveyed by the Charter of Rights and Freedoms, writes Cairns, did not apply to the Québécois but to Canadians whose circumstances impelled them to live in Quebec. In the final analysis, the political culture conveyed by the Charter does not merely shift the place of conflict. It strengthens the minority identities that have no territorial foundation other than the Canadian national community as a whole. In the nationalist political culture of 1982, which Pierre Elliott Trudeau desired, any reference to duality, to the notion of two majorities and a distinct political community in Quebec, was completely eliminated.

If all the Quebec legislators had known about this nationalist dimension in October and November 1981, when the National Assembly debated the constitutional reform, Quebec society could have offered stronger resistance to what was an operation of dubious legitimacy.

QUEBEC LEGISLATORS AND CANADIAN NATIONALISM

Pierre Elliott Trudeau dismisses the interpretation of the 1981–82 events presented in this book. In his eyes, the 1982 constitution fully and completely applies to the whole of Canada. It has the force of law and all the attributes of legitimacy. Trudeau's arguments all rest on a rather simple, if not simplistic, arithmetic. According to him, a substantial majority of the representatives democratically elected by the Quebec people voted in favour of patriating the constitution. Patriation was endorsed by 71 of the 75 Quebec members of the

House of Commons and by 38 of the 108 members of the National Assembly called upon to vote on the question; 109 thus endorsed the project while 70 rejected it.[45]

By this reckoning, 61 per cent of Quebec's legislators ratified the new constitution, repeating in a sense the scenario of the May 1980 referendum. However, contrary to what Trudeau would have us believe, he does not fully account for Quebec's true parliamentary situation in the autumn of 1981. I am compelled to tell him once again that this is not the way to write history. After having set matters straight, I shall draw the conclusions that are necessary for Quebec's political parties in the 1990s.

In the autumn of 1981, the Quebec National Assembly was invited on two occasions to study the proposed constitutional reform. On 2 October the members of the assembly were called on to vote on a government motion denouncing Pierre Elliott Trudeau's unilateral way of proceeding. The motion was debated in the days following the Supreme Court's ruling that the federal government could act as it wished in all legality but that constitutional conventions, and thus legitimacy, required that it obtain the support of a "substantial" number of provinces. At that time it was not known what strategy Mr Trudeau would adopt in the wake of the Supreme Court's judgment. The motion on which the legislators voted read as follows:

The Supreme Court of Canada having decided that the federal proposal respecting the Constitution of Canada decreases the powers of the National Assembly of Quebec and that unilateral action by the federal government, although legal, is unconstitutional, being contrary to the conventions, this Assembly demands that the federal government renounce its unilateral course of action, is opposed to any action that could impair its rights and affect its powers without its consent, and requests the federal and provincial governments to resume negotiations immediately, with full respect for the principles and conventions that must apply to any modification of the Canadian federal system.[46]

This motion was passed by 111 votes to 9. Of the 42 members in the Liberal opposition, 33 supported it, including Claude Ryan, Lise Bacon, Jean-Claude Rivest, Guy Bélanger, and Claude Dauphin. John Ciaccia, Michel Gratton, and Clifford Lincoln were among those who opposed it. I shall return in a moment to the tenor of the debates that preceded this vote, but here I want to point out that when Mr Trudeau makes his scientific calculations, he says nothing about this large October consensus that opposed unilateral patriation. He is referring to the vote that occurred at the National Assembly on 1 December

1981, some weeks after the notorious night when the central and provincial governments, with the exception of Quebec, agreed in Ottawa on a project to patriate the constitution, enhanced by a charter of rights and freedoms. The text of the motion reads as follows (given its importance, I shall quote it in full):

The National Assembly of Quebec, mindful of the right of the people of Quebec to self-determination, and exercising its historical right of being a full party to any change to the Constitution of Canada which would affect the rights and powers of Quebec, declares that it cannot accept the plan to patriate the Constitution unless it meets the following conditions:

1. It must be recognized that the two founding peoples of Canada are fundamentally equal and that Quebec, by virtue of its language, culture and institutions, forms a distinct society within the Canadian federal system and has all the attributes of a distinct national community.

2. The Constitutional amending formula

(a) must either maintain Quebec's right of veto, or

(b) be in keeping with the Constitutional Accord signed by Quebec on April 16, 1981, whereby Quebec would not be subject to any amendment which would diminish its powers or rights, and would be entitled, where necessary, to reasonable and obligatory compensation.

3. Given that a Charter of Human Rights and Freedoms is already operative in Quebec, the Charter of Rights and Freedoms to be entrenched in the Canadian Constitution must limit itself to:

(a) democratic rights;

(b) use of French and English in federal government institutions and services;

(c) equality between men and women provided the National Assembly retains the power to legislate in matters under its jurisdiction;

(d) fundamental freedoms, provided the National Assembly retains the power to legislate in matters under its jurisdiction;

(e) English and French minority language guarantees in education, provided Quebec is allowed to adhere voluntarily, considering that its power in this area must remain total and inalienable, and that its minority is already the most privileged in Canada.

4. Effect must be given to the provisions already prescribed in the federal proposal in respect to the right of the provinces to equalization and to better control over their natural resources.[47]

This motion was passed by 70 votes to 38. All the Liberal members who were present that day opposed it. After having added them to the federal members who had voted in favour of the constitutional reform project in Ottawa, Pierre Trudeau concludes that the majority of Quebec representatives gave their assent to the whole affair, and he asserts that there was thus no problem of legitimacy.

Trudeau's arguments seem fallacious to me in several respects. First, they contravene the most elementary rules of logic. One cannot transform the Liberal members' No to a PQ motion denouncing the patriation project, and specifying under what conditions it could be acceptable, into pure and simple approval of Ottawa's position. In other words, one cannot deduce from the Liberals' No to the PQ that they would have granted a clear Yes to Mr Trudeau's project if the question had been put to them directly. There is no necessary logical link between the two. The Liberal members may well have rejected the PQ motion for partisan reasons, because they doubted the PQ's will to pursue the constitutional dialogue with Ottawa sincerely, and at the same time they may have had reservations about Mr Trudeau's patriation project. Their rejection of the PQ motion could just as easily have corresponded to rapturous enthusiasm, reserved welcome, or even categorical refusal of the constitutional reform concocted at the beginning of November. To know more about it, one must question the people and the texts. For example, during a presentation that I gave before one of the commissions studying Quebec's political and constitutional future, Cosmo Maciocia, a member of the National Assembly in 1981, explicitly corroborated my interpretation. He believed that in rejecting the PQ motion, the Liberal members were not supporting what was to become the Constitution Act, 1982.[48] To find out if this was indeed the case, one must repeat the exercise with all those who, like Mr Maciocia, participated in the debates and National Assembly votes in October and November 1981; for the example of Mr Maciocia shows that Pierre Trudeau's juxtaposition of the votes in Quebec and Ottawa distorts reality somewhat. When probed, the relevant documents confirm this.

To know what the Liberals really thought in the autumn of 1981, one must engage in a more thorough effort than Mr Trudeau's arithmetic and return to the debates of the National Assembly. Readers who are interested in a comprehensive account may also wish to review the whole thing for themselves. I shall highlight just one sample here, which I believe is representative of the Liberal caucus's general opinion. The sample is drawn from statements by Claude Ryan, the Liberal leader at the time. Here is what Mr Ryan said on 30 September 1981, on the eve of the vote on the first motion:

What is at stake is the defence of Quebec's legislative powers, the defence of Quebec's constitutional powers, which are seriously threatened by the project currently put forward by the federal government ...

We must conclude very firmly that each time the National Assembly's essential prerogatives are undermined, the people of Quebec themselves are undermined. To be indifferent to that which undermines the powers of the National Assembly is to be indifferent to, or to treat lightly, the aspirations and fundamental reality of the people of Quebec themselves ...

I personally declare, without the slightest hesitation, that we must, in this situation, act with clarity and courage, without detours, without equivocation, our only concern being to do our duty, which is above all to defend the rights of Quebec and its National Assembly, and also to act with the awareness that when the National Assembly is undermined, the people of Quebec themselves are directly involved.[49]

An attack of the National Assembly, to paraphrase Mr Ryan, is tantamount to violating the people of Quebec themselves. In his harangue against the federal government's unilateral intentions, Mr Ryan took up the Lockean vision of the nature of legislative power, as I presented it in chapter 2. In this context, it is difficult to imagine Mr Ryan agreeing to a constitutional reform that would reduce the powers of the National Assembly without its consent. Several days after the notorious night of the long knives, when Quebec found itself excluded and isolated, reduced to impotence before a constitutional accord accepted by all its partners, Mr Ryan revealed his deepest thoughts:

I firmly hold to the principle that we approved in this House on 2 October, namely that the National Assembly must never be stripped of its powers without its consent, but I maintain on the other hand that there is no reason why the National Assembly and the government should not, for the good of the citizens and the whole country, consent to reasonable adjustments, such as those that we, on this side of the house, are proposing.[50]

In the autumn of 1981, the Liberal caucus and its leader thought that with some good will, the negotiations enabling Quebec to secure its place again in the Canadian constitutional family could indeed be pursued. Mr Ryan's position and that of the Quebec Liberal Party can be summarized as follows: no total rejection, but no blind acceptance either. Let us listen to Mr Ryan again, this time on 24 November 1981:

To conclude, I reiterate that the 5 November agreement in its present form is far from satisfactory, and it will remain so as long as Quebec has not found the right conditions that will allow it to enter by the front door and not the side or back doors. I say to the present government that this agreement contains enough positive elements for us to try, together, in a spirit of good will and collaboration, to improve it in order to make it acceptable to Quebec, to change it in ways that will satisfy Quebec's legitimate demands while at the same time being acceptable to the rest of the country.[51]

I think that the texts clearly establish that the Liberal representatives of the Quebec people did not endorse a patriation project which they deemed incomplete. From this point of view, Mr Trudeau should redo his homework. He has known for three years about my argument, but remains silent. I also think that now people such as Claude Ryan may identify the source of their misunderstanding. He and the Liberal members were wrong about the foundations of Pierre Trudeau's project. I return for the last time to the Liberal leader's performance at the National Assembly, on 10 November 1981:

After having, like all other countries, suffered many injustices over the last 114 years, we now have the chance to establish in Canada a system of rights that would guarantee the individual citizens and minority groups in this country the basic elements of constitutional protection, which it seems to me will in future have to be the hallmark of any civilized country. A charter of that nature, solidly equipped with clauses that take into account other factors that we consider very important here, would not be a step backwards from the vantage point of the ordinary citizens, would not be a hazard. It would, on the contrary, be an immense gain.[52]

I believe we are touching on the heart of the matter. While Claude Ryan found the new constitutional text insufficient, incomplete, and formally inadequate without Quebec's consent, he was nonetheless seduced by the idea of enshrining a charter of rights in the constitution. During his "reign" at Le Devoir, he had distinguished himself in the many positions he took up in favour of individual rights and the protection of minorities. Unquestionably, it was the liberalism of the 1981 reform that appealed to Mr Ryan. The Charter of Rights and Freedoms was and is a liberal document. I would even go so far as to say that it contains a complex balance between individual and collective rights that grants Canadian liberalism a touch of originality when compared with its American counterpart.

What Claude Ryan did not realize during the fall 1981 debates at the National Assembly was that liberalism was especially valuable as an instrument, a means to an end, in Pierre Trudeau's vision. It masked the fundamental objective of constitutional reform, which was driven by the imperatives of Canadian nationalism. According to those who invoke Quebec nationalism to highlight the fact that there is indeed a people, a politically autonomous community, in

Quebec, Claude Ryan committed an error in November 1981. For he claimed that the Canadian project of the Charter of Rights and Freedoms did not endanger Quebec. He did not see that the Charter remains part and parcel of a strategy aimed at corroding Quebec's national identity. As we saw in the preceding section, English-Canadian experts do not conceal this aspect of the 1981–82 constitutional undertaking. Beyond any liberal gains, all the legislators sitting in Quebec's National Assembly should have seen the setbacks and dangers inherent in subordinating Quebec's institutions to the nationalist goals of the 1982 reform.

To end this chapter, I shall inquire whether this reform measures up to the principle of popular sovereignty that lies at the heart of the rhetoric used to justify it.

THE 1982 REFORM AND POPULAR SOVEREIGNTY

Federalism in multinational societies has not had an easy time during the early 1990s. The Baltic peoples, as well as the people of Croatia and Slovenia, have recovered their political freedom. There are many observers who reject any comparison between the past oppression of these peoples and the Canada-Quebec situation. Brian Mulroney recalled in 1991 that the Baltic countries had been forcibly joined to the USSR whereas the Canadian provinces, including Quebec, had freely consented to being integrated into the federal system of 1867. After having spent several years struggling to bring Quebec back into the Canadian constitutional family with honour and enthusiasm, Mr Mulroney knew full well that the 1982 constitutional reform was the main obstacle to the legitimacy of Canadian institutions in Quebec – a situation that in fact justifies the comparison between our federal system and those of Yugoslavia and the USSR.

One could have taunted Mr Mulroney and reminded him that the 1867 constitution did not satisfy the contemporary demands of democratic and liberal political theory (largely inspired by the philosophy of Jean-Jacques Rousseau) any more than the constitution of 1982 did. According to Rousseau, the people's active consent, which is obtained by calling on the rational autonomy and participation of all citizens, is the necessary condition of a political system's appearance of legitimacy. None of this occurred in 1867. In Canada as in Quebec, the political culture of the period owed more to the spirit of Edmund Burke than to that of Jean-Jacques Rousseau. The citizens and peoples of United Canada, New Brunswick, and Nova Scotia were not directly asked, by way of an election or a referendum, whether they wished to join a federal system. The pact of 1867 was concocted by people who had been elected through a voting system based on the poll tax and who had no explicit mandate to transform the constitutional status of their political community. However, the founders of the 1867 system could at least boast of being in harmony with the élitist political culture of their time. The authors of the 1982 reform cannot say as much.

At first glance, there does not seem to be any incompatibility between the 1982 constitutional reform and the principle of popular sovereignty. Alan Cairns, one of the leading experts on the evolution of the Canadian constitution in the community of political scientists, goes so far as to construe the 1982 reform as a "people's package," a real triumph for several categories of citizens. According to him, the inclusion of the Charter of Rights and Freedoms in the fundamental law of the country weakened the tradition of executive federalism, dominated by governments, and gave the constitution back to the citizens. Cairns states that the Charter strengthened the position of individuals in their relations with different administrations and that it had very significant symbolic resonance; it provided a crucial fund of social recognition to women, native peoples, official-language minorities, multicultural groups, the disabled, and visible minorities.[53]

In the debate on the Meech Lake Accord that took place in Canada between 1987 and 1990, several analysts noted that the Canadian population had been excluded from the negotiations leading to the deal that was signed by the prime minister and the provincial premiers.[54] These analysts saw a striking contrast between this exclusion and the vast public consultation initiated by the federal government between 1980 and 1982. The 1982 reform could thus be dubbed "the citizens' constitution" for two reasons: not only did the citizens inherit a whole panoply of rights, but they had an appropriate say in the matter before the legislators adopted the reform. In this view, the 1982 reform initially made possible the exercise of popular sovereignty before consolidating this principle in our laws and political-constitutional customs.

In my opinion, this interpretation cannot stand up to any serious examination of its premises. The 1982 process was miles away from what Rousseau and democratic theory understand by popular sovereignty. Alan Cairns's own work provides evidence of this, when unmasking the Trudeau government's strategy of manipulating the population:

Governments energetically tried to get the people on their side, the better to prove their democratic responsiveness. After the Quebec referendum the federal government brilliantly employed a "people versus power" antithesis to contrast what it sought – a Charter of Rights for the people – with the jurisdictional goals of provincial governments, which were portrayed as selfish aggrandizement. In the subsequent unilateralism stage Ottawa deliberately strengthened the Charter to mobilize public opinion on its side after it became clear that the dissenting provincial governments could not be won over by a weak Charter.[55]

According to Cairns, the 1980–81 public consultation was expertly orchestrated by the government. However, granting individuals rights per se is not equivalent to popular sovereignty. One must also ask the people what they think, and the constitutional reform was never explicitly ratified by the Canadian and Quebec electorates. This could have been done through a referendum, in the best spirit of direct democracy. Short of that, it would have been possible, in accordance with our parliamentary and representative customs, to make the constitution the major issue of an election campaign. But Mr Trudeau's government did no such thing. Today, when popular sovereignty is being affirmed everywhere in the world, we have to admit that the Canadian constitution suffers in this respect from a lack of legitimacy. This is true for the entire country, but it applies even more strongly to Quebec. To consider this more closely, we must return to the works of John Locke.

Like Rousseau's political philosophy, that of John Locke stipulates that the people's consent is always necessary to secure the legitimacy of political authority. Contrary to Rousseau, however, the English thinker believed in the merits of representative democracy; he was prepared to trust the people's elected representatives. In matters of constitutional reform, he believed that this trust could be preserved only through the observance of certain precise rules. The people's consent was even more necessary when the representatives, those entrusted with popular sovereignty, intended to change the very nature of the social pact in fundamental ways. To transform a constitution is tantamount to modifying the social contract, to shifting the foundations on which a political community is erected. The citizens must take part in this process. Yet they did not do so in Canada, especially not in Quebec, between 1980 and 1982.

In Locke's view, the most significant constitutional changes are the ones that affect the nature or extent of legislative power. This is because the legislative power is nothing less than the soul of a society, the most vital organ for its development.[56] To attack the legislative power is to touch a society at its most essential core. Quebec, as everyone knows, lives within a federal system. The people of Quebec delegate part of their legislative power to the National Assembly and another part to the Canadian Parliament. The same division of powers between the two orders of government has roughly prevailed since 1867. The fact that the Constitution Act, 1982, and the Charter of Rights and Freedoms changed the rules of the game without Quebec's consent cannot be repeated too often. The division of powers between the Quebec National Assembly and the Parliament of Canada was considerably altered. Even experts on federalism in English Canada, such as the late Donald Smiley, have acknowledged that Quebec's powers were reduced.[57] According to Locke, when such actions are taken without the formal consent of the people, there is a breach of trust between the people and the government.

A closer look at the changes made to the National Assembly's legislative powers reveals that the breach of trust between the citizens of Quebec and their representatives in Ottawa is a veritable chasm. Since 1982, it has been possible to revise the constitution without Quebec's consent. Then there is the matter of the Charter and its interpretation by the Supreme Court. Nine judges sit on the Supreme Court, and three must come from Quebec. All of them, however, are appointed unilaterally by the federal government. The same applies to judges on provincial superior and appellate courts. In this context, it is widely felt in Quebec that the Charter of Rights and Freedoms, interpreted by persons exclusively nominated by the federal government, has eroded Quebec's powers in the area of justice. The adoption of the Meech Lake Accord would have partially remedied this, though only in the case of the Supreme Court. As well, the National Assembly's prerogatives in the area of language of education have been curtailed by section 23 of the Charter. This section is a fundamental aspect of the Charter and of Trudeau's patriation project, and thus the notwithstanding clause (section 33) can in no way reduce the range of its application to Quebec. Every reader of Locke knows that something terrible is happening when Quebec's legislative power over the language of education is attacked head-on. Considering our situation in North America, to touch this particularly fragile dimension is "Mischief and Oppression ... as the Precedent, and Consequences seem to threaten all."[58]

Yet this is what was sought by the reform that was set in motion at the time. Such was the "spirit of 1982." A constitutional reform modifying Quebec's legislative powers to such an extent, without the explicit consent of the people, is profoundly illegitimate. Canadians imbued with the principles of Liberal democracy should be ashamed of it. From Locke's point of view, pure and simple dissolution of the government responsible should be the immediate consequence of the reform. In a way, there has not been a federal government worthy of the name in Quebec since 17 April 1982.

Serious thought about the political culture promoted by the Charter of Rights and Freedoms, as well as about the context in which the constitutional reform was implemented in 1982, makes it possible to register the depth of the gulf that separates Quebec from the rest of Canada. Some statements made by the former Quebec premier, Robert Bourassa, a few years ago, demonstrate the enormity of this chasm. At the end of the summer of 1991, during a meeting with Mrs Rita Johnston, who was then premier of British Columbia, Mr Bourassa stressed that the crisis stemmed from the inescapable fact that Quebec did not consent to the 1982 reform. Some months later, in an end-of-the-year interview with Pierre Nadeau, he maintained that there had been a misunderstanding between Quebec and the rest of Canada, the latter being unable or unwilling to recall what had transpired in 1982. In mid-January 1992, reacting to Bob Rae's remarks before the Beaudoin-Dobbie Committee, Mr Bourassa once again repeated that one of Canada's founding peoples had not been treated fairly in 1982.

I do not doubt Mr Bourassa's sincerity in his reading of 1982, but I do believe that he has underestimated the scope of the misunderstanding. Quebec's leaders would like Canadians to feel regret for 1982 and then agree that the need to repair the injustice done to Quebec should be the first priority in any further constitutional reform. In other words, we are asking them to "regret" what has become the cornerstone, the founding myth, of Canadian nationalism at the end of the twentieth century, namely, the 1982 reform with its Charter and its talk of equal rights. We would like Canadians to apologize when in fact they would rather celebrate the arrival of their new identity and the institutions that promote it. To me, this is the symbol of the lack of understanding between Quebec and the rest of Canada.

On further thought, Mr Bourassa's statements, which denote a certain ineptness in grasping the subtleties of Canadian political culture, seem surprising. Following the failure of the Meech Lake Accord, Quebec adopted instruments that might have enabled it to make more enlightened political choices. In the next chapter, I shall examine the proposals for renewed federalism through the prism of the Allaire and Bélanger-Campeau reports.

CHAPTER SEVEN

Allaire, Bélanger-Campeau, and Proposals for Renewed Federalism

Every political system is protected by a very great inertia. This is even truer when it comes to a liberal-democratic state like Canada. The British philosopher John Locke, one of the key reference points of this book, liked to repeat that human beings, as citizens, do not readily part with their political customs. It is extremely difficult to get a people to change its political system "even when all the world sees there is an opportunity for it."[1] The federal system can rely on this force of inertia, on the residual sense of allegiance which a considerable number of Quebec's citizens feel towards the idea of Canada. Brian Mulroney played on those feelings in 1992 when he asserted that Quebecers did not wish to give up being Canadians, that they were not prepared to part with their Canadian passports. Ottawa was gambling that the force of inertia would win out in the end, that Quebecers would gradually forget how their government had been rebuffed when it attempted to get Quebec recognized as a distinct society. Jean Chrétien's Liberal government seems to be gambling on the same strategy. The question remains whether such political reckoning is accurate. John Locke warns us against underestimating the force of inertia that saves political systems, but he does not view them as invulnerable for all that. The interpretive consensus that emerged from the Allaire and Bélanger-Campeau reports reminds us that the federalists are far from having succeeded once and for all. My argument is that this consensus will continue to work as a structural element in the debate ahead.

THE ALLAIRE AND BÉLANGER-CAMPEAU REPORTS

Exhaustive research into the Quebec literature on the history of Canadian federalism since 1867 would be long and arduous. Fortunately, I do not believe it is necessary. Two official documents that have emerged in the post–Meech Lake era enable observers to trace the horizons of Quebec's expectations as an autonomous political community inside or outside Canada. The two documents reveal a remarkable interpretive consensus in Quebec concerning the meaning of Canadian federalism. The first of these texts is *A Quebec Free to Choose*, the report of the Constitutional Committee of the Quebec Liberal Party (the Allaire Report), published in January 1991 and adopted with minor revisions by the party at its March conference. The second is *The Political and Constitutional Future of Quebec*, the report of the Quebec National Assembly's Special Committee on the Political and Constitutional Future of Quebec (the Bélanger-Campeau Report), which was published at the end of March 1991 and was endorsed by Robert Bourassa's Liberal government. For those who are interested in the totality of the history I have just evoked, Alain Gagnon and Daniel Latouche have published a book that offers a preliminary synthesis as well as a selection of documents.[2]

Beyond their common emphasis on an appropriate timetable and process, it seems to me that the central theme of the Allaire and Bélanger-Campeau reports is that the Canadian dream of the Québécois was dualism but that, for many Québécois, the dream crumbled with the failure of the Meech Lake Accord in June 1990. Neither report explains systematically the origin of the dualist outlook of Quebec's political and intellectual élites, from Henri Bourassa's dualist nationalism to the detailed interpretation proposed in the Report of the Royal Commission on Constitutional Problems (the Tremblay Report) in 1956. The latter explicitly defined the vision of a federation conceived by two founding peoples, by two nations, which had their own homogeneous identity, built around language, culture, and religion. This is the vision that André Laurendeau so brilliantly took up in the 1960s, when he co-chaired the Royal Commission on Bilingualism and Biculturalism. In Laurendeau's view, mere linguistic duality was an insufficient basis for the "complete preservation of a culture."[3] Canada's two dominant cultures were embodied in distinct societies that had to be recognized as such. Both had to be granted appropriate powers if French Canada, Quebec, was to support the system. The Allaire and Bélanger-Campeau reports present the dualist reading of the history of Canadian federalism as an inescapable reality. They advise their readers that this is how French Canadians, the Québécois, have always thought of their involvement in this country:

In Quebec, Confederation has always been perceived as a solemn pact between two nations, a pact that could not be changed without the consent of the two parties.[4]

The problems engendered by political relations between Quebec and the rest of Canada are not new. Their sources can be found in the past. The Royal Commission on Bilingualism and Biculturalism (Laurendeau-Dunton Commission, 1963) and the Task Force on Canadian Unity (Pepin-Robarts Commission, 1978) focused on a number of their causes and proposed solutions. Essentially, these complex problems concern the political and constitutional expression of the relations between two linguistic groups, two majorities. One province among 10, Quebec, holds the francophone majority.[5]

When the Allaire and Bélanger-Campeau reports were published, some observers, especially in the English-language media, denounced their biased, not to say simplistic, vision of the history of Canadian federalism.[6] At first glance, it is hard not to agree with them. Eugene Forsey was one of the great constitutional authorities and essayists of English Canada. In his memoirs, which were published during the Meech Lake debate, he mocked the historical weakness of the dualist argument. According to Forsey, all the elements needed for a complete refutation of the dualist reading can be obtained from a serious analysis of the origins of Confederation and the operation of the Dominion government in the years following the adoption of the British North America Act of 1867. There was no pact between two nations at the Charlottetown and Quebec conferences, maintained Forsey. Discussions there were not organized along the lines of a dialogue between English and French Canada. In fact, the debate revolved mainly around questions other than language and culture, the two factors so dear to the supporters of the duality argument; and in the British Parliament, language and culture were discussed even less.[7] Another English-Canadian intellectual, Donald Creighton, devoted a large part of his long career to demonstrating that the founders of Canadian federalism wanted as much centralization as circumstances would allow and purposely placed the provinces in a subordinate position.[8]

The critics were right to note that the historical analysis contained in the Allaire and Bélanger-Campeau reports lacked depth. It is true that the authors of these documents made no attempt to refute other interpretations of Canadian federalism, such as those put forward by Forsey and Creighton. Yet from the point of view presented here, Forsey's and Creighton's accounts, as well as the critiques of the Allaire and Bélanger-Campeau reports, leave out what is really essential. On this score, I believe that the late sociologist Jean-Charles Falardeau made an absolutely decisive remark some thirty years ago in a book edited by Mason Wade, the title of which I find very revealing: *La dualité canadienne/Canadian Duality.*

This interpretation of Confederation as a pact still surprises English-Canadians for whom the 1867 Act can only be construed as an act of the Imperial Parliament, which can only be interpreted by sticking closely to the legal texts, which nowhere allude to any pact. Howsoever that may be, the sociologically significant and important thing is that French Canadians have attributed that meaning to the Canadian Constitution since the end of the Nineteenth Century or thereabouts. It is a view that has become embedded in their attitude. It has become a persistent theme, orchestrated in many variations by French Canada's religious and political leaders up to the present day. Whether English-Canadian publicists and legal experts find it acceptable or not, it will persist as one of the most tenacious elements of the way French Canadians define the history of their Canada.[9]

This paragraph, written at the dawn of the Quiet Revolution, reveals Falardeau's premonition of the whole orientation of the efforts of French Canada and Quebec towards renewed federalism. The dualist vision had become embedded in the attitude of our intellectual and political leaders. It was to prove tenacious in their understanding of their Canada's history, whatever the past and present publicists and legal experts of English Canada may think about it. This vision inspired the behaviour of André Laurendeau and Daniel Johnson; it was the vision proposed to the people of Quebec by Claude Ryan, Solange Chaput-Rolland, and the other leaders of the No camp during the 1980 referendum. We could feel it at work in the Meech Lake Accord, in Quebec's attempt to get itself recognized as a distinct society (an expression that was dear to Laurendeau, perhaps the greatest thinker in the dualist tradition) within Canada. From 1960 to 1990, the dualist interpretation played a major role in defining the horizon of our intellectual and political leaders' expectations with respect to Canadian federalism. It enabled them to identify the reforms they would seek to achieve by their political struggles. In 1987, a few months after the signing of the Meech Lake Accord, Léon Dion concluded a book with this magnificent defence of the dualist creed:

I can see the day coming when English Canada will be proud of including Quebec within its political space, to the point of insistently asking it: "What political status can we offer you so that you may be wholly fulfilled? For we now know that it is you especially who are blazing the most promising paths into the future for the whole country." Then, and only then, instead of grovelling to beg a few crumbs of uncertain concessions from our constitutional partner, we shall stand erect, and negotiate the constitutional clauses that will guarantee an equal, happy, proud and prosperous coexistence to two different societies, two distinct peoples – and for a long time.[10]

The Allaire and Bélanger-Campeau reports have in a sense made official the dualist interpretation of Canadian federalism shared by Léon Dion and Claude Ryan, Gérald Beaudoin and Solange Chaput-Rolland, Robert Bourassa and Gil Rémillard. The dualist thesis has been adopted by the Government of Quebec, by Robert Bourassa's Liberal Party, and by Jacques Parizeau's Parti québécois, as well as by the overwhelming majority of the nonaligned members of the Bélanger-Campeau Commission, who represented a broad section of Quebec civil society. The impact and consequences of this consensus have been neglected by observers. Yet it is very significant for the future. Quebec's horizon of expectations, as defined by its élites, will not readily be changed. A sign of this can be found in a 22 May 1991 article in *Le Devoir* by the high priestess of duality, Solange Chaput-Rolland. It is an appeal, a veritable petition, for a return to the spirit of the Task Force on Canadian Unity, which recognized Quebec's distinct character and its need for special powers to affirm it.[11]

Furthermore, analysts have not paid enough attention to a second element of the dualist consensus. The Allaire and Bélanger-Campeau reports did not only say how Quebec has interpreted Canadian federalism. They also took note of the rejection of the dualist argument by Quebec's partners. In the Allaire Report, a document written by members of a party that had invested its entire constitutional capital in the Meech Lake venture, this refusal of duality was received with much bitterness:

The rest of the story is all too familiar! Two provinces failed to ratify the Accord and the exercise ended in failure. A failure that confirms that federalism in its current state is at an impasse: while Quebec was proposing a new vision of Canada based on duality, Canada rejected that vision and was unable to put forward an acceptable alternative ...

In spite of recent efforts by certain provinces to improve services to their francophone population, in practical terms, whole communities are threatened with assimilation and even the notion of two founding peoples is rejected by English Canada, and, sadder still, all this is despite the continuing determination and heroic efforts that have always marked the struggle of francophones outside Quebec ... Support for multiculturalism in Canada works against the francophone population, which is considered by a very large proportion of Canadians as one cultural community among others, meaning it should be treated the same way as the others![12]

The Allaire Report is written in the language of bitterness and resentment of those who voted No in the referendum, who long believed in the dream of a dualist reconstruction of Canadian federalism and were carried by the Meech Lake saga from the heights of joy to the deepest despair that could be experienced in politics.[13]

The tone of the Bélanger-Campeau Report is more serene, more lucid, and more analytical in discussing the causes that led Quebec and Canadian federalism to the current impasse. As we know, this report was rather poorly received by the media and the critics. The anglophone media complained of its biased reading of the history of Canadian federalism, while the Montreal journalists Lise Bissonnette and Lysiane Gagnon spoke of a phony consensus, a pot-pourri of elements aimed at satisfying sovereigntists and federalists in turn, and an agreement on process that concealed deep disagreement on substance. What was the diagnosis proposed by the Bélanger-Campeau Commission? What reasons did it invoke to explain the failure of the Meech Lake Accord and the rejection of duality? What was this interpretation of the state of Canadian federalism that was accredited by Lucien Bouchard and Jacques Parizeau as much as by Robert Bourassa and Ghislain Dufour?

To begin with, the report of the Bélanger-Campeau Commission puts forward a particularly critical synthesis of the political events that unfolded in Canada after the May 1980 referendum. As the report recalls, the Canadian constitution was revised in 1981–82 without the consent of the Government of Quebec, the National Assembly, or the people of Quebec. This revision reduced Quebec's powers over the language of education, and its amending formula made possible further changes that would be likely to affect Quebec's interests. And on top of this, the principle of maintaining and developing Canadians' multicultural heritage redefined the country without any consideration for duality and the specificity of Quebec.[14] The most important passages of the report outline the principles and vision that guided the authors of the 1982 constitutional reform:

The *Constitution Act, 1982* and the principles it enshrines have indeed engendered a hitherto unknown political cohesiveness in Canada. It helped bolster certain political visions of the federation and the perception of a national Canadian identity which are hard to reconcile with the effective recognition and expression of Quebec's distinct identity ... The vision of an exclusive national Canadian identity emphasizes the centralization of powers and the existence of a strong "national" government. This vision appears to have a levelling effect: an exclusive national Canadian identity centred on the equality of individuals actually becomes a prohibition for Quebec to be different as a society.[15]

The authors of the Bélanger-Campeau Report and all those who signed it point to a triple search for equality in the Constitution Act,

1982. The first is the form of equality that prevails among Canadian citizens, who enjoy the same, fully symmetrical, individual rights. In this context, attributing supplementary rights or privileges to some individuals on the basis of their membership in a given collectivity seems completely inequitable. The report draws the conclusion that the 1982 reform "does not make allowance for Quebec society to receive special constitutional recognition."[16] The second form of equality governs the relations between cultures and cultural origins in Canada. In the unfolding of that vision, the French language and its related culture have exactly the same status as all the other elements that make up the Canadian multicultural mosaic. The report concludes: "Many Canadians feel that the notion of 'linguistic duality' and 'two founding nations' do not reflect what they perceive to be the Canadian reality in which they recognize themselves."[17]

The final aspect of Canadian constitutional equality concerns the relations between the ten provinces. The Bélanger-Campeau Report observes that the principle of equality between provinces was sanctioned by the amending formula, which is an integral part of the 1982 reform; this applies to the unanimity rule no less than to the "7–50 per cent" rule. When this principle is applied in a strict fashion, it becomes almost impossible to attribute special status to Quebec; the principle leads ineluctably to a symmetrical devolution to all the provinces of the powers granted to Quebec.[18] As the report says in veiled terms, this is exactly what happened in the case of the Meech Lake Accord.

During the April and June 1987 negotiating sessions, all the provinces were granted what initially only Quebec had demanded. The accord collapsed because of the clause recognizing Quebec as a distinct society. This clause would have provided a principle of interpretation of the whole constitution, including the Charter of Rights and Freedoms, and thus collided head-on with the principle of equal individual rights among all Canadian citizens. To the extent that it reaffirmed the role of the government and the National Assembly of Quebec in protecting and promoting Quebec's distinct society, the clause was a blow to the supporters of cultural equality. Finally, granting the status of distinct society only to Quebec offended those who believed in the equality of the ten provinces of Canada. Bill Vander Zalm, the former premier of British Columbia, provided a good example of the strength of this aspiration to equality when he suggested that the impasse could only be overcome by granting the status of distinct society to each of the ten provinces.

To sum up, the Allaire and Bélanger-Campeau reports give an official status to the dualist vision of Canada that has gradually taken hold in the political class and intelligentsia of Quebec during the twentieth century, and especially since the Quiet Revolution. Both documents note that Canadian federalism has rejected that vision, that it has just about completely purged its institutions of it. Finally, both reports, and especially that of the Bélanger-Campeau Commission, analyse the causes of that expulsion, which has been so deeply felt in Quebec. This analysis has been corroborated, as the previous chapter pointed out, by English-Canadian experts and political scientists. The consensus on duality and the acknowledgment of the current impasse seem to me to be much more decisive than many experts would like to think. Those who reflect on the search for the conditions of a genuine partnership between Quebec and Canada will be guided by this consensus. I shall now examine whether these conditions are present in the proposals for renewed federalism that were published in the fall of 1991 and the winter of 1992 in two documents that provided the foundations for the Charlottetown Accord.

A NEW OFFER OF PARTNERSHIP: FROM *SHAPING CANADA'S FUTURE TOGETHER* TO THE BEAUDOIN-DOBBIE REPORT

As several observers have remarked, the document published by the federal government on 24 September 1991 was very complex. I shall leave to others the task of analysing its second and third parts, on the modernization of federal institutions and the economic union, and will focus my attention here on the first part, which deals with common citizenship and diversity. My comments on the whole document are based on my understanding of the ins and outs of the first part.

In elaborating and presenting Ottawa's proposals, everything was done to give the impression that they were part of a Canada round. Nowhere did the document refer to Quebec's threat to the integrity of the Canadian political system. It never mentioned the referendum that the Quebec government was committed to holding no later than October 1992; but those in the know immediately understood that the federal government had to operate within very tight timelines. For example, the conclusion of the document stated that the special joint parliamentary committee would submit its report by early 1992, after which the federal government would submit to Parliament a plan to reform the country's institutions. A reader from abroad, not being familiar with our recent history, would have had no way of knowing that Quebec was controlling the timetable. This is what was left unsaid in the federal document, and it is symptomatic of how the Canadian system refuses to confront the question of Quebec squarely and honestly.

While the federal government seemed, if only indirectly and implicitly, to agree to work to a timetable dictated by Quebec, it was still a long way from answering the pressing call of necessity. A comparison between Germany and Canada is instructive in this respect. The Berlin Wall came down in November 1989, and eleven months later, in October 1990, the two Germanies completed the process of reunification. Of course, we are speaking of two societies that share the same language and, to a great extent, the same culture. Nevertheless, we have to recognize that the German political leaders faced colossal obstacles. The political and economic systems of the Federal Republic and the German Democratic Republic rested on diametrically opposed foundations. A liberal democracy driven by a market economy had to be fused with a Marxist-Leninist system with a planned economy. The tasks involved in restructuring Canada are incomparably lighter than those Germany faced in November 1989. With some variations, all the actors on the political stage of Canada and Quebec accept the rules of liberal democracy and a market economy. The challenges that lie in wait for our leaders are therefore less terrifying, but they do not – or do not yet – grip those leaders with the same sense of urgency, the same force of necessity.

Proof of this can be found in the sequence of events following the submission of the Bélanger-Campeau Commission's report in March 1991. The commission gave the political class eighteen months to rethink relations between Quebec and Canada. The federal government needed six months to prepare a fifty-page working paper which, in a strict sense, did not bind any of the governments or legislatures of the country. Five months after the publication of *Shaping Canada's Future Together*, the situation was no different. When the Beaudoin-Dobbie committee had finished criss-crossing Canada in all directions and had finally handed in its report, in the midst of well-publicized confusion, on 29 February 1992, everything still remained to be done. In the days that followed, the federal government initiated a round of multilateral consultations with provincial leaders, as well as with representatives of the territories and native organizations, with the aim of coming to an agreement and formulating an offer to submit to Quebec. Yet in July 1992, fifteen months after the Bélanger-Campeau Report had been published, everything still in a sense remained to be done for Canada and Quebec – just a few weeks before the referendum process had to be set in motion in Quebec. None of the obstacles to an agreement had been removed.

The contrast with Germany is striking. In the same period that had witnessed the two Germanies changing their political structures, Canada had in the final analysis simply gone round in circles, unable to resolve the impasse that is paralysing our political life. Are our leaders less gifted than Germany's? I doubt it. Rather, I think they did not yet feel necessity breathing down their necks. I shall return to this point.

The authors of *Shaping Canada's Future Together* could not bring themselves to state directly the question of Quebec, the question of a society that sees itself as distinct and also sees in Quebec a people, a nation, an autonomous political community. A certain view of Canadian nationalism prevents the political system from truly redefining itself in order to seek reconciliation with the visions Quebecers have of themselves – of their society and identity. Yet the authors of the document sometimes showed signs – too rarely and timorously! – indicating that they were not unaware of the real nature of the problem. One small example seems particularly revealing. The preface of the French version of the document says: "Ces propositions visent à circonscrire le dialogue." The same passage in the English version reads: "These proposals are intended to give focus to a national dialogue."[19] Why is not the dialogue "national" in French? Perhaps because the authors were well aware that, for many Quebecers, the national dialogue was taking place within Quebec and that it had been given focus by the Bélanger-Campeau Commission well before the federal proposals came into being.

At its best, *Shaping Canada's Future Together* brought new life into the spirit of 1867. More than a quarter of a century ago, in centennial year, the English-Canadian historian Ramsay Cook wrote that the founders of our country had sought to preserve a balance between the values and the sources of tension which then existed in Canada. The spirit of 1867 means the recognition of diversity, the (at least) tacit acceptance of national differences. Canada's founders dreamed of a federal and pluralistic society, renouncing the ideas of homogeneity and uniformity.[20] True to British political custom, they preferred to have ambiguous texts, which were likely to give rise to divergent interpretations and misunderstandings, rather than having no agreement at all. I would go so far as to say that Mr Joe Clark, – who, as minister of constitutional affairs, was responsible for the federal document – deserves to be considered an heir of the federative spirit of 1867.

Shaping Canada's Future Together declared that the country is strong enough to allow several collectivities to share its institutions without giving up their identities.[21] In recognizing that Confederation was

largely a pact between the leaders of two societies and in asserting
that Canada is the homeland of two great linguistic majorities,[22] the
document also provided openings to the dualist vision that has been
so important to the interpretation of federalism in Quebec. Nonetheless, even though it came out in favour of respecting "authentic
diversity," the document could not go further than the linguistic
dimension of duality when the time came to recognize Canada's
fundamental characteristics. The authors could not bring themselves
to speak openly of cultural duality and national duality, despite the
importance of these categories to those who seek to reconcile Quebec
nationalism with a certain Canadian patriotism, following in the
footsteps of André Laurendeau. As we shall soon see in greater detail,
this document was not touched by the spirit of 1867 alone; it was
also affected by the spirit of 1982 and the vision of Canadian nationalism promoted by Pierre Elliott Trudeau.

Before proceeding to a detailed analysis of the consequences for
Quebec of the distinct society clause and the Canada clause, which
were formulated in the first part of the document on common citizenship and diversity, I would like briefly to consider a philosophical
issue of prime importance. Here is an excerpt from the document:

In the Canadian experience, it has not been enough to protect only universal
individual rights. Here, the Constitution and ordinary laws also protect other
rights accorded to individuals as members of certain communities. This
accommodation of both types of rights makes our Constitution unique and
reflects the Canadian value of equality that accommodates difference. The
fact that community rights exist alongside individual rights in our Constitution goes to the very heart of what Canada is all about.[23]

This principle of reconciling individual and collective rights and freedoms is, moreover, reaffirmed in two of the fourteen elements likely
to find their way into a possible Canada clause. As we have seen, the
recognition of collective rights is not given unanimous assent in political and intellectual circles. In a heavily polemical essay, David Bercuson and Barry Cooper go so far as to claim that Quebec society,
torn between individual and collective aspirations, threatens the very
survival of liberal democracy in Canada.[24] These two University of
Calgary professors no doubt shuddered when they read that the federal government wished to enshrine collective rights in the constitution. The federal government thought that Canada had found an
original way of embodying the tenets of liberal democracy in its
institutions, in part because of the presence of a balance between
individual and collective rights in the Charter of Rights and Freedoms.

The logical premise of this part of the federal document was that the Canadian government recognizes that liberal democracy can take on various guises. In other words, liberal justice is not incompatible with a diversity of approaches, with divergent interpretations of the definition and scope of the rights of individuals and collectivities. To take the analysis a step further, did the propositions contained in *Shaping Canada's Future Together* imply that it would be acceptable for liberal justice in Quebec to take on original forms in relation to the rest of Canada? To answer this question (no doubt one of the most fundamental questions at the present time), we must take a closer look at what the document told us about recognition of Quebec as a distinct society. Here I must make it clear that the Beaudoin-Dobbie Report simply took up the definition of "distinct society" provided in *Shaping Canada's Future Together*. The same is true of the Charlottetown Accord.

By virtue of the Meech-Langevin agreements signed in 1987, an interpretative rule would have been placed in section 2 of the Constitution Act, 1867, stipulating, inter alia, that any interpretation of the constitution of Canada would have to tally with recognition that Quebec constitutes a distinct society within Canada. Line 3 of that section was to specify that the legislature and government of Quebec had the role of preserving and promoting the distinct identity of Quebec. This clause could have served Quebec's interests in the grey areas of the division of powers, as well as in the interpretation of the Charter's section 1, which recognizes the existence of reasonable limits to exercising rights in a free and democratic society. As an interpretive rule, the distinct society clause ratified the principle of asymmetrical liberal justice – that in certain circumstances, which would be defined by the courts, the common good for Quebec would not be equivalent to the common good for the rest of Canada.

At first sight, the federal proposals appeared rather sympathetic to this logic: "[By] ridding laws of discriminatory distinctions, equality rights aim at equality of opportunity for disadvantaged individuals or groups. In fact, the Supreme Court has said that the accommodation of differences is the essence of true equality."[25] However, a closer look reveals that recognition of Quebec's difference had dropped a few notches between 1987 and 1992. This time, the distinct society clause no longer applied to the interpretation of the constitution as a whole, but only to the Charter of Rights and Freedoms. And although it was still to be placed in section 2 of the Constitution Act, 1867, it would be merely one dimension among others in the Canada clause.

It is difficult to view this as anything other than implicit recognition of the subordination of the distinct society rule to the Charter of

Rights and Freedoms. Henceforth, the distinct society clause would be only one of the many interpretive provisions in the Charter. Inasmuch as it repeated the wording of the clause mentioning the objective of promoting multiculturalism, the very wording of the subsection dealing with the distinct society corroborates my reading. Let readers judge for themselves:

25.1.(1) This Charter shall be interpreted in a manner consistent with
    (a) the preservation and promotion of Quebec as a distinct society within Canada;

27. This Charter shall be interpreted in a manner consistent with the preservation and enhancement of the multicultural heritage of Canadians.[26]

With respect to the wording of the distinct society clause, it is worth noting that the word "objective" was not mentioned. As well, the 1987 Meech-Langevin agreements spoke of the "recognition" of Quebec as a distinct society. This symbolically charged word was omitted in 1992. Nor should we neglect the significance of another small semantic difference between the 1987 and 1992 projects. In 1987, the National Assembly and the Government of Quebec were given the obligation of preserving and promoting the distinct society as part of an interpretive rule encompassing the entire constitution. In 1992, not only was the application of the distinct society clause confined to the Charter of Rights and Freedoms, but any explicit reference to a role of preservation or promotion for Quebec's legislative and governmental institutions had been deleted. It would have been up to the courts to take into account Quebec's character as a distinct society in their interpretation of the Charter. In a way, the blueprint of *Shaping Canada's Future Together* transferred the task of preserving and promoting Quebec's distinct society from the National Assembly and the Government of Quebec to federal courts such as the Supreme Court of Canada.

The people who drafted the federal proposals were not content to restrict the application of the distinct society principle. They also made strategic choices when it came to making room for the principle in the Charter of Rights and Freedoms. For example, they could very well have made it a subsection of section 1, which recognizes the existence of limits to exercising rights. In proceeding thus, they would have provided ammunition to those who defend the idea of asymmetrical liberal justice in the relations between Quebec and Canada. But their choice was very different. True to the prevailing view in Canadian nationalist circles, and following the model of a mosaic created by native communities and then made bilingual and multicultural, they made the distinct society rule a subsection of section 25 of the Charter, which concerns the rights and ancestral freedoms of the native people. Quebec's status as a distinct society and the legal consequences that follow from it were thus placed in a symbolically subordinate position with respect to the rights and demands of Canada's native people. Was this subordination fortuitous? I do not think so. The preface of the federal document enumerated the factors supporting another effort to renew federalism. After the first paragraph, which stressed native demands, the document added: "Canada must *also* address Quebec's desire for recognition of its distinct nature and for more control over areas that are inherent to that distinctiveness" (my emphasis).[27] In short, everything turns on this "also," which indicated that the 1992 round of constitutional revision was indeed dominated by Canada's preoccupation with its own identity. In the symbolic order of things, the Quebec question was not officially the Canadian political system's main concern.

In contrast with the Meech-Langevin agreements, the 1991 federal document proposed the following definition of the distinct society of Quebec:

(2) For the purposes of subsection (1), "distinct society," in relation to Quebec, includes:
    (a) a French-speaking majority;
    (b) a unique culture; and
    (c) a civil law tradition.[28]

In the French version, the distinct society was not reduced to the elements that define it, thanks to the presence of the adverb *notamment*:

(2) Pour l'application du paragraphe (1), une société distincte comprend notamment:
    (a) une majorité d'expression française
    (b) une culture unique en son genre
    (c) une tradition de droit civil.[29]

It is important to note that the same does not hold true for the English version, which does not have a higher legal status but is perhaps closer to the intentions of the document's authors, since it was written first and then translated into French. Logically, according to the English version, everything has been said about Quebec's distinct society once the civil law tradition has been mentioned. The difference between the two versions could only reinforce the prejudices of those who regarded this definition, like any definition, as an attempt to pinpoint and limit the scope of a particular object, in this case the nature of Quebec as a distinct society.

In the light of this observation, is it possible to interpret this process as an effort to trivialize Quebec, to transform it into an element of folklore? As we are dealing with an interpretive rule to be used by the judiciary, no definite and sure answer would have been available for several years to come, pending the crystallization and stabilization of the jurisprudence associated with the issue. As with the Meech Lake Accord, Quebec was being invited to engage in a real act of faith in the Canadian judiciary system. The danger of folklorization appears very real when the horizon of discussion is extended to the federal proposals as a whole. Beyond the French language and civil law, an essential dimension of Quebec's distinct society involves a dense, interlocking institutional network, in which not only linguistic and cultural but also economic and social questions play a very major role. Quebec's originality in North America is related to the fact that it is the only society aspiring to embody modernity in all its dimensions principally in French. Quebec's socio-economic institutional network, like its aspiration to be a modern society, was omitted from the definition of distinct society proposed in the federal document. By contrast, the document undeniably wished to reinforce Canada's socio-economic institutional network by way of an ambitious project of economic union. I leave to economists the detailed analysis of this part of the document. However, I would add my voice to those who realized that the promotion of a distinct Quebec society would be threatened by granting new powers to the federal Parliament to pass the laws needed to make economic union work, as well as by the project of elaborating guidelines for improving the coordination of budgetary policy and harmonizing it with Canada's monetary policy. On this score, the definition of distinct society proposed in the federal document increased the danger to Quebec.

By the terms of the Meech-Langevin agreements, the clause recognizing Quebec as a distinct society would have enjoyed an enviable strategic position. It would have been included in section 2 of the Constitution Act, 1867. In reality, as in the symbolic order of things, it would in a sense have reigned supreme over interpretation of the whole Canadian constitution. In the 1991 plan, however, although there was still a desire to grant the distinct society an important position, it was now featured in the broader framework of a Canada clause, in which the proposal to recognize "Quebec's fundamental responsibility to preserve and promote its distinct society" appeared as one of a group of fourteen Canadian values and characteristics.

Thus, in 1991, Quebec's distinct society had become but one of the constitutive facets of Canada's national identity.

The Constitution Act, 1982, and the Charter of Rights and Freedoms have breathed a strong nationalist spirit into Canadian political culture. According to this spirit, there really is a national Canadian identity, which can be observed anywhere in the country. The corollary of this vision is that Quebec and its citizens are full participants in this national Canadian identity. The implicit postulate is that there is no national Québécois identity worthy of the name. I have already shown that the federal offers of constitutional renewal were not ungenerous with respect to Quebec's aspirations. One can sense the spirit of 1867 in them sometimes. Nevertheless, the document remained true to the nationalist spirit of 1982 most of the time. The first section of the first part of the document made no bones about it: its topic was Canadian identity and the common values that define it.

The document recalled what Canadians told the Citizens' Forum on Canada's Future: "They expressed a sense of deeply felt core values which they believe that *all* Canadians share."[30] Equality and equity ranked highest among these values. The rights and freedoms guaranteed by the Charter could be limited only in order to allow everyone to enjoy the same rights and freedoms. Two things are noteworthy in the definitions of citizenship and identity proposed in the federal document. First, Pierre Elliott Trudeau's mark was ubiquitous. Mr Trudeau made the following comment during the Meech Lake debate: "And once again, it means an even greater tendency, a greater weight on the side of provincialism, at the expense of a federal institution or legislation which, up until now, has given Canadians a feeling of belonging to one Canada. In the same way the Canadian Charter of Rights and Freedoms was important to Canadian unity."[31] The following passages are from the Canada clause proposed in the Beaudoin-Dobbie Report:

All those things are important in the sense that they help Canadians to realize that they share with *all* other Canadians, *throughout* the country, the same set of fundamental values. We reaffirm our profound attachment to the principles and values that have drawn us together, enlightened our national life, and afforded us peace and security, such as our unshakable respect for the institutions of Parliamentary democracy ... Therefore we, Canadians all, formally adopt this, our Constitution, including the *Charter of Rights and Freedoms*, as the solemn expression of our national will and hopes."[32]

We have seen what Mr Trudeau's intentions were in founding a new constitutional order for Canada. He wished to strengthen and unify the nation. By virtue of its influence on Canadians' notions of identity and citizenship, the Charter of Rights and Freedoms is the ideal instrument for realizing these objectives. In the previous chapter, I tried to show that these objectives had essentially been achieved among English-speaking Canadians. But after reading – in *Shaping Canada's Future Together* – that those who participated in the Citizens' Forum expressed their attachment to a Canadian identity, I feel that we need to think further and anticipate the consequences this attachment could have for Quebec and for Quebec's concern for its specificity:

For most participants outside Quebec, Quebec's continued presence in Confederation cannot be bought at the price of damaging or destroying those things they value most about the country, and in particular, must not be bought by sacrificing individual or provincial equality ...

Non-constitutional mechanisms might be found to accommodate a number of Quebec's and other provinces' desires for control in certain areas. In the view of participants outside Quebec such agreements would have to be made in the context of a strong pan-Canadian framework of equal rights, national standards, and equal accessibility to programs and services by all Canadians for them to be acceptable.[33]

Following Trudeau's initiatives, the Charter of Rights and Freedoms was set to work fashioning Canadian identity and political culture. It has succeeded so well in this that a majority of English-speaking Canadians would give up the unity of the country before giving in on the question of equal status and rights. This opinion was corroborated by Alan Gregg, one of the leading analysts of the English-Canadian political psyche: "The whole notion of asymmetrical federalism has no chance, just none whatsoever. I can't see English-Canadian public opinion changing sufficiently to make the prospect of giving Quebec anything that is special, unique, different, politically viable. If it was asymmetrical federalism or no Quebec, right now they would probably choose no Quebec."[34]

In the first part of *Shaping Canada's Future Together* there is a certain oscillation between the spirit of 1867 and the spirit of 1982, between generosity towards diversity – including Quebec's national originality – and the search for symmetrical equality based on a uniform notion of Canadian identity. The triumph of the spirit of 1982 is more apparent in the rest of the document. All the provinces, including Quebec, have equal status with respect to changes to the constitution. Even in the case of the double majority required in the reformed Senate's votes on issues of language and culture, any hint of a special status for Quebec is scrupulously avoided.[35] For their part, the proposals for a more integrated economic union, which are full of dangers for the project of promoting a distinct society in Quebec, are completely in line with the Canadian nationalist project: the reader is cautioned that "the Government of Canada will maintain its ability to ensure that all Canadians continue to receive the benefits of Canadian citizenship."[36] The federal government's promotion of Canadian identity is the primary criterion underpinning Ottawa's efforts on the issue of economic union.

The objective of promoting Canadian identity is far from disappearing when it comes to modernizing federalism and clarifying the responsibilities of each level of government. In the area of immigration, the federal government will continue to determine the number of immigrants and to set national standards and goals. The Canadian nationalist outlook emerges even more clearly on the issue of culture. The document first asserts that Canadian identity was born out of a symbiosis of cultures, and having thus bowed to the official concept of Canada as a multicultural mosaic, it recognizes that "the duality of Canada's cultural milieux has contributed to the country's richness and diversity."[37] Which belongs to this duality – the francophone or the Quebec environment? The document is silent on the question. However, having recognized that language and culture have always been the most strikingly original aspects of Quebec society, the document is unshakable when it comes to the need for the federal government to retain responsibility for the cultural institutions "that allow for the expression and dissemination of Canada's identity both within Canada and abroad."[38]

The spirit of 1982, the spirit of a certain kind of Canadian nationalism, can live with the linguistic dimension of duality: an official-language policy enhanced by language rights enshrined in the constitution. This recognition of the duality of cultural environments is just tolerable to these Canadian nationalists as long as there is no explicit reference to Quebec identity or culture, as the September 1991 federal document demonstrated. But the political duality so prized by an intellectual of the calibre of André Laurendeau, the view that two national identities face each other in the dialogue between Canada and Quebec, still remained unacceptable to them. On this fundamental question, the 1982 founders and the authors of *Shaping Canada's Future Together* saw eye to eye. It is worth noting that the references to national standards for Canada were ubiquitous in the Beaudoin-Dobbie Report. And Joe Clark proclaimed throughout 1992 the necessity of protecting Canada's "national" institutions in the multilateral constitutional negotiations.

The spirit of 1982 involves the inability to recognize the national dimension of the Quebec question. In my view, this spirit remained predominant in the federal proposals of September 1991, despite the presence of elements that recalled what was best in the spirit of 1867: the notion of a pact, the reconciliation between individual and collective rights, the virtue of ambiguity (in the definition of distinct society, the word "culture," for example, lends itself to the broadest as well as the narrowest of readings). Can Quebecers allow themselves to hope, in a realistic enough way, for a turnaround that would restore the supremacy of the spirit of 1867? I shall attempt to answer this question in the conclusion of this book, but first I would like respectfully to question two legislators, one in Ottawa and one in Quebec, who had to face difficult choices in 1992: Senator Gérald Beaudoin and the former cabinet minister Claude Ryan.

Senator Beaudoin was at the centre of all the federal constitutional initiatives of the post–Meech Lake era. In 1991, he co-chaired the Special Joint Committee of the Senate and the House of Commons on the constitutional reform process. He subsequently replaced Mr Claude Castonguay as the head of the committee mandated to study the September 1991 federal proposals. Here is what he wrote some fifteen years ago, on the occasion of his induction into the Royal Society of Canada:

André Laurendeau had a particularly lucid and penetrating mind. In his diary, he declared his allegiance to the federative formula. He was not afraid to write that "having roots in a culture presupposes a minimum of separation." Similarly, the individual who desires a personal life, especially an inner life, experiences the need not to belong wholly to his duties or his fellow citizens.

History teaches us that a balanced federalism can be reconciled with more than one culture taking root. By its very nature, it presupposes a minimum of separation – hence the division of legislative powers which is its essential dimension. Federalism can also bring together more than one nationalism. Nationalism among francophones has enabled French culture to survive in Canada from its roots in Quebec where it has flourished. French Canadians constitute a nation.[39]

Senator Beaudoin, the Canadian federalism you are defending, and not without courage, seems to me too obsessed with the spirit of 1982 to be able to combine more than one nationalism. The September 1991 federal proposals and the report that you signed were a far cry from the political duality demanded by that "particularly lucid and penetrating mind," André Laurendeau. You and the other Quebec legislators in Ottawa will have to tell us why you remain federalists when duality and Quebec nationalism have been purged from the Canadian political system. And you will not be alone in having to account for your position.

Between 1987 and 1990, Claude Ryan was one of the most ardent supporters of the Meech Lake Accord. He viewed it as a victory for "those for whom it is possible both to be a profoundly committed *Québécois*, a *Québécois* first and foremost, and a Canadian sincerely and loyally devoted to building a strong Canada."[40] Mr Ryan is not just anybody in Quebec society. *Eminence grise* of the Bourassa government, former leader of the Liberal Party, former editor of *Le Devoir*, he is unquestionably one of André Laurendeau's heirs and has inherited Laurendeau's dualist vision of federalism. Several years ago, in March 1989, during a conference at the University of Quebec, Mr Ryan joined the intelligentsia and the political class of Quebec to honour André Laurendeau's memory. Mr Ryan, who was minister of education at the time, made a contribution to the conference that attracted considerable attention. He recalled that "the major characteristic of [Laurendeau's] thought, in my opinion, was his conviction that Quebec constitutes a nation and not just a province or cultural community."[41] Ryan emphasized the profound incompatibility between Laurendeau's political thought and that of Pierre Elliott Trudeau. Laurendeau was the promoter of political duality, of the two-nations argument, whereas Trudeau, in Ryan's view, "only had sympathy for Canadian nationalism."[42] As Ryan emphasized, Laurendeau's dualist approach in the Royal Commission on Bilingualism and Biculturalism was overthrown. English Canada preferred to listen to Pierre Trudeau: "English Canada simply was not prepared to accept a thorough revision of the structures of Canadian federalism."[43] Laurendeau preferred renewed federalism to the perils of sovereignty, but he insisted on the necessity of reforms that would provide "satisfactory responses to Quebec's genuinely political aspirations."[44]

Mr Ryan, a Canadian federalist and a Quebec patriot, has like so many others been awaiting such answers for more than thirty years. At the end of centennial year, 1967, Mr Ryan wrote a long editorial in *Le Devoir* under the very eloquent title: "The Canadian Political Scene and the Crisis of the Two Nations: End-of-the-year Perspectives." The editorial sent two warnings to English Canada: to declare its intentions about the recommendations in the first volume of the Laurendeau-Dunton Report, which had been published in December 1967, and to say whether it was prepared to recognize Quebec's distinct situation.[45] At the end of the article, Mr Ryan spoke of the exceptional urgency of the situation. Today, Mr Ryan, as you well know, Quebecers are still awaiting a response from their Canadian partners. If I am right, Canada chose Pierre Elliott Trudeau's vision of federalism, to the detriment of André Laurendeau's, sometime between 1982 and 1992. If you should somehow happen to become reconciled with this choice in the current situation, they are many of us who would appreciate an explanation from you.

When a political system and a society arrive at a crossroads, the time is ripe to question in the most radical fashion – to go to the root of the matter. When the future is uncertain, there is a need to return to the beginning. For Canada and Quebec, the return to their origins means going back to the Conquest and to the Treaty of Paris that made it official in 1763.

CHAPTER EIGHT

The Spirit of the Conquest, Lord Durham, and National Identities

Among English-Canadian intellectuals, one of Pierre Elliott Trudeau's greatest allies throughout the Meech Lake debate was Ramsay Cook, a historian at York University.[1] Ramsay Cook is an ardent defender of liberalism and individual rights, and he shares with Mr Trudeau a deep distrust of all forms of nationalism, especially Quebec nationalism. During the federal Liberal Party's leadership race in the winter of 1968, Cook and some of his colleagues in fact organized a petition supporting the candidacy of Mr Trudeau, who was then justice minister.

Much can be learned about Canada and Quebec from Ramsay Cook's impressive body of work. His 1971 book, *The Maple Leaf Forever*, contains a fine passage on the importance ascribed to the Conquest in French-Canadian and Quebec historiography: "The interpretation of the meaning of the Conquest is one of the most important subjects in the intellectual history of French Canada. Each generation of French Canadians appears to fight, intellectually, the battle of the Plains of Abraham all over again."[2]

Cook gives the name "conquestism" to the propensity of Quebec intellectuals to recall and reinterpret the events of 1759–63. In this chapter, I would like to show that Cook's remark applies to our Meech Lake years. Christian Dufour's essay, *Le défi québécois/A Canadian Challenge*, is best read as one of the finest expressions of conquestism in twentieth-century Quebec letters. But if Quebec and its intellectuals have not put the Conquest behind them yet, the same can be said of English Canada and its thinkers. The writings of David Bercuson and Barry Cooper, Janet Ajzenstat's work on Lord Durham, and Ramsay Cook's own output since the Meech Lake Accord was signed in April 1987 all illustrate the fact that Quebec intellectuals have no monopoly on the Conquest fixation. At the end of this chapter, I shall myself venture into the minefield of conquestism by recalling the broad outlines of my reading of the Constitution Act, 1982, and the project of a pan-Canadian "national" referendum as it was conceived in 1992 during the Canada round of constitutional negotiations that led to the Charlottetown Accord, and as it could recur in the near future.

A COUNTRY BUILT ON THE CONQUEST

According to Ramsay Cook, conquestism means the irresistibly seductive power which the decisive events that sealed the fate of French colonization in America have over French-Canadian and Quebec intellectuals. While it is a constantly recurring theme, interpreting the Conquest becomes even more prevalent during political and social crises. When uncertainty grips the heart, when political institutions are tottering, our intellectuals frenziedly immerse themselves in narratives about the Conquest, searching for new readings that would be likely to shed light on the deliberations about our society's destiny. A sampling of Quebec historians preoccupied by the Conquest would include François-Xavier Garneau, Henri Bourassa, Lionel Groulx, and Maurice Séguin and the other members of the Ecole historique de Montréal on the eve of the Quiet Revolution. Léon Dion also gives in to the fashion of resorting to conquestism in a time of crisis in his 1987 book that served as a springboard for an earlier chapter: "To depict in this way the anguish, the fatigue of so great a number of those who write and speak about their society and who feel such deep attachment to it compels one to consider the event that brutally changed the course of fate: the English Conquest. That was the most tangible legacy we received from France, which left us a meagre heritage that we are laboriously attempting to resurrect today.[3]

Ramsay Cook goes on to suggest that Quebec intellectuals are obsessed by the Conquest because they have never really come to terms with it, never really understood it. Does this remark reflect the condescension of a Toronto sage? I do not think we need to jump to such a conclusion. Cook may have touched on the essence of the matter here. In order really to understand the Conquest, it is not enough to express dismay about its consequences for Quebec, for our history and identity. We must also include in our analysis the Conquest's effects on Canada as a whole, on the history of the relations between English Canada and Quebec, on the development of a pan-Canadian collective identity. As Léon Dion recalled in his book, Quebec intellectuals pass on to one another a dualist vision of Canadian federalism. However, they have a tendency to ignore the "other," the Canadian partner without whom there would be no dualist relationship. In the late 1980s, Christian Dufour wrote an essay that addressed this problem directly. In *Le défi Québécois/A Canadian Challenge*, he returned to the beginning, the Conquest, to understand the relationship between the Quebec identity and the Canadian identity, and to shed new light on the Meech Lake debate.

Quebec is the geographical and historical heart of Canada. Christian Dufour clearly establishes in his book that the Canadian identity that developed after 1763 fed off the Conquest which had just taken place:

The problem is that the relationship between the Anciens Canadiens and the Loyalists was established on the basis of the Conquest, which nourished the Canadian identity and on which the Canada of today is still built. The process has accentuated over these past years. Now it threatens the healthy aspects of the relationship between the Canadian identity and the Quebec identity … Habits were borrowed from both sides. And then there was the essential political consequence of any conquest: the conqueror's profitable confiscation of part of the power that stems naturally from the collective identity of the conquered.[4]

The conquered people – the "Canadiens" who spoke French, the Québécois of yore – remained in the majority throughout the formative period of the country that was to become Canada. After the Conquest, they gave haven to the Loyalists who left the United States, just as they defended the burgeoning country against the Americans in 1812. The collective identity of the *anciens Canadiens*[5] remained strong enough after the Conquest to generate much of the new Canada's originality; for example, its political culture. English Canadians were able to thrive in the individualist atmosphere of North America because they were supported by this collective sense of identity. The collective dynamism of the conquered people was transferred to the institutions and political life of the new country.

Canada has changed a lot over two centuries. The descendants of the conquered people became concentrated in Quebec, where they developed a new identity. Canada also evolved, becoming much more complex. Dufour's fundamental argument is that the Canadian identity continues to draw on the collective dynamism of the Quebec identity, but without recognizing that what makes up Quebec's originality should be reflected in the country's institutions. In Canada, the two identities are entwined, but the Conquest has prevented the Canadian side from recognizing the Quebec side. Dufour rightly points out that the English have had a share in shaping Quebec.

Because of the Conquest, though, the Québécois would sooner banish this fact from their sense of identity and political outlook. For instance, to seek to have all signs in French only is to pretend that the Conquest never occurred, that the English did not settle here two hundred years ago and that they have not become a part of us.

Since 1960, events have evolved fast and furiously in the relations between the Canadian and Québécois identities. The former continues to feed systematically off the latter. The language crisis in Montreal in the early 1960s resulted ten years later in the adoption of a symmetrical policy of bilingualism "from coast to coast," which transformed the Canadian identity and increased its originality with respect to the United States. André Laurendeau and a whole generation of Quebec politicians and intellectuals gave voice to a desire for recognition of the country's bicultural and binational character. The result, from 1971 onwards, has been the development of a multiculturalism policy, which some now portray as the fundamental nature of Canada. Every Quebec government since Jean Lesage has redoubled its efforts to modify the constitution and obtain a new division of powers and special status for Quebec. This led to Canada revising its constitution in 1982 without Quebec's consent, and giving itself a new national myth by way of the Charter of Rights and Freedoms.

Christian Dufour sees the Meech Lake Accord as a break in the process whereby Canadian identity "systematically siphons off" Quebec's identity: "The novelty of the Meech Lake Accord was the breach it opened in the principal effect of the Conquest. It was recognized that Quebec constituted a distinct society, and that that had political effects."[6] Writing in 1989, Dufour could already see the causes of the failure of the Meech Lake Accord building up. The exacerbation of provincialism – the dogma of provincial equality, by which each province wants to get everything that is granted to Quebec – is just the latest embodiment of the main consequence of the Conquest. Canada was never able to get over the Conquest in the Meech Lake saga; it has never been able to recognize national dualism, national pluralism. Let us now examine the forms this inability has taken in the intellectual life of English Canada.

LORD DURHAM IS STILL WITH US

According to Christian Dufour, Canada is a country built on the Conquest. The English reaction to the 1837–38 uprisings is the logical sequel of the Battle of the Plains of Abraham:

In the end, the *Parti patriote* wanted independence without having organized the uprising and without having the means to do so. They had forgotten that

England was not just a motherland in need of coaxing: she was also the Conqueror of the Canadiens.

They had also forgotten that, for the first time, there were as many English in Canada as there were Canadiens. Lord Durham would pass down the verdict in the name of the Conqueror. The Upper and Lower Canadas would be united; the Canadiens, soon to be a minority, would be assimilated, and this would lead to the now inevitable self-government of the colony.[7]

Lord Durham's basic idea, and the essence of the 1840 Act of Union, was that duality – or dualism – meant division. Nothing but perpetual conflict could result from two nations, two peoples, two races, or two distinct societies coexisting and being recognized within the public institutions of a political society. It is remarkable to think that a constitutional agreement recognizing Quebec as a distinct society within Canada was signed at Meech Lake in 1987, some 150 years after Lord Durham's intervention in our affairs. Recent work by some English-Canadian intellectuals shows that the results of the Conquest and Lord Durham's influence still have a powerful impact outside Quebec.

Janet Ajzenstat, an English-Canadian political scientist, published a book on Lord Durham's political thought in 1988, when the Meech Lake debate was just beginning. There is not a single explicit reference to the accord in her book. However, its reviewers were able to read between the lines:

Recent critics of the "distinct society" clause of the Meech Lake Accord have not only challenged its vague wording, but many have also questioned the justice of granting special status to any social group in a liberal society ... As a bold revisionist analysis of Durham's political thought and as a clear defence of mainstream liberalism in the face of attempts to enshrine Quebec's distinctiveness in Canadian federalism, Ajzenstat's contribution to what remains an ongoing debate is well worth consideration.[8]

In the vision that Mrs Ajzenstat ascribes to Lord Durham and takes up and makes her own, liberal ideology loses a good portion of its nuances and complexity. It becomes monolithic and coterminous with modernity. According to this perspective, the liberal historical movement would end up creating an aseptic and more homogeneous world, in which loss of diversity would be compensated for by increased civilization, prosperity, and liberty.[9] In a universe that had become totally liberal, individual rights would flourish in commercial and industrial societies, in which political institutions would be reduced to simple instruments subordinated to the desires of individuals.

Monolithic liberalism makes no secret of its view of the fate of national minorities in the modern world: they will inexorably be assimilated. According to Ajzenstat, such a fate is necessary from the point of view of history and it is ethically justifiable.[10] The benefits of modernization ultimately become so attractive that individuals do not hesitate to renounce their specific culture and their particular way of life. The ambitious and progressive subjects of modern society have no use for the "crutches" of cultural protectionism.[11] It is hard not to see a kinship between this liberalism and the doctrine that engendered Pierre Elliott Trudeau's values of a just society. For those policy makers who are still mired in romantic nostalgia, Janet Ajzenstat offers the following counsel: once a society has set out on the road to modernity, to progress, it is useless and vain to wish to protect and promote its specificity.

Ajzenstat recommends Lord Durham's path as the most promising way of ensuring that the process of assimilating national minorities will unfold smoothly. The most enlightened policy consists of adopting intrinsically liberal measures: individual rights and fundamental freedoms, and equal access to the political system and to socio-economic activities for individuals belonging to national minorities. Such a program, based on individual rights and equal opportunities, was adopted by Pierre Elliott Trudeau from the beginning of his political career. His recent assessment of it dispels all doubt on that score.[12] Equipped with similar beliefs, Mrs Ajzenstat claims that policies that grant cultural protection to minorities and give political recognition to minority nationalities are unwise and unfair.

It would be unwise, argues Ajzenstat, to yield to the pressures of the nationalists, since they would constantly demand more. Such a course would also be unfair because it would infringe on the liberal rights of individuals who belong to minority groups, as well as on the rights of other citizens. Liberal justice, in Ajzenstat's view, is synonymous with symmetry in the acquisition and exercise of individual rights. It thus appears incompatible with the granting of any form of special status to national minorities. Individuals will only have access to all the benefits of liberal justice when they are ready to renounce the particular dimension of their identity that falls short of the universal.

In the context of the Meech Lake debate, as discussed in the preceding chapters, this seems an appropriate time to reflect on one of the final sentences of Ajzenstat's book: "The importance of the mainstream analysis is that it tells us that justice is threatened when a particular way of life is privileged."[13] The most important clause of the Meech Lake Accord stipulated that any interpretation of the

Canadian constitution would henceforth have to agree with the recognition of Quebec as a distinct society within Canada. The National Assembly and the Quebec government would have had the obligation of protecting and promoting this distinct character. This was not insignificant. This recognition and these obligations would potentially have given Quebec genuine special status. The distinct society clause would have had an immediate impact on the Charter of Rights and Freedoms. In interpreting the first article of the Charter, which allows for the restriction of rights and freedoms "within reasonable limits and whose justification can be shown within the framework of a free and democratic society," the courts and Quebec could have resorted to this clause. Even without providing any overall definition of it, the distinct society clause did indeed favour a particular way of life. It hinted that the common good of Quebec would not always be identical with the common good of Canada. It was thus unacceptable for those who, from Lord Durham to Janet Ajzenstat, through Pierre Elliott Trudeau, have refused to believe that liberalism could be compatible with dual national allegiances.

Should Janet Ajzenstat's study be regarded as an isolated event that says little about the evolution of the English-Canadian intelligentsia and its attitudes towards Quebec? I think not. The public reception of David Bercuson and Barry Cooper's pamphlet, *Deconfederation*, demonstrates that Lord Durham's resurgence was no mere coincidence. Bercuson and Cooper continued Mrs Ajzenstat's reflection on Durham's liberalism while drawing lessons from it with respect to the Meech Lake Accord: "It was Durham's view that the French must either be left alone entirely or be liberalized and assimilated. The rebellion was clear evidence that they had not been left alone, that they could not be left alone. The option of assimilating the French to a liberal and homogeneous society therefore recommended itself."[14]

In reading Bercuson and Cooper's essay, one gets the impression that they had long believed that the Constitution Act, 1982, could continue Durham's work of liberalizing and homogenizing Canadian society. Hence their disappointment when the Meech Lake Accord emerged:

This clause, which endowed the government of Quebec with special legal and constitutional responsibilities, was utterly unprecedented in Canadian history. It would have given to Quebec alone the authority to "promote and preserve" Quebec's distinctiveness – a clear victory-from-the-grave for Papineau ... Whatever the implications for Canadian federalism, it served to undermine completely one of the fundamental pillars of liberal democracy: equality of all citizens before the law.

The Meech Lake Accord would have been the penultimate blow to Canada as a nation.[15]

Like Lord Durham, Bercuson and Cooper do not believe in the reconciliation of national identities within a single political system, even a federal one. A liberal political association must be based on the consent of the people, the limiting of government power, the supremacy of individual freedom, and equality of all before the law. Bercuson and Cooper hold that the Québécois and their political community have become a threat to the very survival of liberal democracy in Canada, mired as the Québécois are in a nationalism which they claim is founded on ethnic and cultural requirements.[16] Should it prove impossible to fuse both peoples into a single nation, as Lord Durham wished, Bercuson and Cooper would prefer secession over uneasy coexistence. Are the prisoners of the Conquest and the heirs of Lord Durham only to be found around Preston Manning and the Reform Party? Ramsay Cook's transformation seems particularly instructive in this regard.

Around centennial year, Ramsay Cook seemed prepared to break with the legacy of the Conquest and Lord Durham. In 1966 he recognized the principle of cultural duality, of national duality, as the very foundation of Canadian federalism.[17] According to Cook, the founders of Canada wished to preserve a balance between the different values, the sources of tension, in the Canadian society of their day. The best aspects of 1867 federalism were those that gave the minority protection of the things it considered essential for its survival.[18] This federalism depended on its ability to renew itself in the acceptance of national differences.[19] Nationalism seemed dangerous, because it is ruled by a logic of uniformity and centralization, whereas Canada is a federal, pluralistic state. Cook pointed out that French Canadians in the 1950s feared that a strengthened government could become the instrument of a homogeneous nationalism.[20] Even quite recently, Cook analysed in a remarkably lucid fashion the virtues for Quebec society of constitutional ambiguity, as well as ambiguity in terms of identities. He interpreted the perpetual oscillations of the Quebec people, torn between fear of the future and a hunger for freedom, as an ambiguity that was a matter of wisdom more than of cultural fatigue: "It also reflects the shrewdness of a small, determined people who have discovered over the centuries that in the end survival depends on themselves and that no single strategy is perfect."[21]

It seems clear to me that complex federalism, based on the acceptance of national pluralism, on the virtues of ambiguity, and on the refusal of homogeneity, has not, in Cook's case (any more than in

Trudeau's, for that matter) resisted the charms of the new Canadian nationalism that was generated mainly by the Constitution Act, 1982, and its Charter of Rights and Freedoms. Thanks to the Charter and its centripetal force, Canada has been endowed with a national myth, and Quebecers would be wrong to underestimate its powers of integration. To rescue this endeavour to build the Canadian nation, and to conquer Quebec with law and sweetness rather than with arms, Cook has abandoned his earlier analysis of the merits of ambiguity. This is the meaning of his attacks on the imprecision of the distinct society clause during the Meech Lake debate.[22] Cook and his disciples, like Michael Behiels, have had enough of the misunderstandings and difficult balances between interpretive principles, which were so dear to the founders of the Canadian federal order.[23] The Ramsay Cook of 1967 praised ambiguity. The Cook of post-1982 and post–Meech Lake wrote the following in a review of Christian Dufour's book, *Le défi québécois*:

What is especially irritating about Dufour's rather shallow skim over Canada's history is that he ends with another repetition of the woolly demand that "Quebec's specifity be recognized" in a new constitution ... What the last 30 years of constitutional debate demonstrated is that those who still want to talk about "specificity," "distinct identity," "special status," and all the other circumlocutions, are the problem, not the solution ... Pierre Trudeau and René Lévesque devoted their political careers to that demonstration. The authors of the Meech Lake Accord believed that with Trudeau and Lévesque gone, the country could return to the *confused ambiguities* [my emphasis] that dominated debate before 1968.[24]

In post-1982 Canada, Ramsay Cook has come to terms with a vision of Canadian nationalism that has no use for misunderstandings and artfully maintained ambiguity with respect to questions of identity and belonging. He has also expressed great sympathy for the monolithic liberalism of Lord Durham as interpreted by Mrs Ajzenstat: "Finally, and not incidentally, Ajzenstat has provided a clear-headed defence of liberalism at a time when the Meech Lake Accord once again potentially provides an instance where 'justice is threatened' when a particular way of life is privileged."[25]

Lord Durham and his liberalism are indeed still alive in the English-Canadian intelligentsia, as is the Canadian malaise denounced by Christian Dufour, the disease that prevents Canada from frankly and openly welcoming Quebec's national difference while simultaneously accepting that this difference may have repercussions on the operation of the political system. If the effects of this disease were only felt by some English-Canadian intellectuals, there would perhaps be no great cause for worry. Unfortunately, the whole political system is affected by it. To conclude this chapter, I shall try my hand at a small variation in conquestism.

THE NEW COUNTENANCES OF THE CONQUEST

There are several degrees of oppression and injustice in the relations between peoples. One would be wrong to think that these realities find expression only in violence or that they apply exclusively to totalitarian regimes. I am well aware that it would be excessive to compare the fate of Quebec with that of Lithuania and Slovenia. However, I continue to see the 1982 constitutional reform and the recent federal referendum act as unjust and reprehensible measures. I regard them as an updating of the Conquest and as a continuation of Lord Durham's policies by other means. That two Quebecers, Pierre Elliott Trudeau and Brian Mulroney, were the principal instigators of these endeavours can only leave us with a bitter taste in our mouths and a great feeling of sadness.

In Quebec, it was a long time before what had transpired in 1982 was fully understood. For several years, as Léon Dion correctly pointed out, those who denied the legitimacy of the Canadian state were in a way rendered impotent. The same applies to people such as Donald Smiley and Philip Resnick in English Canada, who had the courage to denounce Mr Trudeau's coup and "constitutional Bonapartism."[26] Following the 1980 referendum, after twenty years of numerous upheavals, Quebecers seemed desperate for political and constitutional peace. Indeed, while all Canada was in the midst of an economic recession, Quebecers did not take to the streets to protest against the Constitution Act, 1982. Since the revelations in the Morin affair, we now know that there were many reasons for the post-referendum depression of René Lévesque and the Parti québécois. Whatever the reasons may have been, one fact remains, namely, the passive overall attitude of Québécois public opinion and of our political leaders. Our society accepted the reduction of the powers of the National Assembly, the trustee of the people's authority, with a certain indifference. This is not to say that such popular passivity necessarily legitimizes the whole business. Events over the last few years in Eastern Europe and the former USSR have provided us with numerous examples of situations in which nations bow for a certain period before rebelling against unjust laws and political systems.

The Meech Lake saga brought out what was really terrible and profoundly unacceptable in the spirit that Mr Trudeau breathed into

Canadian institutions in 1982: the desire to break the spine of the Québécois community in the interest of an idealized vision of the Canadian nation. Several experts reiterated before the Bélanger-Campeau Commission that the Québécois see themselves as a nation and as a unique political collectivity, and that their home environment is a specific complete society; yet, having pointed to the existence of the levelling and homogenizing tendencies in the institutions stemming from the 1982 reform, these experts concluded that it would be very difficult to get Quebec's specificity accepted within the Canadian constitution.[27]

As I write these lines, a few days before Quebec's *fête nationale*, everything points to the nationalist and reductive spirit of 1982 continuing to rule over Canadian institutions. After three months of frantic negotiations, the multilateral meetings on the constitution ended up with an interim report that boded ill for Quebec. It seemed that a bowdlerized version of the distinct society clause would be accepted and that a cosmetic operation would be substituted for a new division of powers. The federal government's spending power would be limited only in the case of new shared-cost programs, and provinces would only be able to withdraw from them if they agree to implement programs or initiatives compatible with "national" goals. The different partners of the Canada round (the federal government, the provinces minus Quebec, and the leaders of the native peoples and the territories) agreed that culture should be recognized as an exclusively provincial matter. They hastened to add, however, that the constitution should also recognize the federal government's responsibility for existing "national" cultural institutions. The fundamental assumption of the Canada round remains the existence of a single and unique national Canadian identity. As in the days of Lord Durham, despite all the eloquent words on the importance of authentic diversity, there is a relentless drive to fuse different peoples into a single nation.

In the months that followed the failure of the Meech Lake Accord, while Michel Bélanger and Jean Campeau bore on their shoulders the dignity of the National Assembly whose prerogatives had been held up to ridicule in 1982, one felt that Quebec was perhaps going to have the opportunity to extricate itself from Trudeau's claws and his hostile view of the principle of national duality. Jacques Dufresne captured this situation correctly in a vocabulary akin to that of Machiavelli: "There are, in the history of nations as in those of organisms, opportunities that one must know how to seize in flight, critical moments when the speed of execution becomes as important as the decision itself. In medicine, in psychiatry especially, the word kairos is given to the intuition that enables one to sense these opportunities."[28]

It is now clear that Quebec's leaders were not able, or did not wish, to display such intuition. By dint of wavering and dithering, Mr Bourassa was so successful in calming things that the will to change seems to have worn off in Quebec public opinion. There is a sense of being fed up, a feeling of weariness in the air. In the context of a seemingly interminable economic crisis, the same indifference to constitutional questions as there was ten years ago seems to be taking over in Quebec society. The defenders of the status quo, of the order imposed on Quebec in 1982, are not, however, at the end of their tether.

In every act of conquest, there are strategic objectives. For Pierre Elliott Trudeau and the constitution builders of 1982, the metropolitan region of Montreal was one such strategic fortress. Capturing it seemed essential to the project of building the Canadian nation. It is in Montreal more than anywhere else in Quebec that the national patriotism promoted by the Charter of Rights and Freedoms – as well as the programs of the secretary of state and the Ministry of Multiculturalism and Citizenship, targeting different minority groups – try to foment a primary allegiance towards the Canadian community, to the detriment of identification with Quebec. Montrealers experience the daily clash between national visions and aspirations. If the constitutional mess continues, they will not readily renounce the symbols of Québécois national identity.

One has really felt in the last few years that there are people in Canada who are desperately eager to refight the Conquest of Quebec. A few months before the referendum on the 1992 Charlottetown Accord, federal departments multiplied their public relations campaigns in Quebec, the *belle province* that was to be retained at all costs. They boasted of the value of passport and citizenship, inviting Quebecers to travel in Canada and to celebrate the 125th anniversary of Confederation. "Canada 125" proposed to spend $50 million to this end. Meanwhile, the prime minister of the day, Brian Mulroney, promised to wage a bitter fight against Quebec sovereigntists. Economic terrorism was resurfacing as in the worst moments of the 1980 campaign on sovereignty association.

This desire for a new conquest of Quebec never seemed to me as obvious as in the 1992 debate on the referendum act in the federal Parliament. Once adopted, Bill c-81 would enable Ottawa to organize a "national" referendum throughout Canada, including in Quebec. But to speak of a national referendum in Canada is to presume erroneously that the Québécois subscribe to a pan-Canadian consensus on national identity and national community.

I tried to show in an earlier chapter that the central government of the Canadian federation effected a reform of the Canadian constitution in 1981–82 that reduced the powers of the government and the National Assembly of Quebec, particularly in the area of the language of education. Because the principle of shared sovereignty is at the heart of federalism and because a federal contract on the sacrosanct question of the division of powers cannot be modified without the consent of the parties, the federal government forfeited all legitimacy in Quebec. Its illegitimacy was further deepened by the failure of the Meech Lake Accord, which had been negotiated in good faith by a Quebec government that wanted to play the game of federalism. A referendum on the future of Quebec as a distinct society and national community should never be supervised by a central government that wields its authority on the basis of a constitution that is illegitimate in Quebec. This remains as valid in 1995 as it was in 1992.

The attempt to impose a "national" Canadian referendum in Quebec was another way of pursuing the work of Lord Durham and of fusing the two peoples. The Conservative government for that matter turned down amendments that would have recognized the principle of the double majority (a majority in Quebec and a majority in the rest of Canada). The adoption of such an amendment would have been tantamount to accepting the dualist argument. The amendment contradicted the logic of the 1982 constitutional reform, namely, that the constitution was founded on the principle of the equality of all provinces within a great Canadian nation. Several Quebec members of Parliament and cabinet ministers were absent when the bill was passed at third reading in the House of Commons. One might however ask, like Cicero about Catilina, "until when" the patience of Bouchard, Loiselle, Masse, and Vézina will last with regard to a system that cavalierly dismisses the national dimension of the Quebec question. Although out of office, these figures have, in my mind, an obligation to speak up in the battle that looms ahead in 1995.

The federal government will pull out all the stops to conquer the hearts and minds of the Quebecois in the upcoming referendum. Healthy realism should make us understand that the people in power in Ottawa will be as "reasonable" as people can be who risk losing everything in a large-scale political conflict. In 1965, when Pierre Elliott Trudeau came to Ottawa, he was accompanied by doves, Jean Marchand and Gérard Pelletier. Behind the doves, however, the shadow of hawks could be glimpsed, such as Marc Lalonde and Michael Pitfield, the crusaders who would fight to preserve Canadian national unity, irrespective of the price to be paid. Prime Minister Chrétien will keep the posture of the statesman only as long as he is absolutely certain of the victory of the No forces led by Daniel

Johnson, Jr. If the going gets tougher than expected, he will have no trouble redesigning himself as a street fighter. His adversaries should not underestimate his resolve and sense of purpose.

The political and intellectual leaders of English Canada consider that any attempt to establish a link between the Canada-Quebec situation and that of the federations that collapsed in the USSR and Yugoslavia is a gross exaggeration. It is true that the Soviet regime was totalitarian and that Yugoslavia was not much better, whereas Canada belongs to the world of liberal democracy. It is also true that Quebec, inasmuch as a slim majority of its elected representatives in Ottawa gave their consent, entered freely into Confederation in 1867. One must nonetheless recall that according to the best of Liberal political philosophy, as for instance in the works of John Locke, no people may consent to political authority in any definitive fashion. In 1982 the rules of the federal game were changed, without Quebec's consent. Quebec has had a knife at its throat, to use a popular expression, for more than a decade. Furthermore, like the USSR and Yugoslavia, Canada stubbornly refuses the principle of national pluralism. The history of Quebec and of Canada deserve to be pursued in other ways than by attempts at conquest in which law and the work of reshaping the citizens' identity are used instead of arms. We are not doomed to re-enact Lord Durham's policies by other means, so let us examine the conditions of a real partnership between Quebec and Canada.

The Conditions of a Genuine Partnership between Canada and Quebec

With the death of the Meech Lake Accord, something very profound happened in Quebec. Everybody feels it, but it is not easy to define. For me, the most significant element is that the long-felt ambiguity of the Quebec federalists has been resolved. I do not mean that they are no longer federalists. But the age-old uncertainty about the question of whether it was necessary to make certain changes to the 1867 Constitution or whether we had to remake our structures from head to foot has gone. On 23 June 1990, the 1867 Constitution died morally in Quebec. It is necessary to create anew.

Charles Taylor

Canadian nationalism is the guiding principle which inspired the founders of the new constitutional order in 1982, and which they have sought to inject into political culture and custom. In Mr Trudeau's project, the rhetoric of popular sovereignty (the will to give the constitution back to the people) and of liberalism (the project of enshrining individual rights in the constitution) must be regarded as steps in the grand strategy of building the Canadian nation. Based on the granting of language rights to individuals and on a concept of Canada as a bilingual and multicultural nation-state, Mr Trudeau's project collides head-on with any project of a distinct national society and an autonomous political community in Quebec. In Mr Trudeau's view of things, there is no Quebec nation or people. There is a single, indivisible Canadian nation, and the people of Quebec are Canadian citizens who happen, more or less accidentally, to live in the territory of Quebec. These individuals could live in another province and enjoy the same advantages of Canadian citizenship. Pierre Elliott Trudeau's just society is one that guarantees equal rights and the privileges of citizenship to all citizens on an individual basis. The identity of the people of Quebec has no national, collective dimension. This, in a nutshell, is the spirit of 1982.

This is the context in which the above quotation from Charles Taylor's submission to the Bélanger-Campeau Commission must be interpreted.[1] The ultimate rejection of the Meech Lake Accord made many Quebecers suddenly realize that something very serious had happened in 1982. The events of that year had struck a fatal blow to the compromise of 1867, which was based on the refusal of homogeneity and on implicit acceptance of national duality. The Meech Lake Accord was nothing less than the finest attempt in a decade to breathe life into the spirit of duality. In my view, that is what Taylor meant when he stated that the 1867 constitution had died morally in Quebec on 23 June 1990. That day, what Etienne Parent, Louis-Hippolyte Lafontaine, and Henri Bourassa had hoped for was extinguished forever. Because it is founded on a nationalist dream and ambitions, the Canadian constitutional order will always baulk at recognizing Quebec as a distinct society and national collectivity. The Canadian national identity promoted by the spirit of 1982 seeks to swallow up Quebec, to encompass it in its categories.[2] There is something profoundly unhealthy about this whole business, for Quebec and for Canada.

I do not believe that the constitutional order created in 1982 will withstand the test of time, for it is based on negative aims. What Clarkson and McCall describe as Trudeau's magnificent obsession is not the patriation of the constitution or the adoption of a charter of rights, but the relentless struggle against Quebec nationalism. On this score, I wholeheartedly endorse what Mr Claude Ryan told a conference on André Laurendeau in March 1989 at the University of Quebec in Montreal:

To understand Mr Trudeau's argument, it is necessary first to grasp the view of Canada upon which it is based. Mr Trudeau achieved enormous success by posing as an opponent of nationalism. But in reality what put him off so much was Quebec nationalism. Despite all his anti-nationalist protestations, Pierre Elliott Trudeau has first and foremost been the ardent protagonist of a pan-Canadian nationalism that no longer arouses any emotion in Quebec, but does retain solid roots in English Canada, and whose strongest voice over the past few years has been the *Toronto Star*.[3]

Canada has been forced to undergo immense efforts at institutional and political restructuring over the last quarter of a century, most of the time under Trudeau's leadership. The purpose of this has been to fight Quebec nationalism rather than to build anything positive. Is this reading of events exaggerated and excessively critical? On the contrary. According to Kenneth McRoberts of York University, it is borne out by the historical facts. In a lecture delivered in Toronto in 1991, "English Canada and Quebec: Avoiding the Issue," McRoberts showed that Canada had preferred self-transformation, at the cost of enormous expense and sacrifice, over recognition of Quebec's difference as a nation.[4] In 1969 the political system developed an official-language regime designed to make all Canada like Quebec. Canadian nationalism was the cornerstone of this official-language policy: "In sum, Ottawa's formulation of a language regime for Canada was closely shaped by a more fundamental concern: to counter Quebec neo-nationalism and separatism. Within this 'nation-saving' perspective, a language regime based on the personality principle and defining language rights in purely individual terms was the only acceptable one."[5]

Lurking behind the adoption of a multiculturalism policy in 1971 was the desire to counter the dualist aspirations of Quebec nationalists. With time, and particularly since the basic law was rewritten in 1988, the promotion of cultural diversity has taken on new dimensions. Bilingualism has come to be subordinated to multiculturalism, according to McRoberts, who regards this shift as nothing less than the death of the dualist dream. Meanwhile, the nerve centre of the 1982 Charter of Rights and Freedoms lies in these articles dealing with language rights. The purpose of the articles was to attack Quebec's policies, which were founded on the principle of territoriality. According to Trudeau's biographers, this objective was "coated with layer upon layer of sweetener." It is worth listening to them at greater length:

The notion of an entrenched charter of rights and freedoms would appeal to the legal establishment and civil libertarians among the country's liberal-minded intellectual élite. It would also attract those groups – the ethnics, the feminists, the disabled, the homosexuals, the aged, and the native peoples – who saw themselves as minorities in Canadian society, needing protection against discrimination ... With all these favourable aspects of the package diverting attention, the "constitutionalization" of the official languages law and the entrenchment of minority-language education rights would be camouflaged.[6]

Trudeau's insistence on a symmetrical conception of equal rights has also had repercussions in increasing the uniformity of federalism. As the Bélanger-Campeau Commission pointed out, reinforcing the aspiration to equality among the provinces impedes asymmetrical development towards a special status for Quebec. By dint of its relentless opposition to the project of a national Québécois identity, of its refusal to face up to the Quebec question once and for all, Canada has become exhausted, according to McRoberts. It has undermined the quest for its own identity. In my terminology, Canada has become mired in Trudeau's negative nationalism. Basically, as I tried to show in chapter 6, Trudeau wanted to change human nature. Like Rousseau's legislator, his ambition was to use the Charter to refashion Canadian political culture, to transform the political dimension of the identity of each citizen of this country. However, he did not behave in exactly the same way as Rousseau's legislator. "It is a particular and superior function, which has nothing in common with human empire; because, if he who commands men must not preside over the laws, he who presides over the laws must not have the command over men: otherwise his laws, employed as the ministers of his passions, would frequently merely perpetuate his injustices; and it would be impossible to prevent private aims from defiling the sanctity of his work."[7]

The spirit of 1982 involved some private aims – an obsession with Quebec nationalism – which defile the sanctity of the work, to use Rousseau's expression. Trudeau was too deeply involved in his immediate political fight against the Parti québécois, and against nationalists of all hues in Quebec, to carry out the task of a legislator with the requisite wisdom and prudence. He gave in to the passions of the moment. Despite the valiant efforts of those who prepared and wrote *Shaping Canada's Future Together*, the Beaudoin-Dobbie Report, and the preliminary documents leading to the Charlottetown Accord, these negative private aims remain at the heart of the Canadian constitutional order. The federal proposals added further emphasis to the shift of power within the Canadian political system towards the judiciary branch, a trend that began in 1982. The courts would have been called on to breathe life into the Canada clause, the distinct society clause, and the grey areas of economic restructuring. The Supreme Court would have continued to hold sway over interpretation of the Charter of Rights and Freedoms, a document inspired as much by nationalism as by liberalism.

The experts all stress that the courts have considerable latitude in all these areas. Alain Baccigalupo has demonstrated how great this freedom is with respect to interpretation of section 1 of the Charter of Rights and Freedoms, which recognizes reasonable limits to the enjoyment of rights within a free and democratic society.[8] Over the years, as jurisprudence has evolved, the Supreme Court's attempts to define relatively objective criteria on the nature of reasonable limits have taken nothing away from the judiciary's interpretive freedom. Furthermore, the notwithstanding clause does not constitute a sufficient counterweight to the increase in the judiciary's power. The more Canadian political culture falls under the influence of the spirit of 1982, the harder it will be for governments on a political level to resort to this clause. The federal constitutional proposals of September 1991, which would have lessened the scope of the notwithstanding clause, provided a fine example of this.

The work of experts such as Peter Russell, Rainer Knopff, and F.L. Morton, which I drew on in an earlier chapter, brings to light a further dimension of the courts' great freedom to interpret the Charter.[9] In Canada, the judiciary has the most difficulty in reflecting the spirit of federalism. The federal government alone is responsible for nominating Supreme Court justices. Both *Shaping Canada's Future Together* and in its wake the Beaudoin-Dobbie Report proposed that the federal government should consult the provinces about the nomination of judges, while reserving the final decision for itself. The 1991 federal proposals would not have enshrined the existing composition of the Supreme Court (three of whose members are from Quebec) in the constitution. That would have required unanimous provincial approval. However, the federal government sought to avoid any discussion of areas in which unanimity would be necessary for a constitutional amendment. Every transformation proposed by the federal government, including changes to the Supreme Court, could have been brought about despite Quebec's opposition.

Finally, it must be remembered that the Supreme Court is not the only important court in the Canadian judicial system. By virtue of section 96 of the British North America Act, the federal government has full power to appoint all the judges of the Quebec Superior Court and the Quebec Court of Appeal. Like their peers in other provinces, these judges operate in courts that are the place of last appeal in 98 per cent of the cases. One has to keep this unilateral power in mind and remember these statistics in order to realize just what a leap of faith Quebec was being asked to make in surrendering to the judiciary the power to decide the definitive meaning of distinct society and its relation to the Charter of Rights and Freedoms.

The Canadian political culture that has flourished since 1982 stresses the symmetry and equality of individual rights, as well as the refusal of discrimination. No individual or group ought to enjoy special treatment. As Charles Taylor has shown in a work of seminal importance, there is a vision of liberalism in North America that promotes values similar to those of the political culture that emerged from the spirit of 1982.[10] It would perhaps be more precise to say that the spirit of 1982 is inspired by North American procedural liberalism. Procedural liberalism regards symmetrical equality and invidual autonomy as absolutes. It believes that individual rights and the principle of the absence of discrimination must always rank above the collective goals a society might set. In this view of liberalism, there cannot be a public concept of the common good protected and promoted by the state. The procedural approach, which is individualistic, neutral, egalitarian, and symmetrical, is not the only interpretation of liberal democracy to be found in the Charter of Rights and Freedoms. But until now, this is the view of liberalism which the Canadian judiciary system has favoured. According to Taylor, this bodes ill for a society such as Quebec, which ascribes great importance to collective goals without neglecting individual rights, and which regards the survival and progress of that distinct society as a common good that the Quebec state must protect and promote.[11]

On a practical level, a philosopher such as Charles Taylor can have doubts about Quebec's linguistic legislation, but in his eyes the project of a distinct society in North America, embracing the full experience of modernity mainly in French, is far from incompatible with the principles of liberal democracy:

A society with strong collective goals can be liberal, on this view, provided it is also capable of respecting diversity, especially when this concerns those who do not share its goals, and provided it can offer adequate safeguards for fundamental rights. There will undoubtedly be tensions involved, and difficulties, in pursuing these objectives together, but they are not uncombinable, and the problems are not in principle greater than those encountered by any liberal society that has to combine liberty and equality, for example, or prosperity and justice.[12]

Thanks to the spirit of 1982, the values associated with a certain view of liberalism have become foundations of the Canadian national identity. Canadian citizens have come to feel an affinity with a central state whose institutions, such as the Charter and the Supreme Court, promote the kind of liberalism that guarantees their rights and protects them from discrimination. This helps explain the rhetoric of those who fought for absolute ascendancy of the Charter of Rights and Freedoms over the distinct society clause during the Meech Lake debate. Their position seemed all the more convincing to English Canadians because it blended liberalism and nationalism: "And Quebec saw that the move to give the Charter precedence imposed a form of liberal society that is alien and to which Quebec could never accommodate itself without surrendering its identity. In this context, the protestations by Charter patriots that they were not 'against Quebec' rang hollow."[13]

The view of liberalism that has carried the day in the Charter of Rights and Freedoms, the centralization of the Canadian judiciary system and the courts' immense freedom of interpretation, the negative spirit Mr Trudeau breathed into Canada's constitution and institutions in his fight against Quebec nationalism – all these factors point to the primary condition of a genuine partnership between Canada and Quebec: Quebec must establish on its territory the primacy of its own charter of rights, interpreted by judges appointed by its own governmental and legislative authorities. The Supreme Court of Canada should not have any authority on the territory of Quebec. Nor should Quebec accept the appointment procedures for justices of the Superior Court and the Court of Appeal provided for in the British North America Act. I am fully aware that this primary condition of genuine partnership between Quebec and Canada strikes at the very heart of the spirit of 1982. At the end of this book, I conclude that the Constitution Act of 1982 is tainted by its relentless obstruction of Quebec society's national vision and aspirations. A lasting political system cannot be built on such unwholesome foundations. On this score, I wholeheartedly endorse what Léon Dion said before the Bélanger-Campeau Commission:

Quebec must at long last obtain a right of absolute veto over any amendment to the Canadian constitution. I was heretofore unaware of a consequence that flows from these demands of Quebec. In the final analysis, what I am rejecting is the 1982 constitutional revision in its entirety. English Canada ascribes great importance to the Charter of Rights established by that revision. We should not propose several amendments to it but reject it as a whole.[14]

A second condition flows from what I have said. The ambiguity and misunderstandings that characterized the spirit of 1867 can no longer suffice. The spirit of 1867 was buried once and for all sometime between 17 April 1982 and 23 June 1990. To use one of Christian Dufour's expressions, we have entered a declaratory era, which demands honesty and clarity.[15] Pierre Elliott Trudeau would say that one must compete with one's visor up, that the fight must henceforth be open and above board.[16] This means that the expression "distinct society" has become entirely insufficient as a definition of Quebec. Until now, those who supported the Canadian national project have been unable to look their "Quebec friends" in the eye without batting an eyelid – have been unable to recognize us as their peers, as members of a distinct national community experiencing the adventure of federalism together with them. They have not ceased to slot us back into the categories of the Canadian national project. The spirit of 1982 confirmed them in this attitude. We must smash this front of refusal, this tradition of avoiding the national question in Quebec.

We must ask our Canadian partners the following question: Are you prepared to live within a constitutional framework that recognizes that Quebec is a distinct society – an autonomous political entity, a people, a national community – and declares in its laws and foreign policy that the national identity of Quebec stands alongside the national identity of Canada in this country? This is the question that our political leaders, especially the former premier, Robert Bourassa, should have had the courage to put to our Canadian partners in 1992. Because Mr Bourassa could not bring himself to such lucid firmness, the chances of realizing the conditions of real partnership within the frontiers of a single political community have almost completely evaporated. In the September 1994 election, citizens of Quebec faced the following dilemma: the road to independence, or more or less unconditional surrender to the supremacy of the Canadian national project launched by Pierre Elliott Trudeau in 1982.

There is a Canadian – an English-Canadian – anxiety in North America. There is sometimes despair among those who reckon the odds of retaining a Canadian specificity in the face of the American Leviathan. We Quebecers are well placed to understand this anxiety and despair. To some extent, these feelings help make our Canadian partners unwilling to recognize Quebec's national identity. They refuse the national aspirations of the people of Quebec in order to calm their own fears. Things could have been otherwise. We were well placed to clarify our relations with our Canadian partners, because we too experience anxiety and despair in North America, because Quebec's quest for identity is threatened by the spirit of 1982. The condition of this clarification remains mutual recognition of the national identity of the "other." During the winter of 1992, a new discourse appeared on the intellectual and political horizon of English Canada. On the right and the left, people wanted to see the emergence in North America of a country capable of recognizing three linguistic and cultural communities, even three nations: the First Nations, English Canada, and French Canada or Quebec. The logic of my analysis in this book suggests that the chances of such a discourse succeeding will remain exceedingly slim so long as Canada remains mired in the spirit of 1982, so long as the Constitution Act adopted a decade ago remains the formal and legal basis on which all negotiations will have to take place.

Canadians want their country to remain a member of the Group of Seven, the seven most industrialized countries. They would like their country to continue to wield influence in the Commonwealth, but also in *La francophonie*. From a geographical point of view, they want a country that stretches uninterruptedly from ocean to ocean to ocean. They want their country to be home to an original presence in North America, distinct from the United States, a country respectful of the principle of authentic diversity (to borrow an expression from *Shaping Canada's Future Together*). But if this is what they want, they must realize that they will no longer be able to avoid recognizing an essential aspect of authentic diversity – the existence of a national community in Quebec. For federalism to have any chance at all in North America at the dawn of the twenty-first century, it will have to accept the legitimacy of the national aspirations of Quebec and the native peoples. The period through which we are living has witnessed the disintegration of artificial federations in the Soviet Union and Yugoslavia. They disappeared in part because they dismissed the question of nationalities. They preferred to exclude it with the definition of a single Soviet people or a single Yugoslav people. If Canada wishes to avoid becoming a museum piece alongside these federations, it will have to make up its mind to accept its multinational character.

So far, I have listed two conditions for the emergence of a genuine partnership between Quebec and Canada: the establishment of two distinct judicial systems and charters of rights, and full recognition of the fact that Quebec represents a people, a distinct national society. This adds up to many changes, considering that I have not even touched on the matter of division of powers. But there is another transformation which, if approved, would ease their acceptance and, once and for all, would seal the originality of the Canada-Quebec partnership in the Americas and in the world. At a time when the global political system is undergoing restructuring, we would provide a fine example to the whole world if we gave our political union the name Canada-Québec. We Quebecers are being asked to accept the principle of limited and shared national sovereignty in this era when integration in all of its forms is being reinforced. So be it. But Canada should do no less. Let Canada renounce the sovereignty and monopoly of the Canadian national identity by creating a space for Quebec by its side in the definition of our political system. Philip Resnick, one of the leaders of the English-Canadian intellectual community, has proposed a federal union of Canada and Quebec that would recognize the duality, even the multiplicity, of national identities.[17] All that is lacking in Resnick's proposal, in the current state of negotiations, is a name. I therefore suggest the following name: Canada-Québec.

Some may find my suggestion preposterous. They will point out that English Canadians would never assent to Canada-Québec as a name for their country, nor would they accept two charters of rights, two judicial systems, and so on. To a certain extent, I can understand such scepticism. English Canadians who have been shaped by the political culture stemming from the spirit of 1982 will not accept such a readjustment as long as they maintain the hope of winning Quebecers over to their vision of a homogeneous Canadian national identity. Thus, Quebec's political leaders must find the strength to quash this hope coldly and remorselessly.

The constitutional dialogue of the deaf between Canada and Quebec cannot continue. It has literally been exhausting both communities for decades. A state of political fatigue has spread across the country. More than thirty years ago, Hubert Aquin caustically diagnosed cultural life in French Canada as suffering from ambivalence, incompletion, indecision, and uncertainty.[18] The same condition applies today to the whole of political life in Canada and Quebec. As Gérard Bergeron wrote in 1967, the time has come to put our two tired patiences behind us.[19] The Canadian national project conveyed by the spirit of 1982 is unacceptable to Quebec, so those who wish for a genuine partnership between Canada and Quebec must begin by clearly stating their refusal to submit to this spirit. If our leaders choose silence and inaction, Pierre Elliott Trudeau will congratulate himself for having courted fortune yet again.

As I prepare to lay down my pen, I cannot imagine that those who signed the Charlottetown Accord in August 1992 (who included people open to Quebec's aspirations, such as Joe Clark and Bob Rae) did not realize what they were doing in accepting the principle of equal representation of all provinces in the Senate. They must have known how diametrically opposed this was to the vision of Canadian federalism in vogue in Quebec. Provincial equality in the Senate is the institutional completion of Trudeau's bitter struggle against duality. Solange Chaput-Rolland, Gérald Beaudoin, Claude Castonguay, Arthur Tremblay, and their federalist predecessors in our society had something else in mind when they worked at building the Canadian dream of the people of Quebec. Let us hope they will find the strength required to overcome their sadness. Let us hope, too, that they will devote their energy to the deliberations and actions that are henceforth urgent priorities in our society. As for myself, I consider that to extirpate Quebec from the claws of a negative and unjust constitution – Mr Trudeau's 1982 reform – is the first of these priorities.

Notes

PREFACE

1 Guy Laforest, *De la prudence* (Montreal: Boréal, 1993); Alain Gagnon and Guy Laforest, "The Future of Federalism: Lessons from Canada and Quebec,"*International Journal* 48, no. 3 (1993): 470–91; Guy Laforest and Douglas M. Brown, eds., *Integration and Fragmentation: The Paradox of the Late Twentieth Century* (Kingston: Institute of Intergovernmental Relations, 1994).

INTRODUCTION

1 For a brief history of the different commissions in which the dualist dream crystallized, see Alain Gagnon and Daniel Latouche, *Allaire, Bélanger, Campeau et les autres* (Montréal: Québec/Amérique, 1991), 48ff.
2 See especially André Blais and Jean Crête, "Pourquoi l'opinion publique au Canada anglais a-t-elle rejeté l'Accord du lac Meech," in Raymond Hudon and Réjean Pelletier, *L'engagement intellectuel: Mélanges en l'honneur de Léon Dion* (Sainte-Foy: Presses de l'Université Laval, 1991), 392.
3 Pierre Elliott Trudeau, "La province de Québec au moment de la grève," in Pierre Elliott Trudeau, ed., *La grève de l'amiante* (Montréal: Editions du Jour, 1970), 14 (translation).
4 Gordon Robertson, "What Future for Canada?" in David Smith, Peter Mackinnon, and John Courtney, *After Meech Lake: Lessons for the Future* (Saskatoon: Fifth House Publishers, 1991), 235.
5 André Laurendeau, *Journal tenu pendant la Commission royale d'enquête sur le bilinguisme et le biculturalisme* (Montréal et Sillery: VLB éditeur/ Les éditions du Septentrion, 1990). A selection from the diary has been translated by Patricia Smart and Dorothy Howard, *The Diary of André*

Laurendeau Written during the Royal Commission on Bilingualism and Bicul-turalism, 1964–1967 (Toronto: Lorimer, 1991).

6 Jean Larose, *L'amour du pauvre* (Montreal: Boréal, 1991), 130.

CHAPTER ONE

1 An earlier version of this chapter was presented as a paper at the annual conference of the Canadian Political Science Association at the University of Victoria in May 1990. I would like to thank Professors Alan Cairns, Donald Forbes, and Rainer Knopff for their comments and criticism.

2 Claude Morin, *Lendemains piégés: Du référendum à la "nuit des longs cou-teaux"* (Montreal: Boréal, 1988), 16.

3 See, for example, historian Michael Behiels's introduction to a text by Trudeau, in Behiels, ed., *The Meech Lake Primer: Conflicting Views of the 1987 Constitutional Accord* (Ottawa: University of Ottawa Press, 1989), 47–9. See also Max Nemni, "Le 'dés'Accord du Lac Meech et la con-struction de l'imaginaire symbolique des Québécois," in Louis Balth-azar, Guy Laforest, and Vincent Lemieux, eds., *Le Québec et la restructuration du Canada, 1980–1992: enjeux et perspectives* (Sillery: Sep-tentrion, 1991), 175.

4 Pierre Elliott Trudeau, "Say Goodbye to the Dream of One Canada," in Donald Johnston, ed., *With a Bang, Not a Whimper: Pierre Trudeau Speaks Out* (Toronto: Stoddart, 1988), 8.

5 This argument will be developed further in a later chapter of this book, on André Laurendeau and F.R. Scott.

6 "The stakes were important, because he was gambling both his credibility and his place in history." See Pierre Fournier, *A Meech Lake Post-Mortem: Is Quebec Sovereignty Inevitable?* translated by Sheila Fischman (Montreal and Kingston: McGill-Queen's University Press, 1991), 4.

7 Marcel Adam, "Let Meech Lake Be English Canada's Problem," in Donald Johnston, ed., *Pierre Trudeau Speaks Out on Meech Lake* (Toronto: General, 1990), 111.

8 Ibid.

9 Pierre Elliott Trudeau, "The 1982 Constitution Act Was Not a Bad Bar-gain for Quebec," in Johnston, *Pierre Trudeau Speaks Out on Meech Lake*, 114–15.

10 Marcel Adam, "The Real Question Is: What Was Quebecers' Under-standing of Mr. Trudeau?" in Johnston, *Pierre Trudeau Speaks Out on Meech Lake*, 120.

11 Claude Morin, "Trudeau's Legacy of Bitterness," in Johnston, *Pierre Trudeau Speaks Out on Meech Lake*, 124ff.

12 Pierre Elliott Trudeau, "Pierre Trudeau Replies: 'That's No Way to Write History,'" in Johnston, *Pierre Trudeau Speaks Out on Meech Lake*, 129.

13 Claude Morin, "Let's Try to Have Done with May 1980," in Johnston, *Pierre Trudeau Speaks Out on Meech Lake*, 133.

14 Pierre Elliott Trudeau, "A Last Word from Pierre Elliott Trudeau," in Johnston, *Pierre Trudeau Speaks Out on Meech Lake*, 137.

15 For a thorough introduction to Skinner's approach, see James Tully, "The Pen Is a Mighty Sword: Quentin Skinner's Analysis of Politics," in Tully, ed., *Meaning and Context: Quentin Skinner and His Critics* (Princeton: Princeton University Press, 1988), 7–25.

16 Quentin Skinner, "'Social Meaning' and the Explanation of Social Action," in Tully, *Meaning and Context*, 83.

17 Quentin Skinner, "Motives, Intentions and the Interpretation of Texts," in Tully, *Meaning and Context*, 77.

18 Frederick J. Fletcher and Donald C. Wallace, "Parliament and Politics," in R.B. Byers, *Canadian Annual Review of Politics and Public Affairs 1979* (Toronto: University of Toronto Press, 1981), 29–30.

19 Pierre Elliott Trudeau, "Choisir sa destinée," *Le Devoir*, 22 November 1979, p. A-9.

20 Michel Roy, "La démission de Pierre Trudeau," *Le Devoir*, 22 November 1979. See also Marcel Adam, "La fin d'une carrière exceptionnelle," *La Presse*, 22 November 1979.

21 In Machiavelli's view, when fortune is so generous to a political leader, giving him perhaps one last opportunity to achieve some of his most cherished ambitions, one can expect him to behave in an implacable manner thereafter. Machiavelli both described and prescribed this. The study of history teaches us that many leaders have behaved thus in similar circumstances. Moreover, this is what one ought to do in such an exceptional situation. Machiavelli's views on this issue provide the key to understanding Trudeau's actions during the 1980s. I shall come back to this in the chapter on Trudeau and the Meech Lake Accord.

22 Pierre Elliott Trudeau, "La primauté du devoir sur le désir," *Le Devoir*, 19 December 1979.

23 Lysiane Gagnon, "Trudeau n'abordera pas la question nationale," *La Presse*, 5 January 1980.

24 Michel Roy, "Premiers jalons de renouvellement," *Le Devoir*, 8 January 1980.

25 Richard Gwyn, "What Did Trudeau Really Mean When He Agreed to Run?" *Gazette*, 20 December 1979.

26 L. Ian MacDonald, "Trudeau Throws a Wrench into the Referendum Campaign," *Gazette*, 24 December 1979.

27 L. Ian MacDonald, "Here's Why Trudeau Is Lying Low on Constitutional Question," *Gazette*, 9 January 1980.

28 L. Ian MacDonald, "Why Is Trudeau Avoiding Quebec on Campaign Trail?" *Gazette*, 11 February 1980.

29 William Johnson, "Leaders Hold Tongues on Constitution Ideas," *Globe and Mail*, 13 February 1980.

30 "Clark, Trudeau et Broadbent répondent aux questions du *Devoir*," *Le Devoir*, 12 February 1980.

31 Task Force on Canadian Unity, *A Future Together: Observations and Recommendations* (Ottawa: Ministry of Supply and Services, 1979).

32 Léon Dion, *Le Québec et le Canada: Les voies de l'avenir* (Montreal: Les Editions Québécor, 1980), 82.

33 Constitutional Committee of the Quebec Liberal Party, *A New Canadian Federation* (Montreal, 1980), 13.

34 Ibid., 22.

35 Ibid., 141.

36 See Edward McWhinney, *Canada and the Constitution, 1979–1982* (Toronto: University of Toronto Press, 1982), 32.

37 See the excerpts of Trudeau's speech in *Le Devoir*, 17 April 1980 ("Un plébiscite de tous les jours").

38 Michel Vastel, *The Outsider* (Toronto: Macmillan, 1990), 203.

39 Graham Fraser, *P.Q.: René Lévesque and the Parti Québécois in Power* (Toronto: Macmillan, 1984), 225.

40 Kenneth McRoberts, *Quebec: Social Change and Political Crisis*, 3d ed. (Toronto: McClelland & Stewart, 1988), 326.

41 Trudeau's words are quoted in Fraser, *P.Q.*, 227.

42 *Le Devoir*, 15 May 1980.

43 Skinner, "Motives, Intentions and the Interpretation of Texts," 77.

44 Donald Smiley, *Canada in Question: Federalism in the Eighties*, 3d ed. (Toronto: McGraw-Hill Ryerson, 1980), 22.

45 Peter Leslie, "In Defence of the 'Spirit of Meech Lake': Evaluating the Criticisms," in Behiels, *Meech Lake Primer*, 484.

46 Donald Smiley, "A Dangerous Deed: The Constitution Act, 1982," in Keith Banting and Richard Simeon, eds., *And No One Cheered: Federalism, Democracy and the Constitution Act* (Toronto: Methuen, 1983), 78.

CHAPTER TWO

1 An earlier version of this chapter was published as "La révolution glorieuse, John Locke et l'impasse constitutionnelle au Canada," *Les Cahiers de droit* 31, no. 2 (June 1990): 621–40. The ideas presented here were perfected during discussions with several colleagues. I would like to thank Stéphane and Léon Dion, Rainer Knopff, and James Tully, for their criticism and comments.

2 John Locke, *Two Treatises of Government*, ed. Peter Laslett (London: New English Library, 1965).

3 André Jardin, "Liberté," in Pascal Ory, *Nouvelle histoire des idées politiques* (Paris: Hachette, 1987), 151.

4 See Richard Ashcraft, *Revolutionary Politics and Locke's Two Treatises of Government* (Princeton: Princeton University Press, 1986), 371.

5 Simone Goyard-Fabre, introduction to John Locke, *Traité du gouvernement civil* (Paris: Flammarion, 1984), 20.

6 Richard Ashcraft, the American historian of political ideas, has recently reviewed the new writings on Locke. See his *Locke's Two Treatises of Government* (London and Boston: Allen and Unwin, 1987), 298–305. As Ashcraft points out, the turning point was the publication, some twenty years earlier, of John Dunn's book, *The Political Thought of John Locke* (Cambridge: Cambridge University Press, 1969). Dunn retraced Locke's intentions by genuinely situating them within their historical context.

7 Ashcraft, *Revolutionary Politics and Locke's Two Treatises of Government*, 79.

8 John Locke, *An Essay concerning Human Understanding*, with introduction by John Yolton (London: Dent, 1961). John Locke, *A Letter concerning Toleration* (The Hague: Martinus Nijhoff, 1963).

9 Locke, *Two Treatises of Government*, 401–2, par. 134.

10 John Dunn, *Rethinking Modern Political Theory* (Cambridge: Cambridge University Press, 1985), 52.

11 See James Tully, "John Locke," in J.H. Burns, ed., *Cambridge History of Political Thought* (Cambridge: Cambridge University Press, 1987). See also James Tully, "Governing Conduct," in Ed Leites, ed., *Conscience and Casuistry in Early Modern Europe* (Cambridge: Cambridge University Press, 1988).

12 Ashcraft, *Revolutionary Politics and Locke's Two Treatises of Government*, 228.

13 On the relation between Locke and atomism, see Charles Taylor, *The Sources of the Self: The Making of the Modern Identity* (Cambridge, Mass.: Harvard University Press, 1989), 166–7.

14 Locke, *Two Treatises of Government*, 459, par. 220.

15 Ibid., 420, par. 158.

16 Ibid., 416, par. 155.

17 Ashcraft, *Revolutionary Politics and Locke's Two Treatises of Government*, 300.

18 Julian Franklin, *John Locke and the Theory of Sovereignty* (Cambridge: Cambridge University Press, 1978), 104–5.

19 Locke, *Two Treatises of Government*, 477, par. 243.

20 For an intelligent synthesis, see Gérard Bergeron, *À nous autres: Aide-mémoire politique par le temps qui court* (Montréal: Québec/Amérique, 1986), 20–36.

21 Constitutional Committee of the Quebec Liberal Party, *A Quebec Free to Choose* (Montreal, January 1991), 56.

22 Léon Dion, *A la recherche du Québec* (Quebec: Presses de l'Université Laval, 1987), 24.

23 Stephen Clarkson and Christina McCall, *Trudeau and Our Times*, vol. 1, *The Magnificent Obsession* (Toronto: McClelland & Stewart, 1990).

24 Franklin, *John Locke and the Theory of Sovereignty*, 97.

25 For a general interpretation of the events by an important author, see Claude Morin, *Lendemains piégés: Du référendum à la nuit des longs couteaux* (Montreal: Boréal, 1988), 7.

26 Donald Smiley, "A Dangerous Deed: the Constitution Act, 1982," in Keith Banting and Richard Simeon, eds., *And No One Cheered* (Toronto: Methuen, 1983), 76.

27 Locke, *Two Treatises of Government*, 452, par. 209.

28 Alan Cairns, *Disruptions: Constitutional Struggles, from the Charter to Meech Lake* (Toronto: McClelland & Stewart, 1991), 237.

29 Locke, *Two Treatises of Government*, 456–7, par. 214.

30 Ibid., 401–2, par. 134.

31 Ibid., 464, par. 227.

32 Gil Rémillard, *Le fédéralisme canadien: Éléments constitutionnels de formation et d'évolution* (Montreal: Québec/Amérique, 1980), 1:354.

33 Gil Rémillard, *Le fédéralisme canadien: Le rapatriement de la constitution* (Montreal: Québec/Amérique, 1985), 2:409 (translation).

34 Gil Rémillard, "Legality, Legitimacy and the Supreme Court," in Keith Banting and Richard Simeon, *And No One Cheered* (Toronto: Methuen, 1983), 201–2.

35 Quentin Skinner, *The Foundations of Modern Political Thought: The Age of the Reformation* (Cambridge: Cambridge University Press, 1978), 2:347.

36 Locke, *Two Treatises of Government*, 462, par. 223.

37 Benoît Lauzière and Gilles Lesage, *Le Québec et le lac Meech: Un dossier du Devoir* (Montréal: Guérin littérature, 1987). This anthology presents the text of the agreement in its different versions, as well as a host of commentaries and analyses. The most exhaustive analysis is that of Pierre Fournier, *A Meech Lake Post-Mortem: Is Quebec Sovereignty Inevitable?* (Montreal and Kingston: McGill-Queen's University Press, 1991), 15ff.

38 Christian Dufour, *A Canadian Challenge/Le défi québécois* (Lantzville/Halifax: Oolichan Books/Institute for Research on Public Policy, 1990), 155.

39 Fournier, *A Meech Lake Post-Mortem*, 26–7.

40 Peter Leslie, "In Defence of the 'Spirit of Meech Lake': Evaluating Criticisms," in Michael Behiels, ed., *Meech Lake Primer* (Ottawa: University of Ottawa Press, 1989), 484.

41 See Broadbent's concerns as reported in the *Globe and Mail*, 27 October 1989.

42 Locke, *Two Treatises of Government*, 439, par. 185.

43 Rémillard, "Legality, Legitimacy and the Supreme Court," 203.

44 Locke, *Two Treatises of Government*, 463–4, par. 225.

45 Ibid., 476, par. 241.

CHAPTER THREE

1 An earlier version of this chapter was delivered at the annual conference of the Société québécoise de science politique at Laval University
in May 1990. I thank Alain G. Gagnon for his comments. I would also
like to thank Professor Donald Smith, from the Department of History
of the University of Calgary, and Professor Christian Dufour, formerly
of the Institute for Research on Public Policy, who enabled me to
address their students and thus to refine my ideas on the theme of this
chapter. The same applies to the students in my graduate seminar on
Canadian political thought at Laval University.

2 I am thinking, for example, of the work of Henri Brun, Gérald Beaudoin, and Gil Rémillard.

3 Stephen Brooks and Alain G. Gagnon, *Social Scientists and Politics in
Canada: Between Vanguard and Clerisy* (Montreal and Kingston: McGill-
Queen's University Press, 1988), 116ff.

4 Léon Dion, *A la recherche du Québec* (Quebec: Presses de l'Université
Laval, 1987), 81.

5 Michel Leclerc, *La science politique au Québec* (Montreal: L'Hexagone,
1982), 12.

6 For a recent synopsis, see Pierre Fournier, *A Meech Lake Post-Mortem: Is
Quebec Sovereignty Inevitable?* (Montreal and Kingston: McGill-Queen's
University Press, 1991). See also François Rocher and Gérard Boismenu, "L'Accord du lac Meech et le système politique canadien," *Politique* 16 (1989): 59–86.

7 André Laurendeau, *Artisan des passages*, edited and introduced by
Suzanne Laurin (Montreal: HMH, 1988), 116 (translation).

8 Fernand Dumont, "Y a-t-il une tradition intellectuelle au Québec?" in
Nadine Pirotte, ed., *Penser l'éducation: Nouveaux dialogues avec André
Laurendeau* (Montreal: Boréal, 1989), 68.

9 Charles Taylor, "The Tradition of a Situation," trans. Paul Leduc
Browne, in Taylor, *Reconciling the Solitudes: Essays on Canadian Federalism and Nationalism*, ed. Guy Laforest (Montreal: McGill-Queen's University Press, 1993), 138.

10 Denis Monière, "André Laurendeau et le renouvellement de la pensée
nationaliste," in Pirotte, *Penser l'éducation*, 83–4 (translation).

11 Denis Monière, "André Laurendeau et la vision québécoise du Canada," in
Robert Comeau and Lucille Beaudry, eds., *André Laurendeau: Un intellectuel
d'ici* (Sillery: Presses de l'Université du Québec, 1990), 200 (translation).

12 Paul André Comeau, "Préface," in André Laurendeau, *Journal tenu pendant la Commission royale d'enquête sur le bilinguisme et le biculturalisme* (Montreal and Sillery: VLB éditeur and Les éditions du Septentrion, 1990), 21.

13 Doug Owram, *The Government Generation: Canadian Intellectuals and the State, 1990–1945* (Toronto: University of Toronto Press, 1986), and Sandra Djwa, *The Politics of the Imagination: A Life of F.R. Scott* (Toronto: McClelland & Stewart), 1987.

14 Owram, *The Government Generation*, 150–2. See also Philip Resnick, *The Masks of Proteus: Reflections on the State* (Montreal and Kingston: McGill-Queen's University Press, 1990), 210–11.

15 Djwa, *The Politics of Imagination*, 270, 336–7.

16 Frank R. Scott, *A New Endeavour: Selected Political Essays, Letters and Addresses*, ed. and intro. by Michiel Horn (Toronto: University of Toronto Press, 1986).

17 Denis Monière, *André Laurendeau et le destin d'un peuple* (Montreal: Québec/Amérique, 1983), 16.

18 Djwa, *The Politics of Imagination*, 371–2.

19 Monière, *André Laurendeau et le destin d'un peuple*, 85.

20 Ibid., 110.

21 Michiel Horn, *The League for Social Reconstruction: Intellectual Origins of the Democratic Left in Canada, 1930–1942* (Toronto: University of Toronto Press, 1980), 117.

22 Djwa, *The Politics of Imagination*, 138–9.

23 Scott, *A New Endeavour*, 30.

24 Horn, *The League for Social Reconstruction*, 220.

25 Ibid., 16.

26 Monière, *André Laurendeau et le destin d'un peuple*, 119.

27 Djwa, *The Politics of Imagination*, 183.

28 Ibid., 200.

29 Owram, *The Government Generation*, 172.

30 Ibid., 239–40.

31 Ibid., 252–3.

32 Djwa, *The Politics of Imagination*, 229.

33 Monière, *André Laurendeau et le destin d'un peuple*, 139.

34 Ibid., 143.

35 Djwa, *The Politics of Imagination*, 232–3.

36 Monière, *André Laurendeau et le destin d'un peuple*, 207.

37 Ibid., 313.

38 Ibid., 224.

39 See Michael Behiels, *Prelude to Quebec's Quiet Revolution: Liberalism vs. Neo-Nationalism, 1945–1960* (Montreal and Kingston: McGill-Queen's University Press, 1985), 214.

40 Ibid., 216.

41 Fernand Dumont, "Préface," in André Laurendeau, *Ces choses qui nous arrivent* (Montréal: HMH, 1970), xxi.

42 André Laurendeau, *The Diary of André Laurendeau Written during the Royal Commission on Bilingualism and Biculturalism, 1964–67*, trans. Patricia Smart and Dorothy Howard (Toronto: Lorimer, 1991), 87.

43 *A Preliminary Report of the Royal Commission on Bilingualism and Biculturalism* (Ottawa: Queen's Printer, 1965), 151.

44 Monière, *André Laurendeau et le destin d'un peuple*, 331–2.

45 Djwa, *The Politics of Imagination*, 389.

46 Léon Dion, "Bribes de souvenirs d'André Laurendeau," in Pirotte, *Penser l'éducation*, 53.

47 Claude Ryan, "Il a soulevé les vraies questions et réfuté les réponses toutes faites," in Robert Comeau and Lucille Beaudry, *André Laurendeau* (Sillery: Presses de l'Université du Québec, 1990), 279.

48 André Laurendeau, *Journal tenu pendant la Commission royale d'enquête sur le bilinguisme et le biculturalisme* (Montreal and Sillery: VLB éditeur/ Les éditions du Septentrion, 1990), 111 (passage omitted from Patricia Smart's and Dorothy Howard's translation).

49 Claude Ryan, "André Laurendeau," *Le Devoir*, 3 June 1968 (translation).

50 *Le Devoir*, 3 June 1968.

51 Djwa, *The Politics of Imagination*, 269.

52 "General Introduction," in *Report of the Royal Commission of Bilingualism and Biculturalism*, 1 (Ottawa: Queen's Printer, 1967), 1:xxx, par. 33.

53 Ibid., xxxiii, par. 44.

54 Ibid., xxxvii, par. 56.

55 Ibid., xliii-xliv, par. 77.

56 Ibid., xlv, par. 82.

57 Ibid., xlv, par. 83.

58 Ibid., xxxiii, par. 44.

59 *Constitution Act, 1982*, part 1; Canadian Charter of Rights and Freedoms, s. 1. See "Loi constitutionnelle de 1982," in Gil Rémillard, *Le fédéralisme canadien*, vol. 2, *Le rapatriement de la constitution* (Montreal: Québec/Amérique, 1985), 517.

60 Those who defend the absolute preponderance of the Charter of Rights and Freedoms obviously lay the greatest emphasis on this article.

61 "General Introduction," in *Report of the Royal Commission on Bilingualism and Biculturalism*, 1: xlii, par. 72.

62 Pierre Elliott Trudeau, "Say Goodbye to the Dream of One Canada," in Donald Johnston, ed., *With a Bang, Not a Whimper: Pierre Trudeau Speaks Out* (Toronto: Stoddart, 1988), 8.

63 Henri Brun, "Droits individuels et droits collectifs: Un difficile équilibre," *Relations*, June 1989, 142.

64 *The 1987 Constitutional Accord*, 3 June 1987, reprinted in Johnston, *With a Bang, Not a Whimper*, 147–8.
65 Rocher and Boismenu write that the accord "explicitly attributes primacy to duality over the distinct character of Quebec" (*L'Accord du lac Meech*, 65).
66 "First Ministers' Meeting on the Constitution. Draft Statement of Principles. April 30, 1987."
67 Claude Ryan "Il a soulevé les vraies questions et réfuté les réponses toutes faites," in Robert Comeau and Lucille Beaudry, eds., *André Laurendeau* (Sillery: Presses de l'Université du Québec, 1990), 281.
68 Michael Oliver, "F.R. Scott as Quebecer," in Sandra Djwa and R. St J. MacDonald, eds., *On F.R. Scott* (Montreal and Kingston: McGill-Queen's University Press, 1983), 174.
69 Claude Ryan, "L'Accord du lac Meech permettra au Québec de faire des gains importants et incontestables," in Lesage, *Le Québec et le lac Meech*, 359.
70 See, for example, Donald Johnston's introduction to his *With a Bang, Not a Whimper* (Toronto: Stoddart, 1988), 3–4.
71 This is clearly proven by the wide divergences in legal interpretations, in particularly those of the Judicial Committee of the Privy Council.
72 Michael Behiels, introduction to his *Meech Lake Primer* (Ottawa: University of Ottawa Press, 1989), xxiv.

CHAPTER FOUR

1 The first part of this chapter is a slightly revised version of an article published in 1989. See "Fichte's Reden as a Model: Léon Dion's Addresses to the Quebec Nation," *Canadian Journal of Political Science* 22 no. 1 (1989): 49–62. That article was based on papers delivered during the winter of 1988 at the Political Science departments of the Universities of Calgary and Edmonton. I would like to thank Professors B. Cooper, R. Knopff, D. Carmichael, and A. Noël for their comments. I would also like to thank G. Bergeron and V. Lemieux for their criticism.
2 Jean Larose, *La petite noirceur* (Montreal: Boréal, 1987), 50 (translation).
3 Johann Gottlieb Fichte, *Addresses to the German Nation*, with intro. by George Kelly (New York: Harper Torchbooks, 1968).
4 Léon Dion, *À la recherche du Québec* (Quebec: Presses de l'Université Laval, 1987). Dion's project as a whole is more ambitious than Fichte's, but the first volume of Dion's tetralogy is on national identity, making the parallel with Fichte possible.
5 Larose, *La petite noirceur*, 16; and Daniel Salée, "Pour une autopsie de l'imaginaire québécois: Regards sur la morosité postmoderne," *Canadian Journal of Political and Social Theory* 10 (1986): 114–15.

6 Alain Gagnon and Khayyam Paltiel, "Toward Maîtres chez nous: The Ascendancy of a Balzacian Bourgeoisie in Quebec," *Queen's Quarterly* 93 (1986): 739–40. Dion himself senses a profound malaise in contemporary Quebec society. This was in fact the starting point of his book.

7 Dion, *A la recherche du Québec*, 133.

8 Kenneth McRoberts, *Quebec: Social Change and Political Crisis* (Toronto: McClelland & Stewart, 1988), 400.

9 Friedrich Meinecke, *The Age of German Liberalism, 1795–1815* (Berkeley: University of California Press, 1977), 30.

10 The following list is far from exhaustive: Fernand Dumont, *Le sort de la culture* (Montreal: L'Hexagone, 1987); Gérard Bergeron, *A nous autres: Aide-mémoire par le temps qui court* (Montreal: Québec/Amérique, 1986); Louis Balthazar, *Bilan du nationalisme québécois* (Montreal: L'Hexagone, 1989); Christian Dufour, *A Canadian Challenge/Le défi québécois* (Lantzville: Oolichan Books, 1990); Daniel Latouche, *Le bazar* (Montreal: Boréal, 1989); Hubert Guindon, *Tradition, modernité et aspiration nationale de la société québécoise* (Montreal: Editions Saint-Martin, 1990); Daniel Jacques, *Les humanités passagères: Considérations philosophiques sur la culture politique québécoise* (Montreal: Boréal, 1991).

11 Dion, *A la recherche du Québec*, 28–9.

12 See Gary Caldwell and Pierre Fournier, "The Quebec Question," *Cahiers canadiens de sociologie* 12 (1987): 30–1.

13 But Dion is not blind to the problems of contemporary liberal society. See Léon Dion, *Société et politique: La vie des groupes*, vol. 2, *Dynamique de la société libérale* (Sainte-Foy: Presses de l'Université Laval, 1972), 460–1.

14 Léon Dion, *Société et politique: La vie des groupes*, vol. 1, *Fondements de la société libérale* (Sainte-Foy: Presses de l'Université Laval, 1972), 10–11.

15 John Meisel, "Léon Dion: L'Homme et sa société," in Raymond Hudon and Réjean Pelletier, *L'engagement de l'intellectuel: Mélanges en l'honneur de Léon Dion* (Presses de l'Université Laval, 1991), 504–9, 512 (translation).

16 A. Philonenko, *Théorie et praxis dans la pensée morale et politique de Kant et Fichte en 1793* (Paris: Librairie philosophique J. Vrin, 1968), 168, 178, 185.

17 Fichte, *Addresses*, 166.

18 Ibid., 107–8.

19 Dion, *A la recherche du Québec*, 109–10.

20 Jacques Droz, *Le romantisme allemand et l'Etat* (Paris: Payot, 1966), 116.

21 On this issue, one can rely on the French Fichte experts, who are well placed to understand it. See Martial Guéroult, *Etudes sur Fichte* (New York: Georg Olms Verlag Hildesheim, 1974), 70–1.

22 Dion is influenced by George Grant here. See Dion, *A la recherche du Québec*, 84–5.

23 Charles Taylor, *Human Agency and Language: Philosophical Papers* (Cambridge: Cambridge University Press, 1985), 90–1.

24 Dion, *A la recherche du Québec*, 12, 109.

25 Ibid., 11–12 (translation).

26 Léon Dion, "Bribes de souvenirs d'André Laurendeau," in Nadine Pirotte, ed., *Penser l'éducation* (Montreal: Boréal, 1989), 53 (translation).

27 Meinecke, *Age of German Liberalism*, 99.

28 Dion, *A la recherche du Québec*, 74.

29 Ibid., 164 (translation).

30 Charles Taylor, "Why Do Nations Have to Become States?" in his *Reconciling the Solitudes: Essays on Canadian Federalism and Nationalism* (Montreal and Kingston: McGill-Queen's University Press, 1993), 49.

31 Dion, *A la recherche du Québec*, 49.

32 Léon Dion, *Le Bill 60 et la société québécoise* (Montreal: HMH, 1967), 125. Dion's book demonstrates the astuteness of the Quebec bishops, who proved able to appropriate the language of rights and the liberal discourse.

33 Charles Taylor, "The Tradition of a Situation," trans. Paul Leduc Browne, in *Reconciling the Solitudes*, 137.

34 Dion, *A la recherche du Québec*, 44, 49, 52.

35 Droz, *La romantisme allemand et l'Etat*, 115.

36 G.W.F. Hegel, *Hegel's Philosophy of Right*, trans. T.M. Knox (Oxford: Oxford University Press, 1978), par. 324.

37 Dion, *A la recherche du Québec*, 165.

38 Ibid., 78–9. See Patricia Smart, "Our Two Cultures," in Eli Mandel and David Taras, eds., *A Passion for Identity: An Introduction to Canadian Studies* (Toronto: Methuen, 1987), 187.

39 Léon Dion, *La prochaine révolution* (Montreal: Leméac, 1973), 9. In this book the author lucidly and critically examined the fate of Western liberal civilization in a style reminiscent of Habermas (see 320–2). Such reflections remain highly topical today in this era of conservative, ahistorical neoliberalism.

40 See Taylor, "Why Do Nations Have to Become States?" 49.

41 Dion, *A la recherche du Québec*, 113.

42 Georges-Henri Lévesque, *Souvenances* (Montreal: Editions La Presse, 1988), vol. 2.

43 Solange Chaput-Rolland, one of the great champions of political duality, was particularly eloquent on this score in her testimony to the parliamentary committee on the Meech Lake Accord during the summer of 1987. See *The 1987 Constitutional Accord*, Report of the Special Joint Committee of the Senate and the House of Commons (Ottawa: Queen's Printer, 1987), 139–40. With this book I aim to convince Madame Chaput-Rolland and her allies that political duality is incompatible

with the logic of the Canadian nationalism that flows from the Ccnstitution Act, 1982.

44 This is why Dion proposed an amendment to the clause. See Gilles Lesage, *Le Québec et le lac Meech* (Montreal: Guérin littérature, 1987), 89.

45 Dion, *A la recherche du Québec*, 127 (translation).

46 Vincent Lemieux, "Faire entendre les voix de la population," in *Les avis des spécialistes invités à répondre aux huit questions posées par la Commission*, Working Paper no. 4, Commission on the Political and Constitutional Future of Quebec (Quebec: Editeur officiel du Québec, 1991), 624 (translation).

47 Léon Dion, "Nos institutions: considérations liminaires," in Vincent Lemieux, ed., *Les institutions québécoises: Leur rôle, leur avenir* (Sainte-Foy: Presses de l'Université Laval, 1990), 20.

48 Eugene Forsey, "Changes Quebec Wants Should Get a Careful Look," *Globe and Mail*, 17 March 1987.

49 Pierre Elliott Trudeau, "The Values of a Just Society," in Thomas Axworthy and Pierre Elliott Trudeau, *Towards a Just Society* (Toronto: Penguin Books, 1992), 409, 412.

50 On this subject, see David Elkins, "Facing Our Destiny: Rights and Canadian Distinctiveness," *Canadian Journal of Political Science* 22 no. 4 (1989): 705–6.

51 Alan Cairns, "Political Science, Ethnicity and the Canadian Constitution," in David Shugarman and Reg Whitaker, eds., *Federalism and Political Community* (Peterborough: Broadview Press, 1989), 116–17.

52 Alan Cairns, "The Charter, Interest Groups, Executive Federalism and Constitutional Reform," in David E. Smith, Peter Mackinnon, and John Courtney, eds., *After Meech Lake: Lessons for the Future* (Saskatoon: Fifth House Publishers, 1991), 23.

53 McRoberts, *Quebec: Social Change and Political Crisis*, 400.

54 Léon Dion, "Pour sortir de l'impasse constitutionnelle," in *Les avis des spécialistes invités à répondre aux huit questions posées par la Commission*, Working Paper no. 4, Commission on the Political and Constitutional Future of Quebec (Quebec: Editeur officiel, 1991), 274 (translation).

55 Dion, "Bribes de souvenirs d'André Laurendeau," 53.

56 Dion, "Nos institutions: considérations liminaires," 19 (translation).

57 Stephen Clarkson and Christina McCall, *Trudeau and Our Times*, vol. 1, *The Magnificent Obsession* (Toronto: McClelland & Stewart, 1990), 9.

CHAPTER FIVE

1 For a more exhaustive description, see Pierre Fournier, *A Meech Lake Post-Mortem*, trans. Sheila Fischman (Montreal and Kingston: McGill-Queen's University Press, 1991), and Alan Cairns, *Disruptions:*

Constitutional Struggles, from the Charter to Meech Lake (Toronto: McClelland & Stewart, 1991), 227. I would like to recall what Fournier says about the 1980 referendum campaign on page 3 of his book: "But support won through fear is necessarily fragile, humiliating and temporary." In the mid-1990s, dire warnings about the flight of capital will not succeed in firming up Quebec's sense of belonging to Canada, any more than they did in 1980.

Cairns and I feel the same way about the Meech Lake saga: "The emotion that drives the debate derives its roots in the elemental notions of honour, dignity, truth, shame, and deceit. Passion is further aroused by their linkages with such emotion-laden categories as citizen, nation, and self-determination. The fact that the central actor around whom controversy rages is Pierre Trudeau adds a further inflammatory element."

2 Pierre Elliott Trudeau, "A Last Word from Pierre Elliott Trudeau," in Donald Johnston, ed., *Pierre Trudeau Speaks Out on Meech Lake* (Toronto: General, 1990), 137.

3 Niccolò Machiavelli, *The Prince*, trans. and ed. Robert Adams (New York: W.W. Norton, 1977), 70.

4 Ibid., 42.

5 Ibid., 49–50.

6 Ibid., 75.

7 Ibid., 51.

8 Ibid., 71.

9 Niccolò Machiavelli, *The Discourses*, ed. Bernard Crick, trans. Leslie Walker, with revisions by Brian Richardson, (Harmondsworth: Penguin Books, 1970), 132.

10 Ibid., 175.

11 Ibid., 371.

12 Pierre Elliott Trudeau, "Say Goodbye to the Dream of One Canada," in Donald Johnston, ed., *With a Bang, Not a Whimper* (Toronto: Stoddart, 1988), 10.

13 Ibid., 8.

14 Thomas Axworthy and Pierre Elliott Trudeau, eds., *Towards a Just Society: The Trudeau Years*, with translations by Patricia Claxton (Toronto: Penguin Books, 1992), 433ff.

15 Jean-Jacques Rousseau, *The Social Contract*, (New York: Hafner, 1947), 2:36.

16 Ibid., book 2, chap. 12.

17 Pierre Elliott Trudeau, "There Must Be a Sense of Belonging," in Johnston, *With a Bang, Not a Whimper*, 32.

18 *Toronto Star*, 1 June 1987.

19 Robert Jackson, *Ottawa Citizen*, 11 June 1987.

20 Robert Fulford, *Saturday Night*, August 1987, 5.

21 George Radwanski, "Meech Lake Accord Said Dangerous, Unnecessary to the Unity of Our Nation," *Toronto Star*, 25 August 1987.

22 Alan Cairns, *Disruptions: Constitutional Struggles, from the Charter to Meech Lake*, ed. and intro. by Douglas Williams (Toronto: McClelland & Stewart, 1991), 132.

23 Trudeau, "There Must Be a Sense of Belonging," 34.

24 Pierre Fournier, *A Meech Lake Post-Mortem*, trans. Sheila Fischman (Montreal and Kingston: McGill-Queen's University Press, 1991), 57.

25 Pierre Elliott Trudeau, "We, the People of Canada," in Johnston, *With a Bang, Not a Whimper*, 45–6.

26 Machiavelli, *Discourses*, 114.

27 Pierre Elliott Trudeau, "We, the People of Canada," 46.

28 Ibid., 87.

29 Ibid., 105.

30 Fournier, *A Meech Lake Post-Mortem*, 63.

31 André Blais and Jean Crête, "Pourquoi l'opinion publique au Canada anglais a-t-elle rejeté l'Accord du lac Meech?" in Raymond Hudon and Réjean Pelletier, *L'engagement intellectuel: Mélanges en l'honneur de Léon Dion* (Sainte-Foy: Presses de l'Université Laval, 1991), 398 (translation).

32 Raymond Aron, introduction to Max Weber, *Le savant et le politique* (Paris: Plon, 1959), 33.

33 Max Weber, "Politics as a Vocation," in *From Max Weber*, ed. H.H. Gerth and C. Wright Mills (London: Routledge and Kegan Paul, 1966), 128.

CHAPTER SIX

1 The above quotation is from Stephen Clarkson and Christina McCall, *Trudeau and Our Times*, vol. 1, *The Magnificent Obsession* (Toronto: McClelland & Stewart, 1990), 9.

2 *Report of the Commission on the Political and Constitutional Future of Quebec* (Quebec: Editeur officiel du Québec, 1991), 30.

3 Thomas Axworthy, "Colliding Visions: The Debate over the Charter of Rights and Freedoms, 1980–81," in Robin Elliot and Joseph Weiler, eds., *Litigating the Values of a Nation: The Canadian Charter of Rights and Freedoms* (Toronto: Carswell, 1986), 14.

4 Pierre Elliott Trudeau, "The Values of a Just Society," in Thomas Axworthy and Pierre Elliott Trudeau, eds., *Towards a Just Society* (Toronto: Penguin Books, 1992), 427–8.

5 Clarkson and McCall, *Trudeau and Our Times*, 357–8.

6 Michael Oliver, "Laurendeau et Trudeau: Leurs opinions sur le Canada," in Raymond Hudon and Réjean Pelletier, *L'engagement de l'intellectuel:*

Mélanges en l'honneur de Léon Dion (Presses de l'Université Laval, 1991). For a corroboration of Oliver's analysis, see Wayne J. Norman, "Unité, identité et nationalisme libéral," *Lekton* 3, no. 2 (1993): 47ff.

7 Pierre Elliott Trudeau, "La province de Québec au moment de la grève," in Trudeau, ed., *La grève de l'amiante*, (Montreal: Editions du Jour, 1970), 12.

8 Pierre Elliott Trudeau, "The New Treason of the Intellectuals," trans. Patricia Claxton, in *Federalism and the French-Canadians*, with intro. by John T. Saywell (New York: St Martin's Press, 1968), 175.

9 For a critique of this outlook, see Guy Laforest, "Herder, Kedourie et les errements de l'anti-nationalisme au Canada," in Raymond Hudon and Réjean Pelletier, *L'engagement de l'intellectuel*, 313–37 (this text is included in Guy Laforest, *De la prudence: Textes politiques* (Montreal: Boréal, 1993), 59–84).

10 Oliver, "Laurendeau et Trudeau," 351.

11 Ibid.

12 Trudeau, *Federalism and the French-Canadians*, 43–4.

13 Guy Laforest, "Une joute mémorable et ses lendemains: La conférence constitutionnelle de février 1968," in Robert Comeau, Michel Lévesque, and Yves Bélanger, eds., *Daniel Johnson: Rêve d'égalité et projet d'indépendance* (Sillery: Presses de l'Université du Québec, 1991), 183–201.

14 Dominique Clift, *Le pays insoupçonné* (Montreal: Libre expression, 1987), 184 (translation).

15 Niccolò Machiavelli, *The Discourses*, ed. Bernard Crick (Harmondsworth: Penguin Books, 1970), 2:372. Fortune requires of a person to adapt to circumstances and not be afraid of resorting to exceptional means. See Niccolò Machiavelli, *The Prince*, ed. Robert Adams (New York: W.W. Norton, 1977), 71.

16 Clarkson and McCall, *Trudeau and Our Times*, 181.

17 Pierre Elliott Trudeau, "Say Goodbye to the Dream of One Canada," in Donald Johnston, ed., *With a Bang, Not a Whimper* (Toronto: Stoddart, 1988), 10.

18 Pierre Elliott Trudeau, "We, the People of Canada," in Johnston, *With a Bang, Not a Whimper*, 94–5.

19 Jean-Jacques Rousseau, *The Social Contract* (New York: Hafner, 1947), 2:36.

20 Trudeau, *Federalism and the French-Canadians*, 202.

21 Oliver, "Laurendeau et Trudeau," 357 (translation).

22 Philip Resnick, *The Masks of Proteus: Canadian Reflections on the State* (Montreal and Kingston: McGill-Queen's University Press, 1990), 207–20.

23 Doug Owram, *The Government Generation: Canadian Intellectuals and the State, 1900–1945* (Toronto: University of Toronto Press, 1986), 223–4.

24 Resnick, *The Masks of Proteus*, 211.
25 Philip Resnick, *Letters to a Québécois Friend*, with a reply by Daniel Latouche (Montreal and Kingston: McGill-Queen's University Press, 1989), 15.
26 Peter Russell, "The Political Purposes of the Canadian Charter of Rights and Freedoms," *Canadian Bar Review* 61 (1983): 31.
27 Ibid., 36.
28 Rainer Knopff and F.L. Morton, *Charter Politics* (Toronto: Nelson, 1992).
29 Russell, "The Political Purposes of the Charter," 41.
30 F.L. Morton, "The Political Impact of the Canadian Charter of Rights and Freedoms," *Canadian Journal of Political Science* 20, no. 1 (1987): 44.
31 Peter Russell, Rainer Knopff, and F.L. Morton, *Federalism and the Charter* (Ottawa: Carleton University Press, 1990), 11.
32 Knopff and Morton, *Charter Politics*, 66–7.
33 For a more detailed analysis of this theme, see Katharine Swinton, *The Supreme Court and Canadian Federalism: The Laskin-Dickson Years* (Toronto: Carswell, 1990), 340–1. See also Rainer Knopff and F.L. Morton, "Nation-Building and the Canadian Charter of Rights and Freedoms," in Alan Cairns and Cynthia Williams, eds., *Constitutionalism, Citizenship and Society in Canada* (Toronto: University of Toronto Press, 1985), 170–1.
34 See Patrick Monahan, *Politics and the Constitution: the Charter, Federalism and the Supreme Court of Canada* (Toronto: Carswell/Methuen, 1987), 252. The criteria are presented and analysed by Alain Baccigalupo, "Le système politique canadien depuis l'avènement de la Charte: démocratie ou juriscratie?" in Louis Balthazar, Guy Laforest, and Vincent Lemieux, eds., *Le Québec et la restructuration du Canada, 1980–1982: Enjeux et perspectives* (Sillery: Les éditions du Septentrion, 1991), 134.
35 Ramsay Cook, "Alice in Meechland or the Concept of Quebec as 'A Distinct Society,'" in Michael Behiels, ed., *The Meech Lake Primer: Conflicting Views of the 1987 Constitutional Accord* (Ottawa: University of Ottawa Press, 1989), 153.
36 Michael Mandel, *The Charter of Rights and the Legalisation of Politics in Canada* (Toronto: Wall and Thompson, 1989), 85.
37 David Elkins, "Facing Our Destiny: Rights and Canadian Distinctiveness," *Canadian Journal of Political Science* 22, no. 4 (1989): 85.
38 David Bercuson and Barry Cooper, *Deconfederation: Canada without Quebec* (Toronto: Key Porter Books, 1991), 164. They make a partial exception for native peoples, for reasons that have nothing to do with philosophy.
39 Alan Cairns, "The Charter, Interest Groups, Executive Federalism, and Constitutional Reform," in David E. Smith, Peter McKinnon, and John Courtney, eds., *After Meech Lake: Lessons for the Future* (Saskatoon: Fifth House Publishers, 1991), 21.

40 Alan Cairns, "Constitutional Change and the Three Equalities," in
    Ronald L. Watts and Douglas M. Brown, eds., *Options for a New Canada*
    (Toronto: University of Toronto Press, 1991), 81.
41 Cairns, "The Charter, Interest Groups, Executive Federalism, and Con-
    stitutional Reform," 23.
42 Alan Cairns, "Constitutional Minoritarianism in Canada," in Ronald
    Watts and Douglas M. Brown, eds., *Canada: The State of the Federation,
    1990* (Kingston: Institute of Intergovernmental Relations, 1990), 86–8.
43 Alan Cairns, "Political Science, Ethnicity and the Canadian Consti-
    tution," in David P. Shugarman and Reg Whitaker, eds., *Federalism
    and Political Community* (Peterborough: Broadview Press, 1989),
    127.
44 Cairns, "Constitutional Change and the Three Equalities," 80.
45 Pierre Elliott Trudeau, *Fatal Tilt: Speaking Out About Sovereignty* (Toronto:
    HarperCollins, 1991), 15.
46 *Votes and Proceedings of the National Assembly of Quebec*, Second Session
    of the Thirty-Second Legislature, 116, no. 3 (2 October 1981): 9.
47 Ibid., no. 12 (1 December 1981): 140–2.
48 Quebec, *Le Journal des débats*, Commission parlementaire spéciale, Com-
    mission d'étude sur toute offre d'un nouveau partenariat de nature
    constitutionnelle, no. 16 (23 January 1992): 504.
49 Quebec, *Le Journal des débats*, vol. 25, no. 1 (30 September 1981): 23
    (translation).
50 Ibid., 10 November 1981, 41 (translation).
51 Ibid., 24 November 1981, 379 (translation).
52 Ibid., 10 November 1981, 41 (translation).
53 Alan Cairns, *Disruptions: Constitutional Struggles, from the Charter to
    Meech Lake* (Toronto: McClelland & Stewart, 1991), 166.
54 Ibid., 251.
55 Ibid., 83.
56 John Locke, *Two Treatises of Government*, ed. Peter Laslett (London: New
    English Library, 1965), 401–2, par. 134.
57 Donald Smiley, "A Dangerous Deed: The Constitution Act, 1982," in
    Keith Banting and Richard Simeon, eds., *And No One Cheered* (Toronto:
    Methuen, 1983).
58 Locke, *Two Treatises on Government*, 452, par. 209.

CHAPTER SEVEN

1 John Locke, *Two Treatises of Government*, ed. Peter Laslett (London: New
   English Library, 1965), 462, par. 223.
2 For a preliminary analysis of the contents of the reports, as well as a
   study of the political context that produced them, see Alain G. Gagnon

and Daniel Latouche, *Allaire, Bélanger, Campeau et les autres: Les Québécois s'interrogent sur leur avenir* (Montreal: Québec/Amérique, 1991), 434.

3 *Report of the Royal Commission on Bilingualism and Biculturalism* vol. 1 (Ottawa: Queen's Printer, 1967), xxxvii, par. 56.

4 Constitutional Committee of the Quebec Liberal Party, *A Quebec Free to Choose* (Montreal, 1991), 56.

5 *Report of the Commission on the Political and Constitutional Future of Quebec* (Quebec: Editeur officiel du Québec, 1991), 9.

6 See Gagnon and Latouche, 459, 462.

7 Eugene Forsey, *A Life on the Fringe: The Memoirs of Eugene Forsey* (Toronto: Oxford University Press, 1990), 208–9.

8 Donald Creighton, *Towards the Discovery of Canada* (Toronto: Macmillan, 1972), 71.

9 Jean-Charles Falardeau, in Mason Wade, ed., *Canadian Dualism/La dualité canadienne* (Toronto/Sainte-Foy: University of Toronto Press/Presses de l'Université Laval, 1960), 25.

10 Léon Dion, *A la recherche du Québec* (Quebec: Presses de l'Université Laval, 1987), 165 (translation).

11 Solange Chaput-Rolland, "Esprit de Pepin-Robarts, es-tu là?" *Le Devoir*, 22 May 1991.

12 Constitutional Committee, *A Quebec Free to Choose*, 12, 22–3.

13 See the Report of the Joint Committee of the Senate and the House of Commons, *The 1987 Constitutional Agreement* (Ottawa: Queen's Printer, 1987), 137ff.

14 *Report of the Commission on the Political and Constitutional Future of Quebec*, 28–9.

15 Ibid., 33, 36.

16 Ibid., 34.

17 Ibid.

18 Ibid., 35.

19 *Bâtir ensemble l'avenir du Canada* (Ottawa: Ministère des approvisionnements et services, 1991), iii; *Shaping Canada's Future Together* (Ottawa: Ministry of Supply and Services, 1991), iii.

20 Ramsay Cook, *The Maple Leaf Forever* (Toronto: Macmillan 1971), 213.

21 *Shaping Canada's Future Together*, v.

22 Ibid., vi, viii.

23 Ibid., 3.

24 David Bercuson and Barry Cooper, *Deconfederation: Canada without Quebec* (Toronto: Key Porter Books, 1991), 15–16.

25 *Shaping Canada's Future Together*, 3.

26 Ibid., 14.

27 Ibid., vi.

28 Ibid., 14.

29 *Bâtir ensemble l'avenir du Canada*, 14.
30 *Shaping Canada's Future Together*, 2 (emphasis in original).
31 Pierre Elliott Trudeau, "There Must Be a Sense of Belonging," in Donald Johnston, ed., *With a Bang, Not a Whimper* (Toronto: Stoddart, 1988), 31.
32 *A Renewed Canada: Report of the Special Joint Committee of the Senate and the House of Commons* (Beaudoin-Dobbie Report) (Ottawa: Supply and Services, February 1992), 24.
33 Citizens' Forum on Canada's Future, *Report to the People and Government of Canada* (Ottawa: Minister of Supply and Services, 1991), 53, 58.
34 Alan Gregg, "Rootless and Rudderless," in Knowlton Nash, *Visions of Canada: Searching for Our Future* (Toronto: McClelland & Stewart, 1991), 58.
35 *Shaping Canada's Future Together*, 20.
36 Ibid., 27.
37 Ibid., 35.
38 Ibid., 35.
39 Senator Gérald Beaudoin, Royal Society of Canada.
40 Claude Ryan, "L'Accord du lac Meech permettra au Québec de faire des gains importants et incontestables," in Benoît Lauzière, *Le Québec et le lac Meech*, un dossier du *Devoir* (Montreal: Guérin littérature, 1987), 351.
41 Claude Ryan, "Il a soulevé les vraies questions et réfuté les réponses toutes faites," in Robert Comeau and Lucille Beaudry, eds., *André Laurendeau* (Sillery: Presses de l'Université du Québec, 1990), 277.
42 Ibid., 278.
43 Ibid., 279.
44 Ibid., 280.
45 Claude Ryan, "L'échiquier politique au Canada et la crise des deux nations: Perspectives de fin d'année," *Le Devoir*, 30 December 1967.

CHAPTER EIGHT

1 This chapter was first written for the French edition of the book, in late June 1992, before the agreement that was to lead to the Charlottetown Accord. On reflection, I have left it pretty much intact, in order to preserve the mood of the time. A few more observations are necessary. The Charlottetown Accord itself stopped short of recognizing the principle of national pluralism for Canada. The 1992 referendum came too close to being a "national referendum" for my liking. Although Quebec did impose its own set of rules, the referendum was held everywhere across Canada on the same day, with the same question. The Liberal government led by Jean Chrétien espouses the cause of a

single Canadian nationhood even more steadfastly than the previous Conservative government did. If the Canadian government decides to employ the means of a pan-Canadian national referendum to pre-empt a similar initiative on the part of the PQ government in Quebec, the shadow of the Conquest will be brought back to haunt us.

2 Ramsay Cook, *The Maple Leaf Forever* (Toronto: Macmillan, 1971), 100.

3 Léon Dion, *A la recherche du Québec* (Quebec: Presses de l'Université Laval, 1987), 29 (translation).

4 Christian Dufour, *A Canadian Challenge/Le défi québécois* (Lantzville: Oolichan Books, 1990), 57.

5 *Les anciens Canadiens* is the title of a classic novel of New France by Philippe Aubert de Gaspé.

6 Dufour, *A Canadian Challenge*, 155 (translation).

7 Ibid., 47 (translation).

8 R.A. Rutherdale, "Janet Ajzenstat, *The Political Thought of Lord Durham*," *Canadian Historical Review* 70, no. 2 (1989): 259, 261.

9 Janet Ajzenstat, *The Political Thought of Lord Durham* (Montreal and Kingston: McGill-Queen's University Press, 1988), 25.

10 Ibid., 22–3.

11 It is worth recalling a brief sentence from the preface of Pierre Elliott Trudeau's book, *Federalism and the French-Canadians*. Speaking of the book, Trudeau says: "But it is nonetheless dedicated to the progress of French-Canadians" (xxvi).

12 Pierre Elliott Trudeau, "The Values of a Just Society," in Thomas Axworthy and Trudeau, *Towards a Just Society* (Toronto: Penguin Books, 1992), 401ff.

13 Ajzenstat, *The Political Thought of Lord Durham*, 100.

14 David Bercuson and Barry Cooper, *Deconfederation: Canada without Quebec* (Toronto: Key Porter Books, 1991), 73.

15 Ibid., 100.

16 Ibid., 12–13.

17 Ramsay Cook, *Canada and the French-Canadian Question* (Toronto: Macmillan, 1966), 175.

18 Ibid., 147, 175, 178.

19 Ibid., 164.

20 Ibid., 188.

21 Ramsay Cook, *Canada, Quebec and the Uses of Nationalism* (Toronto: McClelland & Stewart, 1986), 58–9.

22 Ramsay Cook, "Alice in Meechland, or the Concept of Quebec as a Distinct Society," in Michael Behiels, ed., *The Meech Lake Primer* (Ottawa: University of Ottawa Press, 1989), 148, 158–9. See also Ramsay Cook, "The Lament for Meech Lake," *Literary Review of Canada* 3, no. 7 (July/Aug. 1994): 6.

23 Behiels, *The Meech Lake Primer*, xxiv.

24 Ramsay Cook, "From Accord to Ambiguity: In the Aftermath of Meech Lake, All Deals Are Off," *Books in Canada*, Oct. 1990, 38.

25 Ramsay Cook, "Janet Ajzenstat, *The Political Thought of Lord Durham*," *Canadian Journal of Political Science* 21, no. 3 (1988): 610.

26 See Philip Resnick, *Letters to a Québécois Friend* (Montreal and Kingston: McGill University Press, 1989), 61.

27 See in particular briefs by Louis Bernard (pp. 65–6), Simon Langlois (p. 576), Luc Bureau (p. 170), Patrice Garant (pp. 415–16), and Nicole Duplé (p. 323), in *Les avis des spécialistes invités à répondre aux huit questions posées par la Commission*, Working Paper no. 4, Commission on the Political and Constitutional Future of Quebec (Quebec: Editeur officiel du Québec, 1991).

28 Jacques Dufresne, *Le courage et la lucidité: Essai sur la constitution du Québec souverain* (Sillery: Les éditions du Septentrion, 1990), 51 (translation).

CONCLUSION

1 Charles Taylor, "The Stakes of Constitutional Reform," in *Reconciling the Solitudes: Essays on Canadian Federalism and Nationalism* (Montreal and Kingston: McGill-Queen's University Press, 1993), 147.

2 See Guy Laforest, "L'Esprit de 1982," in Louis Balthazar, Guy Laforest, and Vincent Lemieux, *Le Québec et la restructuration du Canada, 1980–1992: Enjeux et perspectives* (Sillery: Les éditions du Septentrion, 1991), 147–64; also Christian Dufour, *Le défi québécois* (Montreal, L'Hexagone, 1989), 76–7.

3 Claude Ryan, "L'Accord du lac Meech permettra au Québec de faire des gains importants et incontestables," in Benoît Lauzière, ed., *Le Québec et le lac Meech* (Montreal: Guérin littérature, 1987), 349 (translation).

4 Kenneth McRoberts, *English Canada and Quebec: Avoiding the Issue* (Toronto: Robarts Centre for Canadian Studies Lecture Series, 1991), 10–11.

5 Kenneth McRoberts, "Making Canada Bilingual: Illusions and Delusions of Federal Language Policy," in David Shugarman and Reg Whitaker, *Federalism and Political Community* (Toronto: Broadview Press, 1989), 162.

6 Stephen Clarkson and Christina McCall, *Trudeau and Our Times*, vol. 1, *Magnificent Obsession* (Toronto: McClelland & Stewart, 1990), 292–3.

7 Jean-Jacques Rousseau, *The Social Contract* (New York: Hafner Publishing, 1947), 2:36.

8 Alain Baccigalupo, "Le système politique canadien depuis l'avènement de la Charte: Démocratie ou juriscratie?" in Balthazar, Laforest, and Lemieux, *Le Québec et la restructuration du Canada*, 133ff.

9 See Peter Russell, "The Charter and the Future of Canadian Politics," in Alain G. Gagnon and James Bickerton, eds., *Canadian Politics* (Peterborough: Broadview Press, 1990), 258.

10 Charles Taylor, "Shared and Divergent Values," in *Reconciling the Solitudes*, 155–86.

11 For a more detailed analysis of this question, see Guy Laforest, "Libéralisme et nationalisme au Canada à l'heure de l'Accord du lac Meech," *Carrefour* 13, no. 2 (1991): 68–90; reprinted in Guy Laforest, *De la prudence: Textes politiques* (Montreal: Boréal, 1993), 85–118.

12 Taylor, "Shared and Divergent Values," 177.

13 Ibid.

14 Léon Dion, "Pour sortir de l'impasse constitutionnelle," in Commission sur l'avenir politique et constitutionnel du Québec, *Les avis des spécialistes invités à répondre aux huit questions posées par la Commission* (Quebec: Editeur officiel du Québec, 1991), 274 (translation).

15 Christian Dufour, "Le mal canadien," in Balthazar, Laforest, and Lemieux, *Le Québec et la restructuration du Canada*, 113.

16 Pierre Elliott Trudeau, "A Last Word from Pierre Elliott Trudeau," in Donald Johnston, ed., *Pierre Trudeau Speaks Out on Meech Lake* (Toronto: General, 1990), 137.

17 Philip Resnick, *Toward a Canada-Quebec Union* (Montreal and Kingston: McGill-Queen's University Press, 1991), 115.

18 Hubert Aquin, "La fatigue culturelle du Canada français," *Liberté* 23, no. 4 (May 1962): 299–325; reprinted in Hubert Aquin, *Blocs erratiques* (Montreal: Quinze, 1977), 97. For a detailed analysis of the political and ideological context in which this article was written, see Réjean Roy's MA thesis, "Etude d'un texte d'Hubert Aquin: La fatigue culturelle du Canada français," Sainte-Foy, Ecole des gradués de l'Université Laval, 1991.

19 Gérard Bergeron, *Le Canada français après deux siècles de patience* (Paris: Seuil, 1967), 258.